# THE CULTURE WAR

## How the West Lost Its Greatness & Was Weakened From Within

## Hanne Nabintu Herland

Christian Publishing House
Cambridge, Ohio

Hanne Nabintu Herland

Copyright © 2017 Hanne Nabintu Herland

All rights reserved. Except for brief quotations in articles, other publications, book reviews, and blogs, no part of this book may be reproduced in any manner without prior written permission from the publishers. For information, write,

support@christianpublishers.org

Unless otherwise stated, Scripture quotations are from *The Holy Bible, Updated American Standard Version*®, copyright © 2017 by Christian Publishing House, Professional Christian Publishing of the Good News. All rights reserved.

*THE CULTURE WAR: How the West Lost Its Greatness & Was Weakened From Within by Hanne Nabintu Herland*

ISBN-13: 978-1-945757-63-1

ISBN-10: 1-945757-63-9

**Cover Photo Credit:** Paul Bernhard

**Translators and Proof Readers:** Lisa Bostwick, Unni Herland, Eleni Smilas, Simon Vincent

# The Culture War

# Table of Contents

In Honor of the Life and Work of Reverend Billy Graham .................. 10

## INTRODUCTION ........................................................................ 11
### An Age of Rebellion ........................................................... 11
### Relativism and Nihilism In the West ................................... 12
### Manifesto ............................................................................ 13

## CHAPTER 1 ............................................................................... 15
## THE CULTURAL REVOLUTION ............................................ 15
### The Frankfurt School: Neo-Marxism Came to Dominate Western Thinking ..... 15
### Progressive Illiberalism Kills Free Speech ......................... 18
### Fearless Speech .................................................................. 20

## CHAPTER 2 ............................................................................... 22
## THE TOTALITARIAN FRENCH REVOLUTION ..................... 22
### The Anti-Religious French Revolution ............................... 22
### Edmund Burke's Disdain for the French Revolution .......... 24
### The Road to Serfdom .......................................................... 28
### Modern Conservatism and Lack of Freedom .................... 29

## CHAPTER 3 ............................................................................... 31
## NIETZSCHE IS DEAD ............................................................... 31
### Secularism and the Misuse of Power .................................. 31
### Optimism on Behalf of the Modern World .......................... 33
### God Is Dead ......................................................................... 36
### Depression on Behalf of the Modern World ....................... 38

## CHAPTER 4 ............................................................................... 40
## THE CHRISTIAN ROOT OF WESTERN CIVILIZATION ....... 40
### The Demonization of Our Christian Heritage .................... 40
### The Triple Cradle of Secular Values .................................. 44

JUDEO-CHRISTIAN ETHICS – DECISIVE FOR HUMAN RIGHTS, EQUALITY AND LEVELLING CLASS DIFFERENCES .................................................................. 45

## CHAPTER 5 .................................................................................. 49

## WHAT IS RELIGION? ..................................................................... 49

DEFINITIONS OF RELIGION ............................................................. 49
MATERIALISM, MARXISM, SOCIALISM – MODERN RELIGIONS ................. 51
A NEW RELIGION AND ITS EFFECTS: SECULAR MESSIANISM ................. 53

## CHAPTER 6 .................................................................................. 56

## SPIRITUAL AWAKENING ................................................................ 56

THE NEED FOR PHILOSOPHY, RELIGION, AND SPIRITUALISM ................. 56
THE POWER OF THE MIND AND THE WILL TO CHANGE ........................ 60
AID FROM THE WORLD OF THE UNSEEN ........................................... 63
THE HUMAN HEART AND SPIRITUAL LIGHT ....................................... 67

## CHAPTER 7 .................................................................................. 70

## SEARCHING FOR PARADISE .......................................................... 70

THEODICY – SUFFERING AND JUSTICE IN THE AFTERLIFE .................... 70
JUDGMENT DAY AND THE JUSTICE OF GOD ....................................... 73
CONDITIONS FOR PARADISE ........................................................... 74
CRITICAL CHOICES IN LIFE ............................................................. 76
RESOLUTION WITH TOXINS OF THE MIND ......................................... 78

## CHAPTER 8 .................................................................................. 82

## THE RATIONALITY OF RELIGION .................................................... 82

RELIGION INFLUENCES MORALITY ................................................... 82
IT IS RATIONAL TO CARE ............................................................... 83
RELIGION AND ITS ETHICS SHOULD PLAY A ROLE IN POLITICS ............. 86

## CHAPTER 9 .................................................................................. 89

## MODERN SCIENCE IS NOT NEUTRAL, NOR OBJECTIVE ..................... 89

| | |
|---|---|
| IS RESEARCH EVER OBJECTIVE? | 89 |
| THE FLAWS OF EMPIRICISM AND POSITIVISM | 93 |
| THE LIMITS OF DARWINIAN EVOLUTION | 96 |
| THE LIMITS OF EMPIRICISM | 100 |

## CHAPTER 10 .............................................................................................. 101

## ANTI-CHRISTIAN ELITES IN A WORLD OF BELIEVERS ..................................... 101

| | |
|---|---|
| A SURPRISING FOCUS ON RELIGION | 101 |
| NATIONAL IDENTITY IN A GLOBALIZED WORLD | 104 |
| RELIGIOUS BELIEF: REMARKABLY RESILIENT | 105 |
| THE NEED FOR UNITY | 110 |

## CHAPTER 11 .............................................................................................. 113

## TOTALITARIAN DEMOCRACY ......................................................................... 113

| | |
|---|---|
| FREEDOM DEFINED AS THE RIGHT TO PARTICIPATE IN THE EXTREME LIBERAL SOCIETY | 113 |
| THE ORIGINAL FORM OF LIBERALISM – JOHN LOCKE | 115 |
| THE ORIGINS OF TOTALITARIANISM | 116 |
| THE FALTERING WELFARE STATE | 119 |
| THE FEAR OF SETTING BOUNDARIES - EDUCATION | 121 |

## CHAPTER 12 .............................................................................................. 125

## FINANCIAL GREED AND ECONOMIC CRISIS ..................................................... 125

| | |
|---|---|
| THE PROTESTANT ETHIC AND THE SPIRIT OF CAPITALISM | 125 |
| THE PROBLEM OF GREED AND LACK OF TRUST | 129 |
| WESTERN CULTURAL DECLINE | 134 |

## CHAPTER 13 .............................................................................................. 139

## CHRISTOPHOBIA IN THE WEST ....................................................................... 139

| | |
|---|---|
| THE RUSSIAN DEFENCE OF CHRISTIANITY | 139 |
| "CHRISTOPHOBIA" | 143 |
| SOCIAL DISORDER AND CHRISTIAN DECLINE | 146 |
| ABORTION – MILLIONS OF UNBORN LOST | 149 |

| | |
|---|---|
| Civilizations Die From Suicide | 150 |
| The Influence of Faith on Health | 152 |
| Revivalism Worldwide | 156 |

## CHAPTER 14 ............................................................................. 159

## THE RISE OF THE ANTI-CHRISTIAN WEST AND ISLAM ........................ 159

| | |
|---|---|
| Extreme Secular Tyranny | 159 |
| Islam Respects Jesus More Than We Do | 160 |
| Islam, Geopolitics and the Refusal of the Extreme Liberal | 162 |
| Humanist Movements – Exploiting Muslims and Harassing Christians | 166 |

## CHAPTER 15 ............................................................................. 168

## HEDONISM, FEMINISM, THE BREAKING UP OF THE FAMILY ................ 168

| | |
|---|---|
| The Value Struggle in Europe | 168 |
| When "feelings" Becomes Slavery | 171 |
| "Feelings," Free Sex and Infidelity | 174 |
| Pornography | 176 |
| The Dangers of Extreme Individualism | 180 |
| Conflict and Rage – The Lifeblood of Feminism | 182 |
| Cultural Downfall | 188 |

## CHAPTER 16 ............................................................................. 191

## FREE SPEECH - TOLERANCE AS TOOLS OF OPPRESSION .................... 191

| | |
|---|---|
| Limitless "Free speech" As a Means to Bully | 191 |
| Voltaire – Founding Father of Modern Intolerance? | 194 |
| One-Way Tolerance – The Repressive Kind | 196 |
| A Culture of Bullying or Rational Debate? | 199 |
| Charlie Hebdo, Terrorism, and Free Speech | 201 |

## CHAPTER 17 ............................................................................. 204

## WHY THE SECULARIZED CHURCH IS IN DECLINE ............................... 204

| | |
|---|---|
| The Definition of a Church and Spiritual Fellowship | 204 |
| Institutionalized Churches Losing Their Appeal | 208 |

CHURCHLESS CHRISTIANS, "CULTURAL RELIGION" AND THE LACK OF SPIRITUAL FELLOWSHIP ................................................................................................211

**CHAPTER 18** ................................................................................................ **216**

**POST-MODERN CHRISTIANITY VERSUS JESUS' SIMPLE MESSAGE** ................ **216**

    CHURCH LEADERS HAVE UTTERLY FAILED ............................................................. 216
    JESUS AS A "MILD, WEAK, MELLOW" CREATURE ..................................................... 218
    CHRISTIAN SELFISHNESS ...................................................................................... 221
    EGOISM AND LACK OF SPIRITUALITY IN CHURCH ..................................................... 225
    TIME TO RETURN TO THE ROOTS OF TRUE FAITH ..................................................... 228

**ABOUT THE AUTHOR** ................................................................................ **230**

**LIST OF REFERENCES** ................................................................................ **231**

*In honor of the life and work of reverend Billy Graham*

# Introduction

## An Age of Rebellion

IN RECENT DECADES, Western culture has undergone dramatic changes. Radical new elites have broken down historical values in order to create a new world order with new sets of ethics. They have pushed for strong anti-traditionalist and globalise world views, and the current establishment now dominates the public through tight control over the media. Many of the values that once made the West a great civilization is now profoundly challenged by an authoritarian liberal extremism.

Just as capitalism won the battle as the ruling economic model, the extreme liberals won the social revolution in the West. They have brutally implemented their ideology since the 1960s, smothering opposition. The hope was to produce a utopian, internationalist society where religion no longer existed, the traditional family was dissolved, national borders disappeared, and everyone lived together in peace and harmony. Today, many grumbles that the opposite happened, we have entered yet another age of feudality, bound to the lords of debt, suffering under the breakdown of marriage while mental and psychological illnesses, drug abuse and family tragedies explode. Society crumbles under the weight of financial crisis, decadence, hedonism, social upheaval and a culture of depression. This is happening while the ultra-rich Western elite assembles the wealth into their own hands. Only a few individuals now own more than half of world assets, according to Oxfam.[1] The same elite owns much of the mainstream media and may easily push the narrative to benefit their own agendas.

---

[1] Oxfam http://www.independent.co.uk/news/world/politics/just-62-people-now-own-the-same-wealth-as-half-the-worlds-population-research-finds-a6818081.html

Many feels that our culture has been hijacked and poisoned by ideologies and collections of beliefs that have destabilized society and weakened the very fabric of who we are. The divide between the elite's perspectives and the people's perspectives are growing, as free speech is increasingly strangled in a culture of repressive political correctness. We have become the victims of our own rebellious age. Is this democracy? How did we end up in such poverty, despite being a society so rich in material wealth and technological progress?

The mainstream contempt for the values that once made our culture world-leading makes it hard even to be proud of historical values. Even celebrating religious festivities such as Christmas and Easter is looked upon with skepticism. We shun away from teaching our children the great stories of the founding fathers and the great kings, the very fabric of what it means to stand together as a culture. Religious values are belittled even if over 72% of European people adhere to the Christian faith[2] and approximately the same number in the US, according to Pew Research Centre Forum.[3]

The new world order seems to unify Western elites across the political spectrum. The traditional Right–Left or Republican-Democrat divide, is increasingly outdated as liberals and conservatives have downloaded the same extreme liberal narrative. The Left is not standing up for its originally constructive anti-war, solidarity with the poor, defending the working-class ideals. The Right silently accepts an increasingly hedonistic way of life combined with a ruthless Capitalism devoid of morality and neoconservative thought with no regard for the sovereignty of nations.

\*\*\*

# Relativism and Nihilism In the West

It is quite clear that the modern definition of liberalism lay far from its original meaning. When John Locke defined the rights of men, he spoke of individual rights and corresponding *duties* and *responsibilities* carried out in society. His "liberalism" was not devoid of morality, like the permissiveness and lack of modesty that now permeate our culture. Tolerance did not mean the right to shut down and silence those who

---

[2] Pew Research Center: Religion & Public Life (August 7, 2017)
http://www.pewforum.org/2011/12/19/global-christianity-regions/#europe
[3] Pew Research Centre Forum on Religion and Public Life, Global Christianity, December 2011.
http://www.pewforum.org/2011/12/19/global-christianity-regions/#europe

oppose the politically correct world view. In its original form, tolerance implied both parties are respecting each other's difference and allowing each other to coexist, with respect for the existing pluralism in the world.

The same is true for Capitalism, asserting the individual's right to own the fruits of his labour. This economic model developed in coherence with the Protestant ethic, focusing on trust, reliability, hard work as a virtue. Capitalism functioned quite well as individuals participating in its free enterprise were largely trustworthy with the aim of helping society prosper. To a large degree, the system self-regulated, the wrongdoer was punished, the liar stopped. Today, we have a Capitalism that is characterized by an acceptance of greed and lack of responsibility. Political leaders remain in office regardless of the magnitude of the "Watergate scandals", which is deeply problematic.

It becomes clear that the current clash of values goes between an extreme, nihilist liberalism and the historical values that once characterized the West. The current nihilist ideology views man as inherently good and traditional morality as a negative structure that prohibits man from liberties. If something goes wrong, man is not responsible, but society is at fault. Consequently, society needs constant reforms away from its traditional values.

In stark contrast, religious thought perceives man as faulty, torn between good and evil. It is his personal responsibility to choose to do justice and that which is right. Classic conservatism asserts that the remedy to problems in society is not revolutions, but subtle and quite careful reforms, to ensure continued growth and stability. Jewish thinking speaks of man as placed on earth with the betterment of society as his normative goal. He is to help God make the world a better place, engaged not only in the pursuit of his own happiness. Evil, defined as acts that are harmful, destructive and cause injury to others, implies the absence of love. Ultimate selfishness is evil and the worst enemy of the fellowship of men. This is a deeply rooted philosophical thought both in Judaism and Christianity.

*** 

# Manifesto

This manifesto does not attempt to examine and present all the intricate pros and cons in the debate on religion and secularization, but rather outlines a generalized critical view as to why traditional values are in decline in the West. It is an angry *Alarm* – in an almost Oriana Fallaci manner, at what our Western culture has become, with a black-and-white approach to the topic. This method is used in order to point out the negative effects of the extreme liberalism that currently penetrates the mainstream. This author refers to books, articles, and references which are also listed alphabetically in the back. Note that the word "liberal" somehow tends to mean "leftist" in the United States, while in Europe it signifies "liberal opposition against the left." The term "extreme liberal" or "liberal extremism" does not signify a negative attitude towards "liberalism" in its original form, but presents a critique of the lack of morality and empathy which characterizes current day nihilism and hedonism.

When speaking about cultural trends and ideologies, a certain amount of generalization is needed in order to visualize the larger picture. Yet, trend analysis and discussions on ideology, culture and comparative studies which do to a certain degree require a broader outlook, tend not to do justice to the myriad of details, minority views, and the plurality within each culture. The following chapters must be read with this in mind.

The monolithic term "the West" is equally complex and generalizing, as it fails to describe cultural complexity, yet I choose to use it to signify the nations that traditionally are viewed as part of the Western Civilization, as opposed to the East, signifying Asia, the South, Africa and so on. The term may describe the broad joint heritage of social norms, ethics, beliefs, cultural customs and technological development that originate in Europe.

This author will specifically choose to cross the boundaries between philosophy, theology, religion, history and various social sciences, attempting to show the coherent development and outcomes within a multitude of fields regarding the impact of ideological change.

It is our aspiration is that the reader will become enthused with a renewed intellectual and spiritual reflection. No man is an island. We are all interconnected and dependent on each other. Freedom has never been the right to abolish empathy and solidarity. Any society that wishes to prosper must be built on justice, mercy and faith.

Many recognize the weaknesses in a society that does not sufficiently appreciate courtesy, civility and respect. We need to re-examine the Western foundational values in a fresh new light, as a source for moral and cultural strength. Let us remember the words of the Catholic Archbishop of Philadelphia, Charles J. Chaput in a *Pro Life* gathering: "Changing the course of Western culture seems like such a huge task. However, St Paul felt exactly the same way. Redeeming a civilization has already been done once. It can be done again." It is this author's hope that these critical philosophical texts can provide a thought-provoking contribution to the debate.

# CHAPTER 1

# The cultural revolution

*The 1700s and 1800s were the era of bloody revolutions. Its subtler Socialist version appeared in the 1900s – the post-war social revolution. The latter was to succeed immensely in demolishing the social fabric of the West from the 1960s onwards and ended up being an illiberal and intolerant force of change.*

## The Frankfurt School: Neo-Marxism Came to Dominate Western Thinking

THE DRAMATIC cultural shift in the West has not happened randomly. Just as novelist and philosopher Ayn Rand commented in a University of Michigan interview, philosophers determine history.[4] They lay out the ideologies that form the basis for cultural development and outline values that are to be considered popular in society. Leading philosophers form a culture's way of viewing the world. Therefore, the choice of ideology and collections of what is to be the "politically correct" belief, is of utmost importance. If the ideological hypothesis, assumptions, and argumentation are faulty and based on models that do not reflect realism, the worldview will end up creating an ongoing misbalance in society with cultural decline as the result. Precisely this has happened.

---

[4] Ayn Rand on Philosophy (Wednesday, August 16, 2017) https://www.youtube.com/watch?v=8hoPo86cErs

# The Culture War

In the West, we have largely completed the objective[5] in *The Communist Manifesto* of 1848, namely, to "melt the solid into air." In the aftermath of the French Revolution, its authors, Karl Marx and Friedrich Engels, saw it as their mission to help shake loose what they felt was cemented in an outdated traditional class society. The Marxists had a desire for a better society more based on equality, where the privileges of nobility did not prevent the advancement of commoners. They analyzed what Capitalism had done to cultural belonging, yet ended up prescribing a radical remedy: revolution. The idea spiraled into tearing down traditional values and the pre-modern family structure, loyalty-based duties, and rights in this "old regime," as Alexis de Tocqueville so eloquently describes it in *Democracy in America*. The movement has been immensely successful in destroying the traditional values and social fabric of Western societies.

Marxism found its revitalized shape after World War II in the Frankfurt School in Germany, an intellectual group connected to the Institut für Sozialforschung *i* Frankfurt am Main before the war. They were interested in analyzing language as a tool of suppression, as seen in destructive propaganda structures, as well as institutionalized language used by an oppressive bureaucracy. As the war broke out, many of them moved to the US.

Martin Jay describes the period well in *The Dialectical Imagination. A History of the Frankfurt School and the Institute of Social Research 1923–1950*. Frustration had for some time dominated the leftist thinkers in Germany, distraught as they were when the Bolshevik revolution implemented Marxism in Russia during World War I quicker than what they were able to do in the West. How could the Soviets grab this vital ideology and make it their own at such a quick pace?

They were left with two choices: either support the Moscow Communism or the more moderate Socialism of the Weimar Republic in Germany. A third choice gradually emerged. German thinkers began re-examining Marxist theory and modernizing it. This became the Frankfurt School which later succeeded in reshaping the social structures in the West. Its disciples acknowledged the need for political change after World War II as National Socialism had utterly failed.

The possibility of the elite abusing its power rightfully worried the post-war Frankfurt School intellectuals, given that the bureaucratic institutionalized society that marked modern democracy had made Nazism function so well in the German state. It was precisely the excellent organization within the institutions and the state-controlled bureaucracy

---

[5] In the West, we have largely implemented the essence of The Communist Manifesto of 1848, and successfully melted down the traditional, Western values.

that made Nazi Germany so efficient. The hope was to avoid such a development in Europe in the future.

Yet, the intellectuals of the Frankfurt School remained Marxist, looking for ways to moderate the Marxist pre-war ideology in order to make it more applicable. What many do not reflect on, is that the leading intellectuals in Europe did not change their ideology after the World War II. The pre-war ideology continued, now only slightly modified. Philosophers such as Theodore W. Adorno, Herbert Marcuse, Friedrich Pollock [6] and Max Horkheimer launched the concept of "critical theory," implying that science should not just describe, but also change oppressive conditions in social structures. The idea was that if the critical theory were applied, misuse of power would be avoided. The original agenda was to establish a just society where minorities were no longer oppressed. They felt that the facilitation of a critical public transparency would make it possible to force a dialogue with elites and governmental powers to avoid misuse of power. In this manner, the ruling system's underlying intentions could be exposed.

Post-war intellectuals, such as Adorno and Marcuse, became the intellectual founding fathers of the student rebellions of 1968, the New Left in America and its liberal attitudes towards drugs and narcotics. This became the early days of free sex, abortion and the revolt against traditional religion. Children were no longer regarded, to the same extent as before, as pure blessings from God, but rather as "obstacles to individual success."

Adornos "*point de depart*" asserted that the process of modernity had failed to free people from the bondage of the past and instead further enslaved them. Adorno exemplifies some of the depressive mood after the war on behalf of modernity. The influence of the initially positive neo-Marxist thinking began permeating the American university structures.

Critical theory sought to expose "the offender," so to speak, and fight for those who were victimized by the bourgeoisie. They were correct in stating that the traditional bourgeois elite structures in Europe needed reforming and more power given to the people. The deep-felt need for critical thinking and intellectuals who posed questions to those in power, was as important then as it is now. They set out to reform that which was not working, but the movement ended up, fundamentally changing the historical European value systems.

---

[6] Pollock, Friedrich (1894-1970) (August 11, 2017) https://www.marxists.org/glossary/people/p/o.htm#pollock-friedrich

***

## Progressive Illiberalism Kills Free Speech

After the war, many of these philosophers returned to Germany and continued their work in Frankfurt and other institutions. Maybe the most famous of these was the German philosopher and Europe's arguably most influential philosopher and social scientist, Jürgen Habermas, who initially continued the work of – and was inspired well into the 1960s by – Marcuse and Adorno. Yet eventually, as we shall see, Habermas seems to have departed from Marxism altogether, turning to Immanuel Kant and communicative ethics.

Kirsten Powers points out in *The Silencing. How the Left is Killing Free Speech* that the increasingly illiberal Left's silencing campaign is a form of "repressive tolerance," arguing that Marcuse openly spoke of the need to curb freedom of speech in pursuit of left-wing ideological goals. Marcuse found it important to change oppressive conditions, - defined as the ideas of the bourgeoisie, the Christians, and conservatives. These groups became the enemy.

Marcuse's words reveal the hidden authoritarian pursuit in this kind of thinking, stating that repressing other worldviews is both necessary and defensible. A lack of respect for different opinions and the democratic process becomes apparent. Suppression of "regressive" policies – defined as the views of non-Marxists – was the prerequisite for the strengthening of "progressive" ideas – understood as his own or those of his particular social movement. Some of the later issues with neo-Marxist critical theory have been precisely the prevalent force by which its philosophers tend to demand uniformity and consensus. Marcuse's words on the need for suppression illustrates the lack of respect for free thinking rooted within critical theory, a tendency that later was to bloom into what we today experience as a regressive, illiberal Left.

As we see, the very foundation of this movement was stained by authoritarian and nondemocratic views. Diversity was to be suppressed through controlling free speech and limiting tolerance towards the "unwanted" groups in society. The Left's campaign for conformity was coupled with strategies of demonizing and defaming its opponents, hoping that this would silence the opposition. Kirsten Powers argues that to this day delegitimization through demonizing and intimidation remains the Left's most successful tactic against political and ideological opponents.

Socialism – coupled with a German elitist nationalism – that failed under Hitler was now moderated and introduced in a brand new version. Intellectuals continued the push for Socialist thinking, both before and after the war. Yet, Socialist intellectuals still failed to recognize the weaknesses within Socialist structures itself, which tended to lean towards precisely the kind of centralization of power that put too much power in the hands of political elites in the first place.

In this environment, the EU was born as a steel and coal union-funded by the same German capitalists that had dominated Hitler's Germany, and the work towards a Europe with a strong centralized government began. In many ways, the EU represents a *Regional Socialism* as opposed to the National Socialism that failed in Germany. Both National Socialism and now *Regional Socialism*, sought to control the European region, both bearing in common a radical dislike towards the bourgeoisie and traditional and religious European values. The work to feverishly erase the memory that intolerant Nazi Socialism was, in fact, left-wing, has been most successful. This has been pointed out by many, among them author Jonah Goldberg in *Liberal Fascism*. The Nazi Party stood for a strong centralization of government and power, a rigid culture of consensus, few individual liberties and strong media indoctrination with heavy use of propaganda.

Few seem to recall that the Nazi party was a form of Socialism. It was an abbreviation for *The National Socialist Labour Party* in Germany. Again, the NAZI party was largely left-wing, not right-wing. Communism, Socialism and National Socialism were all influenced by the root-ideology. At the time, Hitler fought Communist Russia, often referring to its ideology as the enemy, yet pure Marxist thinking influenced both ideologies. Hitler steadily spoke about the importance of the Socialist approach in National Socialism, as the solution for Germany.

Hermann Rauschning, who knew Hitler personally, wrote in *Hitler Speaks: A Series of Political Conversations with Adolf Hitler On His Real Aims*, a work that was first published in 1939 and has been thoroughly researched since, that Hitler felt profoundly indebted to the Marxist tradition, stating that he had learned much from Marxism. Hitler said that his differences with Communists were more tactical than ideological, stating that National Socialism itself was based on Marxism.

Hitler also spoke, as stated in the memoires of his friend Otto Wagener *Hitler: Memoires of a Confidant,* of the importance of ending the age of individualism and transcending into a Socialist state without destructive revolutions such as that of Lenin, which turned the Russian people into a gray, indifferent mass. The route of revolution quenched the educated bourgeoisie, Hitler felt, thus the need to enforce a strong National Socialist state without removing the structures of the elite. His slogan "Crusade against Marxism" may be understood in this light. As pointed out by George Watson in *The Independent*, this early account of Hitler's opinions, show that he initially believed in Socialism without civil war.[7] It has been quite an accomplishment by the European left to cunningly hide the fact that Hitler belonged to the European left-wing.

It is true that Hitler deviated from Marxism by accentuating the importance of racial heritage. He also emphasized nationalism – the belief in the fatherland, rather than "the internationalist proletariat," the classical Marxist ideal of a borderless society.

Eventually, as the advocates of critical theory reached the peak of their own institutional power, they too became infected by the same virus that had plagued the bourgeoisie before them. Power tends to corrupt and "absolute power corrupts absolutely," as historian Lord Acton put it. The ideological inbred push to oppress oppositional voices grew among the new, neo-Marxist elites. The once "oppressed" Marxists, - then Socialist underdogs fighting for "justice for the worker," became the new oppressors who were just as skillful as the previous generation in securing power and influence at the expense of others. They became the new, Western elite.

The same individuals who once participated in the rebellion against the bourgeoisie elite, today constitute the political upper classes of Western societies. The roles changed. Robin Hood became the Sheriff of Nottingham. Or more along the lines of Victor Hugo's *Les Misérables*. Jean Valjean has become Inspector Javert. The left has become the negation of its own ideals.

✷✷✷

# Fearless Speech

Michel Foucault spent a lifetime studying how words may become tools of oppression in the public realm. He studied the language of public institutions and documented the techniques of domination inherent in the institutionalization of words. He looked closely at the way language, and choice of words come across in official documents and forces adversaries to

---

[7] INDEPENDENT: Hitler and the socialist dream (Wednesday, August 16, 2017) http://www.independent.co.uk/arts-entertainment/hitler-and-the-Socialist-dream-1186455.html

compromise and comply. For example, how state institutions implemented a complicated, official language which deterred many in the working class from objecting or posing critical questions. Both Foucault and the father of multiculturalism, who sought to dissolve traditional Western values through his own method, deconstruction, Jacques Derrida, attempted to expose precisely the propaganda techniques through which the elites ruled.

As strong believers in "critical theory," they ended up attacking the misuse of power within traditional Europe but failed to see how the breaking up of traditions and religious values dramatically weakened European culture itself.

Egoism tends to fuel the human heart and abusing power definitely seems to be a tendency in us, regardless of political, ideological standing. It appears to be an innate temptation that faces the atheist, the religious, the agnostic alike. This is precisely why it is the role of scrutinizing intellectuals remain vital, to attempt to minimize the abuse of institutional powers given to the political and financial elites.

In *Fearless Speech*, Foucault explains why it is so essential that society permit critical thinking. The problem being, as stated, that when the neo-Marxists who first engaged so bitterly in the fight against traditional values came to power, they actually became the new elite. Thus, the critical questioning stopped.

Linguist and social scientist, Noam Chomsky, recently named USA's most important intellectual and the most cited living scholar in the humanities, believes that freedom of speech and the right to communicate one's ideas and opinions is far more restricted than people think, particularly in democracies. In *Necessary Illusions: Thought Control in Democratic Societies* he questions how free Western democracies really are, claiming that the media is increasingly an instrument for Western propaganda. The press is, particularly in democracies, manipulated by political-ideological elites with a rising need to control popular opinion. The reason is simple: in a democratic country, the people's opinion determines the results of democratic elections. They go to the polling stations to vote for the politician of their choice. Therefore, control of popular opinion becomes extremely important under such circumstances.

Thinkers such as Marcuse and Adorno, and later disciples such as Jacques Derrida, Michel Foucault thus ended up leading the attack on traditional European thought and ended up weakening the very core of Western civilization.

# CHAPTER 2

# The Totalitarian French Revolution

*Edmund Burke spent much of his life explaining why it is important to maintain Europe's political and moral philosophical traditions, precisely those which made Europe a great civilization: individualism's emphasis on independence and opportunities for all, the value of equality, law and order, as well as the Protestant work ethic - the culture of conscience.*

## The Anti-Religious French Revolution

The sharply anti-religious French Revolution came only years before Karl Marx and Engels wrote the famous thesis *The Communist Manifesto*. Europe was buzzing with radical ideas. Marx and Engels fought to break free from limiting cultural systems, for the "workers of the world to unite" across borders in an economic system in which the people would own the production line. The idea was not that bad: if the people own the industry, the factories, and the capital, wealth may cease to amass only into the hands of the few. Yet, the people need benevolent leaders. It may be argued that the system ended up opening up for the state to administer the capital and the production line, only distributing a "fair share" to each one. A new leadership was formed - the Communist elite. The state and its Communist leaders ended up resuming the responsibility for the citizen's well-being, "the state" becoming the provider to all. They were opposed to the Capitalist structure which sought to reduce the size of state ownership and bureaucratization. Furthermore, Capitalists stressed the need for private company ownership and individuals to own the means of production and the fruit of their own labor. Yet, the market Capitalist economic system clearly also has its flaws.

Marxism was introduced only a few years after the French Revolution and its rebellion against the corrupt French authorities. It is true that before the Revolution, the French ruling classes did little to alleviate poverty and other challenges in a society experiencing corruption and internal unrest. Its wealthy kings failed to address painstaking issues that made life miserable for ordinary citizens. Injustice and discontentment among the people have in history tended to be the root cause of many a revolution. Yet, the idealization of brute revolution somehow created the notion that the victim was defined as "the people," while the bourgeoisie chronically portrayed as "the offender".

Furthermore, the new radical French leaders who spoke so gloriously about "liberty, equality, and fraternity" soon proved to be far more ruthless than their bourgeois predecessors. A few years after the rebels had ousted the king's court, they constructed a power-elite that became vastly more tyrannical than the aristocracy they had removed. This enhanced a brutal tyranny of the mob that to this day remind Europeans of our continent's ruthless legacy of authoritarian intolerance draped in the disguise of liberty and freedom.

Under the French revolutionary leader, Maximilien de Robespierre, guillotines were set up on almost every street corner in Paris. People were executed at the smallest hint of opposition; orgies were organized in churches as a direct move by radicals to spite religion. Robespierre summarized his totalitarian logic, stating that there are only two types of people in France, the people and their enemies. Anyone who opposed the revolution was to be eliminated. Priests and the well-educated were beheaded and killed by the thousands without trials or examining evidence; their bodies were thrown into the streets. Nobody cared about the rule of law in the midst of this so-called glorious revolution. Churches were locked up; priests were killed, it was the end of religious freedom in France.

The anarchy during the French Revolution and its early implementation of democracy – the rule of the people - gave criminals the opportunity to exercise all kinds of violence freely. Its new consensus-oriented politicians were driven by a deep resentment, not only against religion but against all traditional values. In the "New France" no violation of the strict radical consensus was tolerated. Conservative intellectuals, religious dissidents, kings, anyone of authority who did not submit to the new rulers, were ruthlessly killed.

The French Revolution was essentially a disaster for France. It resulted in total anarchy. There was no peace until Napoleon Bonaparte seized power and restored the rule of law. He ended up saving the French "government of the people" from their own merciless spiral of violence against the population. It is quite remarkable – this is how modern Western democracy first was implemented in Europe, by brutal force and authoritarian, illiberal new elites. It was Napoleon who brought back a functioning legal system, restored freedom of religion, the protection of minorities such as the Jews and reinstalled respect for the clergy.

The French Church was not reinstated until Napoleon came to power. He understood how vital this traditional force was for the upkeeping of morality and order. He allegedly even forced his atheist marshals to attend Church and pay their respects. Napoleon was acutely aware of the dangers of hypocrisy within the Church, having attended Catholic schools and seen much of the injustice within the institutionalized Church systems, yet he still believed that religious values such as "love thy neighbor" were ideals that needed to be taught in society in order to uphold social order. He had come to understand that the local churches provided the historically cultural focus on solidarity with the weak, perhaps the most Christian ideal of all.

In *Demonic*, bestselling author Ann Coulter points out that the French Revolution was an uprising of a peer-pressure oriented nihilistic mob, further characterized by irrationality, violence, and destructive social attitudes.

✳✳✳

# Edmund Burke's Disdain for the French Revolution

There were definitely those who were critical of the French Revolution. Nations went to war against France. In England, politicians and intellectuals questioned the rationality of the uprisings, as they watched it unravel in all its horror in Paris and all over the country. The growing modern Conservative movement in England suggested that society needs to maintain laws and regulations, and not too easily fall prey to the passionate call for revolutions. They spoke of the need for moderate reform in order to avoid the type of anarchy that was now plaguing the French.

Many believed that to keep a certain order is necessary since man has an inherent tendency to exploit others to his own benefit. Man needs to control his selfish desires, whether he is rich or poor, among the elites or among the suppressed, regardless of gender and ethnic background. Hence the need for an ethical foundation of society to firmly establish respect for the natural diversity which exists in any given society. It was stated that the goal was to avoid anarchy and ensure the right of the individual to live in a society where his welfare was protected and transgressors punished.

The English philosopher, Edmund Burke, who lived in the 1700s was a strong voice for these ideals. He is described by many as the founder of modern conservatism. In *The Conservative Mind*, historian Russel Kirk describes Burke's strong dislike for the French Revolution, as he fought fiercely against it. In no way, did he want a similar process to take place in England.

In his pamphlet *Reflections on the Revolution in France*, Burke warned against the effects of dramatically changing the values and structures of society. He warned of democracy itself. If democracy means rulership by the mob, he stated, the nations are in trouble. He felt that it was vital that leaders were skilled and properly educated, fixed on serving the people, in order for the system to work.

To Burke, a society without a hereditary nobility and highly educated and capable elites, lacking an established church and continuous traditions, meant dangerously playing with the very fabric of Western society. He examined the inherent problems of injustice and abuse of power among the elites but found completely different answers than Karl Marx.

He fervently stated that the radical French philosopher, Jean-Jacques Rousseau was wrong in arguing that the social contract should be between the sovereign state and its people. Burke referred to the partnership between generations, even incorporating respect for the dead and the yet unborn, as the true source of stability, loyalty, and growth for a nation.

Burke felt that bloody revolutions, civil wars, and horrors such those experienced by the French, were not the way to go about it. This would not lead to prosperity and stability. Within the framework of law and order, he sought to reform society gradually rather than rapidly, and stop the abuse of power without heading towards civil war. Until the day he died, he advocated that change is not always for the better.

According to Ian Harris, in *The Cambridge Companion to Edmund Burke*, Burke firmly believed that religion is one of the main foundational pillars of society. He criticized deism and atheism and maintained that Christianity was vital to maintain in order to push for social progress, both for man's soul on the personal level, as well as for political arrangements and the preservation of constitutional and civil liberties.

The idea of limited governmental authority was viewed as essential, the necessity of independent institutions, the need for the secular separation of church and state to ensure a free, democratic society. Burke strongly believed in the liberty of the people and the need to protect them against the political elites' abuse of power. He felt that only with a full understanding of history, could one avoid repeating mistakes of the past.

Professor at Yale University, David Bromwich points out in *The Intellectual Life of Edmund Burke* that Burke wished for a society built on trust, and felt that democracy in its modern form could easily mean the end of the loyalty between the generations and the breaking away of social bonds between family structures and cultural roots. Burke believed that democracy would lead to new heights of misuse of power, that modern society could end up seeing crimes committed on a terrifying scale precisely under its democratic rule. The same criticism has later been voiced by intellectuals such as Noam Chomsky, as we have seen.

Burke's analysis of the French Revolution anticipates the later Russian Revolution of 1917 and the atrocities of the leaders of the Soviet Union, both Lenin at first and Joseph Stalin later, in the 1930s. Not to mention the time prior to the World War II, which saw Adolf Hitler come to power in a Western democratic nation, heavily controlled by mainstream media propaganda. The people were silenced by the strict ideology of National Socialist consensus that engulfed Germany at the time.

Burke's almost prophetic analysis of the future of democracies, makes him a refreshingly different voice to this day. In many ways, he was against international militarism and definitely against a ruthless colonialism, and advocated for the respect of national sovereignty - refreshing thoughts today.

Bromwich points out that Burke was heavily engaged in criticizing the British Empire and especially the East Indian Company, which he felt misused its economic power and subdued Indians in a way that never would have been accepted if it was done to Englishmen. He was one of the very first, if not the first, to discuss international justice at length, and the need for Britain to keep its responsibilities towards the citizens of India, which it had colonized. Today, the anti-war movement is largely identified as Leftist, yet Burke demonstrated a clear-cut conservative voice who fought for international justice. He discussed freedom in terms of national sovereignty and the need for respect for differences and respect for those one governs.

One of the lessons of the French Revolution was that the revolt of the people occurred because contemporary political elites lost the ability to solve the problems of the people adequately. If authorities are all about elitist camaraderie in a Capitalist structure that only makes the few rich, "democracy" more resembles a dictatorship. Alternatively, rather, an oligarchy where the people are ruled by the interests of the very few.

The nineteenth-century philosopher, Alexis de Tocqueville deeply admired Edmund Burke. He also expresses in *Democracy in America* deep concern for the evolution of modern democracy, stating that democracy could easily become a tyranny of the mob characterized by extreme peer pressure – an *ochlocracy*, as the Greeks called it – an extreme egalitarianism, breeding political forces that gradually transform society in a totalitarian way. In essence, a return to a system that is strikingly similar to the balance of power prior to the French Revolution. He foresaw the rise of the welfare state, where a state rule promises to ensure the economic rights of citizens but demands a rigid obedience and conformity to the opinions of the prevailing political elites.

The rise of totalitarianism in democratic states has worried Europe's intellectuals for a long time. The initial hope of secularism was, in the 1600s, as we shall see, to end religious leaders' misuse of power by instituting the separation of church and state. Secular leaders endeavored to ensure that Europe would avoid more dreadful wars in the name of God. However, no century in history has produced as many genocides and as much humanitarian horror as the twentieth century – often labeled as "the atheist century."

Under the banner of different forms of Marxist ideologies such as Socialism, Nazism or Communism, Vladimir Lenin, Josef Stalin, Adolf Hitler, Pol Pot and Mao Zedong ruthlessly annihilated "unwanted groups." In *What's So Great About Christianity*, author and analyst Dinesh D'Souza point out that during the Middle Ages, inquisitions, witch-burning, and persecutions killed about 200,000 people in total, over a time span of several centuries. Compared to the millions and millions killed by atheist rulers in the 20th Century, this remains a small number.

In the ancient Greek democracies, political leaders had to be responsible for their decisions and resign from office if they did not solve the nation's challenges in a satisfactory manner. Corrupt and incompetent leaders were exiled, some executed. When they entered into office, they knew this could be the outfall if they did not perform. Yet today, we stand far from the early ideals of Greek democracy and far from the values of Edmund Burke.

## The Road to Serfdom

The problem with growing government control in democracies has been addressed by many. In 1944 Friedrich August von Hayek, one of the 1900s most influential economists, wrote a book entitled *The Road to Serfdom*. Its main aim was an outline of the opposition to growing government authority with a firm belief in the need to uphold the individual rights to personal freedom of choice. The book aroused enormous interest.

In short, Hayek argued that Socialism and social democracy eventually would lead to a totalitarian custodial state that chokes freedom of citizens. Where the Socialist government systems develop, elites also seize power and develop an increasingly centralized authority. Hayek lived during the rise of National Socialism in Germany. He watched its grip on the people, its stern propaganda, the culture of fear and consensus, the desire to quench intellectual dissidents.

The collapse of the Soviet Union and its aftermath has somehow pushed for the current Russian resurge towards traditional roots, and cultural strength marks an ideological shift in the nation's current political leadership. Pictures of Russian President Vladimir Putin in churches, attending mass, traveling to Mount Athos in Greece as the spiritual center of the Orthodox Church, illustrate the Russian political push towards a reimplementation of traditional, historical values. The Western 1960s social movement has pushed Western culture in the opposite direction, as we have launched a culture war against Christianity and European historical traditions, to cite Pat Buchanan in *Suicide of a Superpower. Will America survive to 2025?*

While the West seems to be turning to the stringent rule of "statism" and borderless relativism, Russia is becoming a traditionalist, religion-friendly, Capitalist society that remembers its history and honors its historic heroes. In some ironic twist of history, it seems that the West is embracing the kind of thinking that Russia now seeks to rid itself of.

Hayek's vital point is that the citizen's economic and personal freedom is a guarantee against what he calls Socialist forces transforming society towards totalitarianism, recalling how Nazi Socialist roots lie in an anti-Capitalist ideology. He cites Leon Trotsky who aptly pointed out that in a country where the sole employer is the state, resistance against the existing regime means starvation.

The old principle that he who does not work shall not eat is replaced by a new one: he who does not obey the state, shall not eat. It is very hard to be a free-thinking, critically-minded intellectual in such an environment. The minute the scholar writes an article that "the state bureaucracy" doesn't like, he is called to the dean's office and questioned. How is he to further his career in the university systems if he is "disobedient" towards the politically correct ideal? The next time he applies for funds for research, somehow his application is rejected. To many this is painstakingly familiar, having slowly realized that the aim of academics today is mainly to write articles that uphold and maintain the current paradigm.

The same is happening to an increasing number of journalists, when writing an article about, for example, foreign affairs from another angle than the politically correct mainstream dictate. He will face criticism, be called in to defend himself, and easily find himself without a job. Journalists are fully aware of this phenomenon; they are to write within the framework dictated by the establishment. The control is not even subtle.

It is very easy to limit the freedom of thinking in Western democracies. Freedom of speech has become the citizen's right to concur with the arguments of the establishment. As we see, the Marxist goal to remove the power-hungry bourgeoisie elite led only to the emergence of a new, neo-Marxist ruling upper class who in many ways departed from their initial goal of supporting the working classes, fight for international justice and solidarity. It seems to be evident that power corrupts, regardless of class, gender or religious affiliations.

*** 

# Modern Conservatism and Lack of Freedom

Today, little is seen of true conservatism in the West. The respect for sovereign nations that characterized founding conservatives like Edmund Burke stand far from the sentiments within, for example, the US Republican Party. Or in the words of Roger Stone – political strategist and former advisor to presidents such as Nixon and Reagan – in a 2016 interview about his book *The Clintons' War on Women* in the TV show *Sophie and Co*: "The Republican and the Democratic party in this country have become one party. It is the Endless War party, the party of the erosion of our civil liberties. It is the Big Debt and Big Borrowing party. It is the party of high taxes; it's the party of Wall Street, both parties are infected with Wall Street money."

In *Liberty and Tyranny*, bestselling American author Mark Levin offers quite a brilliant understanding of what modern conservatism should be. The task of the government, he states, is not to make decisions for people, but to facilitate a society with as much individual freedom as possible, while still safeguarding collective interests. This implies that each person should be made aware that he or she has a duty and a moral responsibility to do their best to better society. To be conservative is to fight for the rights of the individual to make his own choices and not be choked by a custodial state. Levin describes conservatives as people who value tradition and want to preserve the originally constructive, cultural ideals.

Discussions on how to limit the abuse of power in democratic societies are addressed by early philosophers such as Charles Montesquieu (1689–1755). He spoke of the need for the separation of powers between the legislative, the executive and the judicial branches of government, thus limiting the elites' possibility of corruption and abuse. If too much power is in the hands of the very few who disregard the Constitution, a democracy may easily slip into totalitarianism. In order for a democracy to function properly, the courts must be free; there must be a free press, an independent private sector, an independent parliament where various perspectives are respected, and temporarily elected governments whose power is limited.

The ideal is not conformity, but a pluralistic society where individuals are allowed to explore their talent and succeed, to the betterment of society, states Levin.

# CHAPTER 3

# Nietzsche is dead

*There is a grim, ongoing culture war between mainly two forces. Western culture is torn between those who think that it is rational to keep traditional and historical values and those who think that the only sensible thing is to alter society in an increasingly anti-Christian, extreme liberal direction.*

## Secularism and the Misuse of Power

THE WARS OF RELIGION in sixteenth-century Europe were an important reason for the development of the ideal of a secular society. Religion was to be excluded from the public and relegated to the private sphere. It was an understandable reaction. People were tired of political and religious leaders whose geopolitical agendas, again and again, led to war on the continent. Protestants fought Catholics who fought sectarian groups and the whole of Europe suffered.

Many Church leaders seemed to use the opportunity to secure their own privileges, rather than tending to the welfare of the largely Christian European population. It was in this stage that the Peace of Westphalia was implemented in 1648, which laid out treaties for respect of national sovereignty and each country's right to determine which cultural, religious and national values it would pursue. This did not end all wars, but still created a foundation for the modern concept of respect for national sovereignty and international law that forms the theoretical basis of, for example, the United Nations.

One of the driving forces behind secularism and allowing religion to be a private matter which would not interfere with the state was that Europe finally would be rid of the conflicts between Protestants, Anglicans, Catholics, Quakers, Puritans and other groups. With the original concept of secularism, religious freedom for all was implemented. The secularism practiced respected religious freedom and in fact ensured it. The point being that a secular state would protect different religious group's right to coexist, without one dominating the other.

The attempt was to ignite a positive secular system, an effort to bring respect *for* religious differences. The idea was that different religious or non-religious groups were to tolerate each other, allowing differences to coexist. However, the point was *not* to use "secularism" to persecute believers and ridicule religious faith but to end persecution by implementing secularism as the protector against persecution.

New secular worldviews eventually came to the forefront among European intellectuals, views that attempted to provide meaning to life in the metaphysical and philosophical cultural vacuum left by Christianity: liberalism, Marxism, Darwinism, and nihilism among them. Many of which were pursued with just as much "religious" zeal as any traditional religion before them.

During the 1800s, a widespread optimism on behalf of the scientific and technological progress of modern society was predominant. The flaws inherent in scientific materialism and the belief in the human ability to solely act with reason went unrecognized. European culture became disconnected from its historically moral and religious anchor, without implementing a sufficient substituting moral codex.

The quest for relegating Christianity out of the public sphere overlooked vital points that today are at the forefront of the debate: Removing religious ethics from the centerfold of society ended up, to many secularists' surprise, to weaken vital ethical principles in society. This gradually became evident in the 1970s onward. Intellectuals in the Western hemisphere did not realize that by removing the focus on Christian philosophy from public awareness, as the elites increasingly grew hostile to religion as a whole, the founding ethics of solidarity were no longer preached to the same degree as before. It was not fashionable anymore to speak about the ten commandments as vital ideals to maintain stability, order, and empathy in society. Today, many scholars assert that secularism simply has not been able to motivate individuals to care for one another sufficiently. To a large degree, egocentrism and materialism have become socially acceptable, while solidarity, selfishness, humility, and spirituality lost ground.

As we have seen, the original understanding of the word secularism has been used as a tool to redefine this concept to mean something completely different. Today secularism is often understood as a political strategy that seeks to outroot religion as a whole. To be "secular" now implies to be against religion, while in its original meaning it was an effort to bring respect for religious differences.

***

# Optimism on Behalf of the Modern World

European civilization was probably at its height in the very early 1900s, before the Great War and before Great Britain lost its economic and colonial empire. The economic growth was world leading, prosperity sifting down to a rapidly rising middle class. Optimism on behalf of Western economic achievements was booming.

The late 1800s was the European heyday of conquest, international trade, and colonialism. At the time, modernism represented the epitome of human development, the survival of the fittest society – the best the world had ever seen. Western secular society scored highest on the scale of development, and the urbanization process caused people to move *en masse* from the countryside into the cities. Industrialization gave new hope; the middle class grew all over Europe. Market Capitalism – the economic system in which capital and property are privately owned, and prices for goods and services are set by forces of supply and demand in the market, making the art of competition and hard work essential – gave ordinary people a possibility of unprecedented economic growth.

Between 1870 and 1950, economic revolutions helped improve the Western standard of living immensely, providing electric light, household appliances, cars, radios. Many moved to North and South America and other colonies and found a new life based on better conditions.

The British Empire was world dominating. This was the Golden Age of Imperialism. Darwin's biological theories inspired a strong Social Darwinism within the humanities and cultural studies. From the late 1800s onward, as we have seen, the dominant understanding increasingly viewed history in light of Social Darwinism. This theory became the dominant social paradigm, as the British Empire ruled the world. The broad assumption was that the Western civilization would always remain at the "top of the ladder" of civilization. The progressive mindset tends to assume that reforming society always represents an improvement. Social Darwinists at that time also believed that the world continually moves in the direction of progress. History is viewed as linear, pointing upwards – not circular and thus implying that history repeats itself, though in different time spans and ages.

Modern secular society, therefore, stands, according to this worldview, higher in the hierarchy of development than traditional collectivist societies. Western European democracies were seen to be at its highest level of development, and African, South American and Asian people as the most underdeveloped.

Today we readily profess that the paradigm of Social Darwinism is well behind us, but truth be told, it still fuels our view of history just as it did one hundred years ago. It dominates the progressive universalist view that all cultures should embrace the "liberal Western democracy," an ideological view that implies a stern lack of respect for national sovereignty of other nations and their right to govern their own regions.

When describing the process that led to the growing anti-Christian sentiments among Western intellectuals in the 1900s, it is easy to overlook the contributions done, for example, by the British Empire, of which the United States of America of today is a continuing part. In regions such as Asia, Africa, Australia and the Americas, the British trade influence ended up forming protectorates and colonies, brought infrastructure, well-functioning British institutions, schools and universities as well as hospitals and trade. It is probably not possible to underestimate the value of the development that the British brought to continents such like Africa.

The industrial revolution and technological progress had brought immense optimism coupled with a strong belief in secularism. At one point, Westerners controlled almost three-fifths of the surface of the earth, and accounted for three-quarters of global economic output, as stated by historian Niall Ferguson in *The Great Degeneration: How Institutions Decay and Economies Die*. This was the height of Social Darwinism – defined as the application of biological Darwinian evolution to social fields, which came to the conclusion that the European civilization marked the evolutionary high point in history – Europe's growing might and prosperity led to an intense Western emphasis on materialism.

A hostile attitude towards religion lay buried within this frame: the more modern man becomes, the less faith in God he will have. He will gradually understand that the concept of God and a supernatural world above us are relics of old superstitions. The German philosopher Georg Wilhelm F. Hegel supported this view. He saw religion and the history of the spiritual as a continuous development towards illumination. To Hegel, philosophy was the highest form of thought that would eventually surpass the role of religion.

With optimism regarding the human mind, religion tended to be increasingly deemed something that belonged to the "lower cultures" and primitive peoples who had yet to enter the "Age of Western Enlightenment" and its scientific revolution. Western societies were widely regarded as "developed" or "advanced," while other societies or cultures were viewed as "backward" and "unintelligent." With the new, secular society implemented came a growing consciousness of the division between believers and non-believers. Although the idea of secular governance did not originally imply a society that marginalized believers, but rather one that empowered all citizens, "secularism" now increasingly became an anti-Christian movement.

During the 1800s, a deeper divide between believers and agnostics/atheists had already become imminent. The latter position was considered the more prominent stance among the political and intellectual elites, yet the European people remained essentially deeply religious. This is puzzling. Even today, after a century of an extremely aggressive atheism, which often frankly ends up bullying and belittling Christians, Muslims, and other religions, surveys still show that approximately 72% of the European population still call themselves Christians, as stated earlier. There seems to be a deep divide between the ideological, anti-religious elites and the people.

Increasingly anti-religious thinkers became the new atheist clergy who preached about reason, freedom, and tolerance, implying that these values were opposed to traditional religion. They spoke of a universalist view of human history, which was thought to evolve into an inevitable world triumph of Western principles and institutions. The popular sentiment among the elites was that man needed no God, and if he had to believe in something, he should at least not speak about it publicly.

By the early 1900s, the intolerant version of "secularism only" came to dominate nearly all branches of science. Religion and its traditions were by now unpopular among the intellectuals – increasingly politically incorrect, forming the atheist notion that rational, intelligent and modern people did not believe in a God and the spiritual dimension.

At its metaphysical core, this also implied a major revolt against the idea that God is the Creator of all things, residing high above man and will one day judge him. It implies a fundamental opposition against the concept of the Eternal Eye. Consequently, if God is no more, man needs no morality. At least, he needs not to fear the judgment that religion states lie ahead. If he needs morality, it is only to the degree it helps him get a better life than he otherwise would. He exists for himself and for his own benefit only. He needs to concern himself with the afterlife no more, as "nothingness" awaits him there.

Atheism attempts to remove man of the burden of what he must face after death, allowing man to do as he pleases without fear of the consequences of his actions. Omitting God from the equation of life relieves man of the eternal obligation towards his fellow man and the spiritual "burden of solidarity." The moral implications are evident. In such a system, man is obliged to do good to no one, but himself. There is no God Almighty, a Creator to whom one must be thankful for the gift of life. Humility and respect for the divine disappear. In short, man took the place of God in the new, Western ideal of morality as the West headed towards its new destiny.

* * *

## God Is Dead

The philosopher Friedrich Nietzsche was among those who pursued the progressive Darwinian world-view that fought for a world without traditional, European values and pushed towards radical change in the Western social fabric. He defined his worldview in books such as *Thus spoke Zarathustra* and *Beyond Good and Evil*. Nietzsche's theories about the übermensch - the super human -[8] was one of the concepts in his thinking that later became important to National Socialism and its elitism as it found its form under the leadership of Adolf Hitler.

He proudly declared that the human condition was meaningless, in stark contrast to the Christian message that "God so loved the world that he gave his only begotten Son." Nietzsche questioned of the rationale of the Christian faith, embedded in the notion that man may do well on his own, freed from the chains of a religiously motivated morality. The world was an existentially empty vacuum where each individual was left alone, to Nietzsche – who, by the way, ended his life in an insane asylum. Cosmos was deemed to be empty, with no spiritual forces, unable to help anyone on earth with anything. Nietzsche confidently proclaimed that "God is dead" – as if an Eternal Creator would "die" just because some mortal

---

[8] Nietzsche's idea of an overman and life from his point of view (Wednesday, August 16, 2017) https://ccrma.stanford.edu/~pj97/Nietzsche.htm

philosopher said so. In Nietzsche's view, no God was watching from above, only empty space.

The whole concept of the Creator that will hold us accountable for our own actions, was not only ridiculed by Nietzsche, but also by the earlier Karl Marx, who stated that religion is the sign of the oppressed creature, the heart of a heartless world, just as it is the spirit of a spiritless situation. Religion was, to Marx, the opium of the people and he thought up a remedy: Communism. The French existentialist, Jean-Paul Sartre later followed the same thought process.

Nietzsche maintained that religion developed a slavish mentality whereby people performed rituals only to keep in good graces with gods and other supernatural powers. His conclusion was that people would only become mature and independent in "the scientific stage" when the reference to one's "conscience" dissipated. He sought to free himself from that which he labeled the constraints of the conscience; and hailed a nihilistic way of life, which advocates a hedonistic morality that offers no constraints on the individual.

Men like Nietzsche vehemently proposed the ultimate revolt against religion and its morality. This became a force that pushed society in the direction of what we see today, a modern permissiveness, extreme liberalism and its remarkable disdain of boundaries. It took a strong stance for the legitimization of selfishness and promiscuity which now engulf Western culture.

The revolt against God was given a seductive, philosophic veneer and justification. Sigmund Freud called religion an illusion. In *The Future of an Illusion*, Freud described spiritual belief as an infantile, subservient safety net from which people should liberate themselves.

Evil may be defined as morally wrong acts that cause harm, injury, pain, and destruction to others. When examined closely, evil is closely interlinked to selfishness as a characteristic of humans who only care about their own well-being, and disregard their action's harmful and destructive effects on others. Being immoral thus implies acting without consideration of the social effects of one's actions has on others. Legitimizing evil becomes a serious business. It is but natural that the first step in order to go "beyond good and evil" is to get rid of the conscience.

We often state that hatred is the negation of love, but the true enemy of love is ultimate selfishness, the quality in egoistic men who only care about their own pleasure. In this environment, all kinds of evil breed: complacency, carelessness, murder, rape, theft of other people's property, adultery, envy, deceitful behavior, a lying tongue, selfishness, lack of humility and respect for one's fellow humans. It all stems from a lack of love.

The atheist–nihilist doctrine ended up shaping the new Western paradigm. The intellectual elites perceived Christians as reactionary parts of an undesirable, unfashionable past, an unenlightened part of history where Christian philosophy denied man his right to do as he pleased. Intellectuals smiled condescendingly at believers. To the increasing hedonist European elites, it was only a question of time before the Christian era ended in Europe. History was later to prove them wrong, as the 2000s became a century of major religious revivals – both within Christianity, Islam, and other religions. None of the hard-line atheists had thought this possible.

✽✽✽

## Depression on Behalf of the Modern World

Challenges associated with globalization and individualization have led to intense reactions against modernism from within the culture itself, as pointed out by Andrew Heywood in *Global Politics*. Communitarian theories have criticized the modern form of liberalism with its inherent tendency to legitimize selfish individualism and become anti-traditionalist. If the individual is seen as logically outside of the community, liberalism ends up legitimizing a selfish behavior that downgrades the importance of solidarity within a collective identity.

When the first wave of optimism on behalf of modernity subsided, many started to notice that secular society also presented dilemmas. Even in the early 1900s, before the Great War when the decline of the British Empire took hold, the sociologist Emile Durkheim worryingly declared that rapid social change caused considerable uncertainty as values increasingly became individualized. The eventual breakup of the collectivist family structure with its growing number of bachelors turning to the cities to find work, the lack of anchoring in old traditions and social regulations, left the individual vulnerable. Society was in a quick spiral of change. Modern man was now more or less alone, in a new structure that broke away from the tight family ties of the pre-modern, collectivistic era.

In *Suicide,* written in 1897, Durkheim investigated the reason for the higher number of suicides in predominantly Protestant states in Europe as opposed to Catholic countries further south. He pointed out that in countries where the ideal is to uphold respect for historical norms and values, solidarity correlated with low rates of suicide. In Protestant countries, where individualism and revolt against old rituals stood stronger, the trend was an increased number of suicides. In Catholic countries, that to a greater degree maintained traditions and traditional religious rituals, Durkheim observed the opposite. In these countries, far fewer experienced life as meaningless, which according to him was the main reason for its lower suicide rates. He found disturbing trends in societies where the traditional family structures and social frameworks fell apart. Durkheim's term *anomie* signifies a condition in which society provides little moral guidance to the individual, in a breakdown of social bonds between an individual and the community. This produces a fragmentation of social identity and a rejection of self-regulatory values.

Durkheim explains *anomie* as a state of derangement that arises from a mismatch between personal and community standards, as well as from the lack of a joint social ethic. The term attempts to describe the confusion of identity that typifies modern people, a sense of inner bloodlessness, striving to find his place in society, but without a clear social ethic he never really succeeds and never understands why. Durkheim's analysis of the social conditions for suicide attempted to measure the effects of individualization and the legitimization of egoism. Where solidarity was strong, Durkheim found lower suicide rates. Although many remain critical of parts of Durkheim's analysis, it is a study that attempts to analyze the consequences of breaking away from traditional social systems and disentangling the individual from the group.

# CHAPTER 4

# The Christian Root of Western Civilization

*The anti-traditionalist movement has distorted the view of European history to such a degree that many have forgotten its greatness and foundational values. Ideas that people now consider secular are deeply rooted in Christianity. For example, it was Christianity that introduced humanity the principle of equality and the value of a human being, regardless of class, gender, and race.*

## The Demonization of Our Christian Heritage

THE TERM "WESTERN VALUES" is often used when describing historical and secular ideals and cultural traditions that are perceived to be vital in defining the European civilization. The term "Western values" is broadly generalizing, and discriminatory towards the massive varieties within Western culture. Yet, it is still useful to describe the joint heritage of ethical values, spiritual beliefs, customs and practices as found in cultures connected historically to Europe, – as opposed to those found in the East, in Islamic countries and so on.

If you pay attention to the way the term is currently used, it is easy to assume that modern Western values were invented in the Enlightenment period - the 1600s – with its emphasis on secular civil rights. Many take for granted that these ideals are of a secular, "neutral" origin and do not stem from historical religious ideals, but rather grew out of the growing critical approach to Christianity. This is a highly flawed assumption.

Many also believe that the philosophers in the 1600s who studied scientific rationalism and reason automatically were non-believers, while the opposite is the case. Others mistakenly believe that the modern view of humanity was invented by secularists and atheists, while these Western values clearly are derived from the Judeo-Christian religion. The quest for rational debate and arguments has indeed been a primary philosophical question, ever since the beginning of Christianity and the early Christian thinkers and up through the Middle Ages.

The 1776 American Revolution and the 1789 French Revolution only revived ideals concerning the rights of the common man – ideals that had previously existed and been developed during the Christian Middle Ages. Most of the intellectuals in the so-called "Age of Enlightenment" – the philosophical trend in the 1600s that centered around reason as the source of authority – were devout Christians. They examined scientifically the great works of God in nature and were not hostile towards religion as modern day historians have portrayed them to be.

In order to see how the cultural aspects of a religion can become embedded into the social fabric of a civilization, one need only look to Christianity and the influence it continues to exhibit even on the secular West, including on those who most disavow it. Middle East expert and author Raymond Ibrahim points out that tolerance, human rights, a desire for peace, and being "kind to everyone," all concepts championed by today's liberals did not develop in a civilizational vacuum, but rather from the singular teachings of Jesus of Nazareth. Over the course of some two thousand years, these have had a profound influence on Western epistemology, society, and culture, to the point that they are now simply taken for granted. Jesus, who was Jewish, continued much of the same teaching that is to be found in Judaism, its Ten Commandments, the Torah and other important writings that have ended up greatly shaping Western civilization.

Let me take a few examples. Early Christian philosophers such as St Justin, who lived in the first century AD, strongly emphasized the rationality of creation, its reasonability, arguing that every human is a rational being and that God himself works precisely through rationality. Each man carries within him a "seed" of the eternal, through which he may see parts of the eternal truths. This is why a Christian should be open to any rational argument, regardless of the speaker's creed, race or origin. Man is to be humble enough to perceive the light of God wherever it shows itself, as a rational choice in the search for truth and the best possible life.

St Augustine, who lived in the fourth century AD, clearly states in *Contra Academicos* that reason is a founding principle within the Christian faith, as faith and reason should not be separated or placed in opposition. He wrote that faith and reason are both forces that lead us to knowledge, both about the world, as well as about the reality behind perceivable matter.

Clement of Alexandria, who lived in the third century AD also pointed out that to gain knowledge from contemporary worldviews and philosophies, such as the Greek, was an important dialogue to have, in order to attain higher knowledge. Life is a journey through which we are to attain wisdom and a deep understanding of the world in which we live so that we end up bettering it.

So, for the development of science, monotheism was essential. Western science itself grew from the idea that the universe was rational and orderly constructed with natural laws, with a creative intelligence or a Creator behind it all. Melanie Phillips points in *The World Turned Upside Down* to the early, Christian thinkers such as Anselm of Canterbury and Thomas Aquinas who believed that since God created the world and gave man such a rational mind, the universe itself must be supremely rational.

It is remarkable to read the early thinkers, whose writings so greatly influenced European philosophy both during the Middle Ages and later, to see how focused they were on explaining how philosophy is God's rational tool, explaining why man will benefit from choosing morality and a life in respecting others. It is one of the founding principles of the Christian faith that rationality and its philosophy should be at the forefront defending the faith.

God has provided us with two books, the book of Nature and the Bible – to be truly educated one needs to study both, as argued by the English philosopher and statesman, Francis Bacon. Descartes searched for natural laws and felt that they had to exist because God is perfect. The German mathematician and astronomer, Johannes Kepler, was convinced that the goal of science itself was to discover the rational order which God had imposed on it.

Galileo Galilei stated that the laws of nature are written in the hand of God but in the language of mathematics. He was, as we know, hired by the Church to investigate the universe in order to gain more knowledge about God's creation. It was religion, not secular thought, that pushed for the view that nature is founded on a deep rationality which connects all the elements together and allows us to study these. Therefore, states Melanie Phillips, it is atheism that is innately hostile to reason.

The fourth century famous theologian and bishop, Augustine of Hippo or St Augustine, asserted that reason is indispensably linked to faith. The believer was, in his view, to purify his heart in order to receive the great light of reason. Medieval thinkers simply wanted to find out more about the wonderful world of reason, as God created it to be. Phillips also refers to the medieval Jewish thinker, Maimonides, who brilliantly wrote that conflicts between science and the Bible came about either from a lack of scientific knowledge or a lack of understanding of the Bible.

It seems that scholars have wished to change the memory of how religion impacted history and willfully omit certain historical facts, so that history may fit well into the politically correct, anti-religious ideologies of the present. This has been happening for a long time in the West, and strongly impacted our culture. One almost gets the feeling that all Christianity ever did was harm the European society, oppress the people, quench the hope of freedom, abuse women, harass men and turn the common man into a Church slave, as if Christian history only represents a long list of irrational arguments, superstitions, and atrocities against the innocent.

For example, Jürgen Habermas cites in *The Dialectics of Secularization: On Reason and Religion* that Christian theology in the Middle Ages and Spanish scholasticism as the origins of what we today call human rights. Who knows this today? That Catholic Christian monks and priests were the ones who laid the foundation of human rights in the Middle Ages? All we seem to hear about the Middle Ages is that it was dark, gloomy, full of the Church injustice, horrible popes, and witch-burning priests.

In truth, the Middle Ages was one of the most advanced periods in European history. There was exploding development all over the continent which lay the foundation for the Renaissance and the Age of Enlightenment with its focus on rationality, science and technological improvement. In the 1600s, philosophers and rationalists continued building on the same Judeo-Christian ideals that the learned monks and scholars in European monasteries earlier had reflected on. A religious set of ethics were grounded in the heart of European philosophy, that at the height of its golden age fostered Capitalism mixed with the Protestant Ethic that brought growth and prosperity to the whole Western civilization. European culture has undeniably strong ethical roots in one specific religion: Christianity. To say otherwise is to deny history.

From this perspective, it may be argued that there is an irrational element in modern secular society when it insists on keeping religion outside the public sphere. It rather displays the intense desire from an extreme-secularist and atheist thinking of crushing the role of religion and quelling traditional ethics altogether. It deliberately uses a twisted definition of secularism – implying that secularism means the implementation of an anti-religious system, and uses this system in order to impose repressive, intolerant ideologies.

The underlying idea, of course, being that religion is irrational and incompatible with "secular, modern society", – thus the need to remove this old-fashioned superstition from intellectual debate. Ironically, as stated, it was Christian thought that initially brought the quest for rational explanations of faith as a vital part of understanding the world. As God is rational, man's ability to be rational was an important point to the early Christian thinkers.

***

## The Triple Cradle of Secular Values

Generally, the threefold origin of Western values is found in the Greek, Roman and Judeo-Christian heritage. The main Greek contribution was the understanding of democracy, concepts on political freedom and a marketplace culture of debate where citizens and philosophers discussed public matters, not to forget art and architecture. The Roman contribution includes excellent organizational skills in administration, government, and law that greatly influenced the West; and lastly, the Judeo-Christian contribution to humanist thought was vital – human rights, tolerance and the concept of equality. Its spiritualism and religious world-view also fuelled European thought ever since its early beginnings.

It is unquestionable that the ancient Greek philosophers and religious men provided ground breaking philosophical analysis and thinking. In the Eastern Orthodox Church, Plato and Aristotle are regarded as early prophets who spoke spiritual truth to their generations. Greek philosophy brought, apart from its richly advanced moral philosophy and cognitive thinking, the idea of government by the people. However, Greek democracy differed substantially from modern democracy. Only adult male citizens had the right to vote, not women, foreigners or slaves. They had a high education and participated actively in public debates. In around 400 BC, the city-state of Athens suffered from political instability. The search for justice and better governance led to the development of the Greek ancient form of democracy. The purpose of common education for Greek citizens was to supply the state with a source of skilled political leaders. Through the formation of good habits and knowledge-based insight, education and the search for wisdom was thought to provide the means for men to govern the Greek city states in the best possible way.

It is apparent that the philosophers such as Plato and Aristotle were both critical of democracy and only supported a democracy for selected male citizens. They feared that democracy easily could turn into the rule of the mob. The Athenian structure thus had the form of a state based on an oligarchic, democratic government, in which state officials, the military, and philosophers comprised the leading political elite in society. Yet, slavery remained an institution in Athenian society. Women and children had second-class status.

The Roman contribution to what we today understand as Western values consist mainly of the development of a highly disciplined administrative system, Roman law, and the concept of the dutiful citizen, is best exemplified by the Stoic emperor Marcus Aurelius. Roman law worked on the basis that no human custom is necessarily right, but that there is a universal law, that will be acceptable to all men since its standard rises from human nature and reason, Robert R. Palmer and Joel Colton points out in *A history of the Modern World*.

Through an authoritarian administration emphasizing military control, the Romans continued the Greek elitist definition of what it meant to be a "citizen." The organization of the state reached its zenith under Roman law, and the military system was equally effective. Even though philosophers like Cicero and Seneca made contributions to the concept of humanism, in reality, the Roman Empire was negligibly concerned with individual rights and personal freedom.

\*\*\*

# Judeo-Christian Ethics – Decisive for Human Rights, Equality and Levelling Class Differences

The radical Hebrew–Christian contribution to the concept of Western values differed from both the Greek and Roman ideals in several important areas. Professor at Yale and Harvard, historian Robert R. Palmer and Joel Colton state in *A History of the Modern World*, one of the most highly praised history texts ever and adopted in more than a thousand schools, that Christian philosophy was revolutionary in that its definition of humanity was inclusive of all people, an altogether new sense of human life.

While the Greeks demonstrated the excellence of the mind, the Christians explored the soul and taught that in the eyes of God all souls were equal. They taught that human life was sacred and inviolate, and spoke of worldly greatness and beauty as subordinate values. While the Greeks contemplated much on the beautiful and thought ugliness to be bad, the Christians saw spiritual beauty in even the most unpleasant exterior and sought out the diseased and those in need. Even suffering itself, states Palmer, was proclaimed as in a way divine, since God himself had suffered on the Cross. Christians worked to relieve suffering as none before them, protested against the massacre of prisoners of war, against slavery, against gladiators who killed each other and so on. They taught humility and that all men were brothers.[9]

Palmer says that it simply is impossible to exaggerate the importance of Christianity's influence on the development of Western values. It was Christianity that introduced the principle of equality, which unleashed the revolutionary idea that each man, regardless of class, gender, and race, has a unique value. Despite the fact that this viewpoint would later be seen as a secular idea and one of the cornerstones of secular society, there is no doubt about its religious origins.

Christianity came into existence, marked by revolution, and developed among the lower classes of society, with a radically new view of the poor and the lower classes. This is symbolically well illustrated by Christ being born in a manger. He lived among the poor, spent his childhood in Nazareth – which was a despised small town, disliked by the Jewish elite. The radical Jesus, went starkly against the political and religious elite associating himself freely with the feeble, the sick and even broke the Jewish customs regarding how to engage with women.

This new view of humanity was based on an unprecedented principle of equality that recognized the value of women, children, and slaves in a way that contrasted sharply with the Greek-Roman definition of a citizen. This may be said to be the ultimate cradle of the Western women's liberation movement, a freedom that the later Church was sometimes to fight even if its founder, Christ, strongly embraced it.

*Ennemis Publics*, co-authored by the French-Jewish philosopher Bernard-Henri Levy and French atheist Michel Houellebecq paints a lively, visionary picture of the cradle of human rights. The authors proclaim that they are convinced that we would never have had human rights without the originally Jewish and later Christian hypothesis, the incredibly bold idea about a blessed creation formed in the likeness of God, and therefore also sanctified.

Hugh Cunningham, professor of social history at the University of Kent, remarks that Roman brutality, for example concerning child slavery

---

[9] R. R. Palmer; Joel Colton; Lloyd Kramer, *A History of the Modern World* 9th Edition (New York, NY: McGraw-Hill Humanities, 2001)

and abuse, did not cease until the early Christian movement gained ground in the Roman Empire. He discusses this in *Children and Childhood in Western Society since 1500*. Emphasis on the family as an arena for care and nurturing was reinforced. The status of children improved.

In the early 400s, the Roman empire was in decay – at this stage rampant with hedonism and lack of justice, reeking with disorganized and greedy emperors – it was on the verge of collapse as a regional superpower. The first Christian Emperor, Constantine, then moved the capital to Constantinople in today's Turkey. Here the East Roman Empire continued to build on a strong focus on Christian values and spirituality for another thousand years.

From Constantinople, the Orthodox Church grew and is to this day the main denomination the Christian Middle East. It is highly likely that the Roman Empire would not have survived in its Eastern parts had it not been for its strong links to Christianity, reinforcing morality, philosophy, and order within its borders.

Christian ethics became the source of human rights and one of history's most important contributors to the leveling of class differences. Socialism took several of its most famous values from the pool of Christian thought. Communism's idealized dignity of the worker, the willingness to fight for the rights of the common man and those with lower income not to be degraded by rich landowners, clearly reflect Christian attitudes. Respect for all, regardless of rank is a genuine Christian idea.

Even the origins of the Western belief in the individual, has religious roots, as noted by a professor at Oxford, Larry Siedentop in *Inventing the Individual*. It did not emerge in opposition to religion in the early modern era but is rather an offspring of the Church. The original idea of secularism itself is one of Christianity's gifts to the West, he asserts. Through St Paul's important philosophical work on the concept of equality and the unique value of each human being, Augustine reconfirmed the importance of man's independence as he searches for contact with the divine. He sought God on a personal level and found answers to his philosophical questions about the meaning of life. These were the ideas that were further developed during the Middle Ages and re-emerged as a trace within secularism itself.

Siedentop asks us to rethink the evolution of ideas that built Western civilization, and states that the belief in individual freedom, moral equality and a representative form of government were pioneered by Christian thinkers of the Middle Ages who drew on inspiration from the early Church.

The sociologist Peter Berger asserts that it was in Judaism and ancient Israel that the radical new ideas of how humans best should conduct themselves appeared, and later influenced both Christianity and the Western world on a massive scale. Here we find God as a Creator outside the cosmos, yet acting within history and giving, out of his concern for humans, ethical commandments to guide them through the hardships of life. Individualism itself is born here, the thought that man is a unique individual who is responsible for his own actions, providing a religious framework for individual dignity and freedom of action.

Melanie Phillips points out in *The World Turned Upside Down* that both Berger, Hegel and Max Weber saw Judaism as the main victory of rationality and secularization over paganism. Secularization is a complicated term, as we shall see that generally refers to the early academic assumption that the more modernized society becomes, the fewer people believe in God and a spiritual world.

Traditionally, biblical history and religious scientists searched to understand the cosmos, in order to comprehend its complexity rationally. They incorporated moral philosophy, theology, history, astronomy, astrology, politics and a range of disciplines in order to search for the order of God in the universe. It becomes quite clear that the myth of the objectivity of secularism and the neutrality of its values simply is seriously flawed.

# CHAPTER 5

# What Is Religion?

*Religion teaches that man needs to understand what is the right thing to do. He needs to stop his "inner devils" and choose to better himself and become more thoughtful of others. He should abstain from selfishness. Thus, the need to cultivate inner values that will lead him in the right direction, towards a life where he may have much to give to others.*

## Definitions of Religion

Let us take a step aside and examine the definitions of religion. Scientific definitions of religion arose with the development of disciplines such as anthropology, sociology, and psychology in the 1800s. This was at a time when Western researchers began traveling the globe, studying foreign societies and their structures. Some have viewed religion as a revelation from God; by others as a common human experience, a primitive misunderstanding; or as a human construction of a social or psychological nature. There are many interpretations. Religion may be said to deal with gods and powers, it is not just a clerical phenomenon, but an integrated part of people's everyday life. Religion also deals with the distribution of power in society.

Functional definitions of religion examine how religion functions in society and how religious belonging affects people culturally, socially, and psychologically. Sociologist Emile Durkheim studied religion according to this approach. He attempted to prove that religion is a social phenomenon and part of man's survival techniques. How religion functions in society were, therefore, more important to him than its spiritual origin.

These explanation models were popular when evolutionist anthropologists investigated animistic cultures in Asia and Africa, in the early 1900s. They found that elements in nature such as animals, stones, and trees, were considered to be deities with spiritual powers. Upon returning to Europe, academic discussions focused on the exotic customs of "savages," professors and researchers were fascinated by the perspectives and tried to understand the social role of religion in foreign societies.

The social meaning of religion, its function in the community and individual worship became increasingly popular. It was felt that to understand the origin of religious ideas was important in order to understand man, society and cultural developments better. Researchers studied it from a distance, focusing at large on the role religion played in people's lives, examining how it influenced what they ate, how they intermingled, married, how they spoke to each other, how they handled gender differences, myths, and taboos, as well as many other issues.

Sociologist Max Weber claimed that the need to find the meaning of existence addresses the question of what it means to be human. To Weber, the world's great religions are bearers of explanative models that corroborate the significance of human life. To see life in a larger context, entailing a deeper understanding of existence after death, becomes religion's forte. Religion may offer a deeper and fundamental meaning that also brings new depth and perspectives to regular day-to-day happenings.

A more traditional way to define religion can be summarized in the substantial model. Here, religion is characterized by its spiritual origin, its belief in supernatural creatures and transcendental influences on the human condition. Anthropologist Edward Burnett Tylor (1832–1917) defined religion as the belief in spiritual creatures. He maintained that religion begins when man becomes aware of his soul. This is what separates us from animals. Our ability to sense our soul thus becomes the origin of religion. He felt that religion was a philosophy that man had developed through his natural reflection on what it meant to be human and what it means to live in the world.

In his classic work, *The Sacred and the Profane,* the well-known historian of religions, Mircea Eliade attempted to understand the phenomenology implicated in the spiritual dimension. He assumed that every religious, historical document bears witness to a holy revelation, an emotional and spiritual encounter, for the writer involved. The holy was to him therefore dependent on man discovering it, in his own way. Eliade regarded religious faith as a complex and fundamental part of being human, an inevitable influence on every living soul. The consciousness of a notable spiritual presence, of something outside of the self that comes near, this all ties man to his spiritual soul and prompts a desire for a pure conscience.

The yearning for an existential inner peace is at the essence of religion. "The heart has come to stand for the center of the moral, spiritual and intellectual life of a man. It is the seed of a man's conscience and light," said Billy Graham in his Madison Square Garden Crusade in 1957. From the heart flows his life. The understanding of the essence of what it means to be religious and the plurality of driving forces that make us religious, contribute to an explanation of why faith has such a great influence in the lives of men, both in ancient times as well as today.

\*\*\*

# Materialism, Marxism, Socialism – Modern Religions

The German-American theologian and philosopher of religion, Paul Tillich has defined religion as "that which is man's true concern." Whatever is most important to man, thus becomes his religion, his passion, – his everything. Again, according to Eliade, religious faith is a fundamental part of being human, an inevitable influence on every living soul.

Whatever is most important in someone's life, whatever he desperately believes in and advocates for and cannot live without, may be labeled his religion. In the *Large Catechism*, Martin Luther summed it up by stating that whatever your heart clings to and confides in, is really your God. Or, in Christ's own words, for where your treasure is, your heart will also be.

Considering this definition, one may suggest that religion plays a role in everybody's life, whether they are aware of it or not. Even the nihilist is religious in this sense as he believes that there is nothing above and beyond us.

The German philosopher Martin Heidegger, one of the most influential thinkers of the twentieth-century, once said in a German TV interview: "I would say that men, for example, Communists, have a religion when they believe in modern science. They believe absolutely in modern science. And this is absolutely faith, that is, the trust in the certainty of the results of science, is a faith, and is, in a certain sense, something that emanates from people, and is therefore a religion. And I would say no one is without religion, and every person transcends himself, in a way, that is they are dispatched."

# The Culture War

In the old classic, *Thought and Belief*, the Danish sociologist of religion, Rudolph Arendt adds a twist by defining religion as man's ultimate goal. Man's religion is his all-absorbing attitude towards existence, the foundation upon which he rests his life. According to his view, religion may be found in the transcendental realm, in traditional religions with the belief in God and the supernatural, or it may be found in the material or physical, profane world. Arendt emphasizes that according to such a broad definition of religion, there is no such thing as a non-religious man or a nonbeliever. We all strongly believe in something. That which you find to be the very most important thing in your life is your religion. Your encompassing, all absorbing beliefs and ideals, that which is at the core of your being, at the heart of your desires, the goal of your life.

By this substantial definition, almost any strong belief in something can be called a religion: materialism is the religion of people who put money above all else desirable. An extreme focus on diet and exercise may be the religion of people whose ultimate goal and most important concern in life is a beautiful body and good looks. Hedonism clearly may be defined as a religion – the search for bodily pleasure without moral constraints. Atheism, may in this sense be a person's religion, his all absorbing faith in that there is no God or spiritual beings, none above us to whom he will be held accountable. This forms his foundation and passionate ideology or worldview.

Man's religion becomes whatever is the most important element in his life. It could be materialism, money, atheism or a deep urge to prove that God does not exist; it may be a religion such as Shintoism or Zoroastrianism, or it may be the cult of worshipping Hollywood stars – which may be compared to the ancient worship of gods. Our modern world seems filled with "modern" myths and religious affiliations. The tendency is remarkably strong to search for a "religion," an idea to believe in, an ideological concept to trust – someone to worship. It seems to be a trait of what it means to be human.

In the music industry, we see the tendency of "worshipping" the relationship between man and woman, as "love" is hailed as the solution to almost everything, the end point, as if every problem in life meets its end the moment "girl meets boy." The search for eroticism and romantic love, defined in a Hollywood manner as the very goal in life, clearly has religious undertones.

If one defines religion this way, one may also consider soccer or football as a religion, for that matter. Students of religion have done their master's degree on such topics. Football has its rituals, its myths, and experiences of social cohesion in the tribunes, with grand outlets of emotion as the congregation, hails its heroes on the field.

It is puzzling to see how much both Marxism, Fascism, Socialism and other "-isms" contain strong, religious elements. These ideologies try to explain the existence of man and solve his problems with almost the same religious zeal as traditional religions, focusing on the belief that Man – not God – is at the heart of it all. It was Man who is to bring salvation to himself, Man who is the Saviour of the World.

In *The Law of Peoples,* philosopher John Rawls identifies Nazism as a National Socialist religion that perversely offered a type of salvation and liberation for its members. Ideologies and strong systems of belief such as Marxism, Communism, Capitalism, Liberalism, and Socialism thus may be viewed as religions. "Secular people" may definitely be defined as much more religious than they believe themselves to be.

*** 

# A New Religion and Its Effects: Secular Messianism

As the traditional belief in religion has been met with increasing skepticism among the elites, the media, and academia in the West, the development of a structural lack of moral strength has worried leading philosophers. The atheist Jürgen Habermas is part of this trend. At one point, he changed his view on the role of religion, stating that his previous assumption of its irrelevance in secular nations was wrong.

Habermas points out in *Europe: The Faltering Project* that modern moral philosophical and political theory pays a high price for excluding the very ethics that first provided explanatory strength to the moral form with the ability to motivate the individual to perform just actions. He reminds us that genuinely active traditions often remain hidden in culture. Only in bad times, when they are in danger of disappearing, does its real greatness become visible.

In *Christianity and the Crisis of Cultures*, Pope Benedict XVI seems to concur with the views of Habermas, stating that after years of emphasis on scientific and technological progress alone, European culture now suffers from a lack of emphasis on moral energy. This is the greatest threat to contemporary European culture. Without solidarity, individuals become destructive. Democracy itself depends on citizen solidarity in order to avoid becoming the tyranny of the mob. The whole culture has sunk into a state of apathy and lethargy.

# The Culture War

The Dutch psychiatrist, J. Van den Berg, points out that the modern culture of godlessness has oppressed an important part of being human: consciousness of God and recognition of the transcendental. The collective denial of essential aspects of being human weigh heavy on contemporary society. In *Handling on the faith in an age of disbelief*, he speaks about how few address the alarming level of psychological and psychiatric illnesses that infect contemporary anti-Christian society. Psychiatric suffering at epidemic levels, combined with serious drug abuse. Way too few attempts are made to limit divorce rates, abortion rates, even though we know the amounts of family tragedies, depression and abuse that spin out of these socially destructive trends.

The growing strength of spiritual Islam in the West is but a consequence of Western inability to keep its own structures together. Human beings tend to need a faith to hold on to. Since we are bent on disliking Christianity, many will turn to other religions in search of inner peace and healing. Islam will only grow the coming years; already the mosques are filled with praying believers all over Europe on Fridays.

The Nobel Peace Prize winner His Holiness the Dalai Lama highlights the fact that economic and technological progress is both desirable and necessary. It would be naïve to believe that we could solve the problems of the modern world if we stopped technological progress. He makes an important comment in *Daily Advice from the Heart* warning against the tendency to let it proceed without direction. Technological development must be followed by a development of moral values. It is our duty as humans to make certain that both these tasks are performed to similar degrees.

Dalai Lama calls this the key to our future. A society where material and spiritual development goes hand in hand is a society that bears a promise for the future.

The 1992 book by Francis Fukuyama, *The End of History and the Last Man* sums up precisely this gloriously self-proclaimed state of mind that so strongly captivated and consumed the self-assured West. The final proof of the omnipotence of the West was, to Fukuyama, marked by the end of the Cold War. All the enemies of progress had now been conquered. Western liberal democracy was claimed to be the best form of government the world had ever seen – or would ever see. Again, "we are at the top, all others beneath us." The West against the Rest.

Social Darwinism paired with the idea of scientific progress, opens society up for an ideology which Pope Benedict XVI calls "Secular Messianism." In *Values in a Time of Upheaval*, he points out that the modern, almost desperately zealous, political vision is to perform social change continually. The assumption is that revolution and its more subtle partner, reform, idealistically will lead to the goal of peace on earth. This way of thinking implies a belief in the inherent goodness of man, and that mankind will prove its ability to win the battle of history without the help of any God. Marxism advocates, as we know, for a view of humanity that considers man as innately good. If something goes wrong, it is society, and not the human, which is to be blamed. The state is to solve the problems, take care of the young, the old, give benefits to whoever may need it.

Religions like Taoism, Buddhism, Islam, and Christianity offer different answers to the same existential questions. Christianity states that man is forever divided between good and evil. Evil is the man who acts only in terms of his own selfish needs and pleasures, with no regard for the harmful and destructive effects his behavior has on others.

In that sense, it becomes an illusion to believe that the world will become an oasis of peace. Humanity remains divided between good and evil at the core of its being and needs spiritual fulfillment and a salvation that lies outside the cosmos in order to properly face the chaos of existence and provide justice and rule with wisdom.

# CHAPTER 6

# Spiritual Awakening

*In the West, many search for the meaning of life but fail to reach peace. The spiritual knowledge that once was embedded in our culture is no longer there. Many are denied even the most basic knowledge of spiritual wisdom. In the increasingly de-Christianized West, man is considered to only be a physical body, with no regard for his soul or spirit. A state of inner poverty is the sad result.*

## The Need for Philosophy, Religion, and Spiritualism

LET US TAKE A STEP aside and look at religion itself – defined as belief in God – and how the spiritual realm is connected to individuals and the material world. For centuries in the West, religiously-aware people have reflected on the meaning of life and how man's existence, both today and tomorrow, in life and in death, is inextricably tied to Almighty God and the spiritual world. He is the source of creation – science is his handmaid. The great Jehovah is the mastermind behind it all. This chapter attempts to explain the metaphysical truths of the Christian faith, from a believer's angle.

The Romans were the first to use the Latin word "religio," which derives from "re" meaning "again," and "lego" – signifying "go over again" or "consider carefully." The main focus of spiritual religion should in a way be precisely as the ancient Greek philosopher Socrates argued, that an unexamined life is no life for a human being to live. He humbly believed that each man has access to the truths of life, as they are deep within himself. The soul and the mind are chambers of hidden treasures. Man needs to open these inner rooms and bring forth the treasures that may help him achieve balance, wisdom, and virtues in life.

The early Christian thinkers and philosophers, such as St Justin, embraced Greek philosophy, stating in his *Second Apology* that whatever rightly said and done among all men should be studied by the Christian community, as it contained "seeds" of truth. He stated that as the Old Testament was inspired by God, so was Greek philosophy. Man should listen to both, and search for the "seed" of truth in the writings of spiritually-aware men and women.

St Augustine, who lived during the decaying years of the Roman empire, of which he spoke in *Confessions* and works such as *City of God*, stated that if Plato says that the wise man is the man who imitates, knows and loves his God, and that participation in this God brings man happiness, what need is there to examine the other philosophers? There are none, writes Augustine, who come nearer to Christianity than the Platonists.

Clement of Alexandria said that the ethical ideals of ancient Greek philosophy, liberation from the passions, precisely help man achieve his God-given goal by bettering himself and loving his fellow man, by refusing to attend to his evil carnal desires. In other words, as Pope Benedict XVI states in *Great Christian Thinkers*, "faith itself builds true philosophy," as we diligently work towards the goal of achieving perfection – in a sense the Christian "nirvana" and goal of the human life. Or as St Augustine writes in *City of God*, steadily referring to the need for "true religion" as opposed to "false religion" – the former always leading men to loving others and diligently working for the betterment of the fellowship of men. Augustine famously wrote that knowledge is valuable when charity informs it. Without charity, knowledge inflates: that is, it exalts man to an arrogance which is nothing but a kind of windy emptiness.

Clement of Alexandria points out that the rational purpose of life, the ultimate destination, is to become more similar to God, more knowledgeable and more filled with the love of God towards one's fellow man.

The deep-rooted essence of religion rests on the fact that man is created by, and profoundly dependent on God's benevolence to exist. It is God, outside time and space and the narrow scope of understanding the universe that has created man, it is He that establishes the premises for life. Man is to consider this carefully, as well as choose the right path and examine the way he lives to ensure that he may have a rewardingly fruitful life on earth, as well as reach a better place after death.

The idea is that God knows us far better than we know ourselves, and is able to guide us through the complicated landscapes of life in the best possible way, giving supernatural strength to withstand trials and tribulations. This is why man ought to listen to God's advice, as presented to him through the Holy Spirit in his inner man, through the body of religious texts that have withstood the test of time, as well as through spiritual priests and teachers whom he is led to consult.

Man needs to be humble, willing to learn, stretching his consciousness beyond the shortcomings of this world and reaching for God. The French philosopher, Jean-Jacques Rousseau famously stated that morality is our following of a voice of nature within us. This voice is often drowned out by passions or pride. Thus, the path to moral redemption becomes to turn back to the intimate moral contact with the heart.

This same view penetrates several of the world religions – the essence is to try to bring man closer to the spiritual realm where man will be able to find a deep sense of inner balance, satisfaction, and peace. The message is that the world is, whether we like it or not, governed by quite remarkably specific principles. It does not matter if you belong to Hinduism, Taoism, Islam, Christianity, or atheism – the latter may be defined as the religion of those who believe in the abilities of mankind, and that man is able to solve the problems in the world without help from any spiritual realm. These laws apply to everyone, whether they believe in them or not.

The nontheistic religion of Buddhism teaches, for example, about "the Four Noble Truths," namely that all things are temporary and unsatisfying, though still, we cling to them. Once we stop greedily craving the things of this world and follow the right inner path, we may end or lessen our suffering. The rise of cravings is the proximate cause of the rise of suffering. The point is that the right way of living will help end the suffering of life. This is a quite fascinating view which uniquely correlates to Christian teachings.

The ancient Greek philosopher, Epicurus' teachings take it for granted that humans strive for minimizing pain and maximizing pleasure. His goal seems to be to strive for the absence of pain and suffering in order to have a more pleasurable, tranquil life in peace with others, enjoying life in freedom from fear of the gods.

Epicurus warned extensively against overindulgence, for example, as he stated that it would lead to even more pain. Precisely the ability to choose to endure some pain in the now, by refraining from acting on that which seems pleasurable in the short run, yet in the long run will produce even more pain, precisely this helps you to make the right choice. In a sense, fear of failure becomes the helper that motivates you to act according to that which will benefit you in the long run. This choice will lead to even greater benefits. This, exactly, is the same goal of the religions, which also seek to advise man as to what is the best path in life with as little suffering as possible. At the time, Epicurus was accused of not fearing the gods, adhering to a nihilist worldview, but this implies twisting his teachings.

Buddhism also speaks at length about the poisons of the mind: envy, greed, sexual greed, gluttony, bias, hatred, arrogance and more. The point is that the life that is destroyed is your own when you allow these qualities to prosper. Likewise, Christianity warns of the effects of" - pride, greed, lust, envy, gluttony, wrath, and sloth found described in the book of Proverbs 6.[10] Haughty eyes that look down on others and think too highly of oneself, pride instead of humility, a lying tongue that makes a person impossible to trust, or hands that shed the blood of the innocent.

Billy Graham talks about pride quite harshly in his famous speech at the Madison Square Garden in 1957, saying that:

> More people stay out of the Kingdom of God because of pride than any other sin. You are too proud, you do not want to humble yourself, so you rebel. It is a humbling thing to come to the foot of the cross and repent of your sins and receive Christ, but no man shall enter the Kingdom of Heaven unless he comes. There must be a self-emptying, a self-crucifixion. Yet, we don't like to do it, because we are all egocentric, we don't like to humble ourselves, we don't like to say we are wrong, we don't like to confess that we are sinners, but God says you must do it before you can enter the Kingdom of Heaven.

Graham points out that:

> The only remedy that the Christian faith prescribes is to give one's life to Christ for him to place in it a new heart. He demands that you deny self, take up the cross, take up His unpopularity, take your place with him in suffering. In turn, he will make you a new man.

What is to be avoided is a heart that devises wicked schemes – a premeditated wish to hurt others, according to *Religion Facts*, an eagerness to do evil, quick to spread rumors and easily to react with rage and hysteria. The scriptures from Proverbs warns against being a false witness, someone who brings dissent among brothers, who speaks of rumors as if they were true. *The Christian Post* most interestingly describes this problem. Some say

---

[10] Duane A. Garrett, *Proverbs, Ecclesiastes, Song of Songs, vol. 14, The New American Commentary* (Nashville: Broadman & Holman Publishers, 1993), 97–98.

especially women are guilty of this. Out of the fear of confrontation, many do not speak about the issue at hand in honesty to the person it involves, but rather pretend that all is well and rather fuel hatred and suspicion by addressing the issue to others, behind their backs.

This destroys good relationships and creates an atmosphere of deceit and dishonesty. Proverbs 6 calls these actions elements that God abhors. They poison families, pour lies into a community, produce distrust, solidarity withers, it creates dissent and war mongering and makes people pull away from each other. These are the issues that destroy relationships with bitterness and rancor. It kills whatever was good in a community or family. Low self-esteem is one of the effects on the personality when a person knows that what he is doing is wrong. There is an inner feeling of guilt, and rightly so. This inner feeling – which may be called the conscience – guides him to stop before the envy grows even more, and the evil circle of bad words, deceitfulness, rumors, lying, lack of good self-esteem, lack of loyalty and flaring anger starts all over again. If he chooses another path and starts abstaining from evil, he will reap another fruit and consequently feel better about himself.

\*\*\*

# The Power of the Mind and the Will to Change

There are laws in the universe that we simply do not fully understand. Man is too frail to grasp the depth of existence. He cannot even see through a wall and what goes on in the next room. He is not able to grasp the grand scopes of reality that comprises the observable, let alone that which lurks in the darkness and moves in the spiritual world.

We also seem not to fully comprehend the power of the mind and the eternal weight of our own choices. If we did, we would have been much more careful to observe them and strive much harder to do that which is right – or produce the least pain in the long run. Yet, that takes self-discipline, hard work, and perseverance. The spiritual laws of cause and effect state that we will suffer from our own choices, and may only be relieved from this suffering if we do the right thing.

St Augustine said that the road to God is the passing through our own self-awareness. Or, in Charles Taylor's words, our moral salvation comes from recovering authentic moral contact with ourselves. The essence of religion is that, based on your own choices, you will consequently be rewarded or punished. You choose which plants to plant in your own garden, in the life you are in charge of. It is your responsibility to magnify your talents to the best of your abilities and for the benefit of human kind. In Judaism, this is a religious duty. Jews often say that God created the world, but it is imperfect for the time being. It is man's duty to help the Almighty to improve everything. Life should be spent doing just that.

It is self-evident. If you plant the seed from an apple, you will eventually have an apple tree. If you plant an olive, you will have an olive tree. If you plant wheat, you will *not* have a field of barley. At the heart of Christianity, are valid teachings that may help man choose the right seeds for his garden so that it bears an abundance of fruit. At the center of this is the love of God, who is the giver of power to overcome the destructive forces in the world.

You reap what you sow. You do not reap what others sow. They reap what they sow, in their own lives. In life, each man chooses how he approaches the world and its difficulties, how he handles injustice, scorn, hatred, love, lust, temptations to do evil towards others. He decides on the qualities that he wishes to pursue, those he hopes will bear good fruit in his life. It is in his hands to decide on infidelity and deceit or – on the opposite scale: face the problems by honoring honesty, loyalty and standing up for what is perseverance and compassion.

Hinduism speaks about self-restraint and generosity as important virtues. Taoism highlights the three treasures: compassion, moderation, and humility. The quality of humility is highly underrated in current-day Western society which to a saddening degree has taught man to rebel against the order of the spiritual world.

In one of famous Madison Square Garden Crusades, Billy Graham repeats the Christian verdict by saying that the heart is the seat of a man's conscience and light.

> The Bible says that the heart of man is full of evil imagination. It says that the heart is desperately wicked.[11]

---

[11] First, it should be noted that Graham is paraphrasing Jeremiah 17:9. Second, Scripture also tells us that fallen man and woman are mentally bent toward evil, viewed as acts that separate us from God and his Presence. (Gen. 6:5; 8:21, AT) Prior to acting in a way that God had prohibited, Adam and Eve were in perfect tune with the Almighty, and in perfect harmony with their inner person. There are three helps that enable the Christian to control their destructive, inner inclination. First, the Christian has the Holy Spirit inspired Word of God. (Deut. 17:19; Josh 1:7-8; Ps. 1:1-3; 2 Tim. 3:16-17; 2 Pet. 1:21) Second, the Christian has reliable Bible study tools [Note that there many unreliable study tools], meaning that they are accountable for getting a the accurate truth of God's Word. In addition, God has put spiritual leaders and wise shepherds in the Church whom the believer might consult and get spiritual advice from, through the teaching of the Scriptures. (Acts 20:28; Eph. 5:15-16; Heb. 10:24-25;

Even Jesus confirms this grim prospect and says that "people honour me with their lips, but their hearts are far from God." Therefore, the Christian message requires that man humble himself and seek repentance under God in order to better himself.

Graham further states that:

> Sin is rebellion against God. It's selfishness; I am going my own way, I don't want anyone telling me how to live. I don't want God dictating his terms to me, I will live my own life. And then, isn't it strange to see how some people who have troubles, burdens and difficulties, will try anything *but* God? You'll go to anybody else for advice, but God, the Creator himself?

"Make peace with yourself, and both heaven and earth will make peace with you," states one of the Eastern Orthodox Church saints, St Isaac the Syrian. Christianity teaches the individual to forgive oneself and to forgive one's enemies as a way to personal freedom. Some look at forgiveness as a weakness, that to forgive means to allow him or her to take the stronger position. The opposite is the case.

Bitterness is the true seed that poisons your life. Forgiveness frees you from the bondage of hatred. Letting go of bitterness sets you free from destructive attachments to others. Bitterness and strife are weeds that will hinder progress. When forgiving, you root out the weeds of hatred in your own garden. This is one of the rational elements in Christianity, the wisdom of letting go of hatred.

The idea is that since God is the avenger of all evil, He is the Eternal Judge who one day will call us forth in order for each one to be judged by his own actions. We are to leave the revenge to Him. The New Testament is clear on this subject. This is why man should forgive others as he also wishes to be forgiven by God. No one is a better and more just Avenger than God himself – justice is one of God's main qualities.

The dogmas of Christianity try, on a philosophical and spiritual level, to lead people to a better life by teaching man a set of spiritual and mental skills that will help him along the way. These skills may help the individual to take control of his own life, not for others to control him, but for him to take charge of his "garden" and fulfill his destiny. Others might influence

---

13:7) The believer is, though, responsible for making sure that which he is being taught really is the Word of God, lest he be pushed into religious bondage by the Christian Pharisees of today. (Heb. 10:19-25) Third, the Christian has the Holy Spirit that guides him or her by God's Spirit inspired word as the way he or she should go. (Gal. 5:16-26)

your life, but only you control how you respond to their actions. Self-esteem is deeply interlinked to this picture. Somehow, if you do good, you end up feeling good. If you do evil, you feel evil. Be careful of what you sow, because you will reap its fruit.

We come from different walks of life. Some had an easy childhood, but a harsher adult life. Others had a bad childhood, but then things smoothened out. Their parents almost destroy some, some learned almost nothing good from theirs, and some were taught excellent skills on how to handle life. We are all different. The beauty is that the principles of true religion may help us all. The Holy Scriptures clearly say that God will consider all the above. That is why we should not envy others. God sees to the heart, but man judges from appearance. So, we should all remain humble, and not crush the small plants around us, trying to grow.

We should rather help one another into a better situation wherever we see the need. The example of Jesus shows us that he especially had the heart for the weak and oppressed. Those who are quick to call themselves strong and pure will be judged even harder, as more is expected of them. To whom much is given, much will also be expected.

✵✵✵

# Aid From the World of the Unseen

A spiritual person rises above the everyday earthly realm and that which is visible to the naked eye, and fervently reaches out to God in cosmos, in faith, in something – non-material and non-empirical – as the metaphysical blood of Jesus Christ cleanses the human soul and connects it through the Holy Spirit to God.

The cosmic story of the Christian faith seeks to explain how evil came into the world and the implications for humans. In Christianity, God's advice to us all on how to live is summed up in the sentence: "Love thy God and love thy neighbor." That is, do good to others. Billy Graham, who may be said to be one of the most balanced and sound-minded Christian leaders – if not the most important spiritual leader in our age, explains in one of his 1957 sermons: "The Christian faith is vertical – Thou shall love thy God with all thy heart, but also horizontal – love thy neighbour as thy self. When your heart is right, you have the ability and the capacity to love your neighbor properly."

To do what is good may mean standing up for honesty, showing kindness, compassion, unraveling hypocrisy, being just, yet generous, forgiving and asking for forgiveness when it is needed. A fundamental Christianity idea is the concept that God's love for his own offspring, the created, is greater than man can ever understand. He simply cannot comprehend how the Creator longs for fellowship with the created. He seeks each of us with a burning and intense spiritual love.

Christianity dramatically proclaims the possibility of a new life – spiritual help, capable of providing the strength necessary to overcome difficulties, of prevailing over hatred, bitterness, and evil– the spiritual love of the heavens, delivered from the Creator through his Son, Jesus Christ. The Bible teaches that there is a cloud of witnesses and an army of creatures, demons and angels, that support man in the cosmic battle between good and evil. Faith is a choice, to surrender, a submission to God, a yearning for existential peace where His gift is received through faith in the invisible. In faith lies the hope of conquering evil with goodness.

According to the Bible, Satan and his angels were condemned to earth when they were cast out of God's heaven. They reign in this realm, in this darkness, and here transpires the battle, with all the qualities of any "science fiction" movie – both in the heavens above us and in the hearts of men, the battle between good and evil. No one is untouched by it, and not surprising that wars and conflicts overwhelm the world, considering the massive, cosmic forces that are active in and around the earth. In fact, it is surprising that we even have even the little peace that we do.[12]

Separated from the Almighty's goodness, man will remain existentially lonely, cold and frustrated. It is like a father who loves his son: without each other, they are both distraught. The force of the cosmic rebel, named Lucifer or Satan, shapes man and drags him slowly and cunningly into self-destruction.

Satan or Lucifer has many names. He was once one of the chief personalities in the Heavens; he was a musician, artist and a wonderfully

---

[12] We live under the influence of the spirit of the world, and each one of us is drawn away and tempted by his own desires. (Jam. 1:13-18) Man's problem is the evil in his own heart, which draws him away from God and makes him feel that God is distant. This applies to the religious and non-religious alike, as submission under God and obedience to Him is the only element that will release man's soul from the dominion of the demonic forces in this world. The spirit of this world naturally proceeds from the Satanic ruler of the world, according to the Bible. (John 14:30; 2 Cor. 4:3-4; 1 John 5:19) The worldview of Satan's human society is in stark opposition to the will of the Creator of the world, whose main message is that we are to love one another. Under Satanic influence, the individual will submit to selfish desires and lifestyle, in a roaring hatred towards that which is holy, which places him in opposition to his celestial Father and thereby opposed to reasonable and rational thinking. – 1 Corinthians 2:6-16.

beautiful creature, the Scriptures say – one of the sons of God. Yet, in his heart grew envy of God's omnipotence; he sought to take his place, and so he rebelled. The celestial, cosmic story then goes on to tell how he was branded and ruined by his rebellion against God, and one-third of the angels in heaven fell with him. This story is told both in the Old as well as the New Testament.

Satan had freely chosen to rebel against God, in time, he was ousted out of heaven to the earth, the area around our planet and does so still today. These constant forces of evil are felt by man throughout his life, as he struggles to fight in order to survive life. This is where the search for spiritual light becomes vital – search for the source of wisdom - as man is locked in a battle with Evil and needs help from the celestial Light. This light is only provided by God since only God is pure. *He is light.* This is at the core of the Christian faith and a tangible reality to the believer.

For generations, man has attempted to liberate himself from his spiritual origin. He has announced God's death and apotheosized man as the source of perfection in His stead. However, none of this rebellion against The Almighty has led to a condition of complete inner peace. We are more at war than ever. People are still, even after the rise of atheism and denial of God, hopelessly trapped in time and painfully lonely, incapable of bringing the world closer to a permanent condition of harmony. However, one of religion's fundamental truths is that the bright flames of the eternal light of God can never be extinguished.

We progress slowly but steadily, in the current war zones on so many levels, towards the apocalyptic end of the world – an Armageddon in which nation will stand against nation, people against people, in a cataclysmic collision. The Bible explains this on several levels, both allegorically, symbolically and as a fact in history. Then Christ will return and re-enter the earthly realm, establish his kingdom in Jerusalem and rule the world according to principles quite the opposite to those of today's power-hungry, greedy, international political and economic elites.

The Messiah will then – probably to the great joy of conservationists of the environment, animal lovers, and the anti-war movement – create peace and restore the healthy balance of the earth so that the world will experience years of cosmic balance and prosperity, not only for the wealthy but for all.

Those who in life maintained that the Christian faith was nonsense, are of course dead at this point. They will neither experience the restitution of the earth nor what follows after that: the creation of a new heaven and a new earth where justice will finally prevail and the curse of evil eternally broken.

Throughout European history, leading philosophers, authors, architects, poets, artists, actors, politicians and clergy have been concerned with these existential metaphysical and philosophical topics. In *Thoughts*, Blaise Pascal describes human choice as a gamble – if God exists and eternity is a reality, there is absolutely everything to gain by faith. If God does not exist, nothing is lost by moral actions and kindness shown towards others during your life; either way, death is a state of eternal silence. The natural focus is life itself; the choice becomes our own.

Thus, spiritual, Christian thought fundamentally breaks off from the notion that the only thing that exists is the materially and physically tangible world. Christian thought explains the spiritual laws that create the relationship between heaven and earth, man and man, man and God. Christianity addresses these questions which relate the earthly to what we cannot see, yet exists every day of our life – this cosmic turmoil that colours the world and hurls us towards insanity, accidents, war, strife and discord, contempt for those who are different, war at home, war at work and in the newspapers, suicide, depression, murder, envy and conflict everywhere.

In this chaos, where evil tries to torment us, the spiritually aware rises towards the extra-terrestrial and the cosmos and the spiritual journey – like a Hollywood 'Interstellar' experience – where the possibility of eternal life defines the future reality. To him, this life is but a test, in which his choices determine the destiny in the next life. He becomes Plato in search for the origin of all things, as the world as it appears to us through our senses is defective and filled with error. The more real and perfect realm populated by forms or ideals are eternal, changeless, as explained by Stanford Encyclopedia of Philosophy.[13] Among the most important of these are goodness, equality, unity, change, and changelessness. As previously stated, Plato is regarded as one of God's prophets by the Eastern Orthodox Church, stating that much of what he wrote is in clear accordance with the teachings of the Bible.

Eternal life – life in the perfect, eternal realm without sickness and frailty - is the life that follows these few struggling years we have on a planet where the struggle for survival and certain death awaits us all. Establishing contact with the spiritual domain is the aim of spiritually aware individuals, as they seek help from God who is the creator of all things, He who resides outside of cosmos, on "the other side."

Encouraged by the Holy Saints who died before us – those who belong to the Church and watch us from above – the believer yearns for the

---

[13] Stanford Encyclopedia of Philosophy (Wednesday, August 16, 2017) https://plato.stanford.edu/entries/plato/

communion with the Creator. The point of contact is in Christ, who restores man's dignity and equips him with the spiritual weapons necessary to overcome this world.

\*\*\*

# The Human Heart and Spiritual Light

Let me continue the explanation of some of the central truths found in Christian spiritualism. Jesus was widely engaged in society. He did not withdraw from it, but went to all kinds of gatherings, engaging in conversation with high and low, rich and poor. He encouraged people from all walks of life to enter the path to spiritual light, regardless of religion, ethnicity, politics, gender or class. He stated that the path into his Kingdom is by rebirth, a transcending spiritual experience in which man is reincarnated into a new dimension and a new awareness –from now on he lives with a new source of strength and light within him, to guide him to a healthy and balanced life.

This requires repentance of sin – defined as "missing the mark." It requires an application of will, a change of the heart. In this regard, Christ described the road as "narrow."

As St Porphyrios writes:

> Sin makes a person exceedingly psychologically confused. Moreover, nothing makes the confusion go away – nothing except the light of Christ. Can you understand the truth? Then you are out in the sun, in the light; you see all the magnificence of creation; otherwise, you are in a dark cave, like Lazarus before the stone was removed from his grave. Light and darkness. Which is better? To be meek, humble, peaceful and to be filled with love, or to be irritable, depressed and to quarrel with everyone. Unquestionably the higher state is love. Our religion has all these good things and is the truth. However, many people go off in another direction.

This life is a gift. Grace is like gasoline in the car on the road trip of life. We cannot detour around atonement and continue blithely on the highway of selfishness and impurity. Christ is adamant that repentance is critically important to reaching the destination of spiritual liberation.

Precisely here lies one of the most significant points: the reason for pursuing the existential peace promised to the believer, is not that he should live complacently without care for those who live in the world around him. In such unproductive waters, his faith will rot, as egoism is one of the enemies of love. The focus should not solely be on his own blessings and contentment in life. Those in contact with the spiritual dimensions of God will be gripped by a pervasive love and compassion for their fellow human beings. They will engage socially in society, just like Jesus did. It will be impossible not to be touched by the warm vitality of spiritual compassion and kindness.

Again, St Porphyrios:

> Love always understands the need to make sacrifices. Whatever is done under coercion always causes the soul to react with rejection. Love attracts the grace of God. When grace comes, then the gifts of the Holy Spirit come. The fruit of the Spirit is love, joy, peace, long-sufferance, gentleness, goodness, faith, meekness, self-control. These are the things which a healthy soul in Christ should have. With Christ, a person is filled with grace and so lives above evil. Evil does not exist for him. There is only good, which is God. Evil cannot exist. While there is light, there cannot be darkness. Nor can darkness encompass him because he has the light.

Jesus Christ pointed out that 'Truly I tell you, whatever you did for one of the least of these brothers and sisters of mine, you did for me.' (Matt. 25:40) strongly implying that the spiritual person should engage in society and meet the needs of those around him show kindness and justice. "For I was hungry, and you gave me food. I was thirsty, and you gave me drink. I was in prison, and you visited me" – all the conditions of the human experience, of those in need. The hope of friendship, kindness, for fellowship, for instruction and correction, for discipline and wisdom, the necessity of deep recognition, the need to feel loved.

The simple command to love has in the course of history often drowned in ecclesiastical power intrigues, monetary questions, the pursuit of elite privileges and other impurities that do not make God great, but instead blaspheme his name. All quite contrary to the fact that Christ said that he who will be greatest, must be the servant of everyone. When humility vanishes, the flame of the Spirit is extinguished, and all manner of religious demons overwhelm the church with their theological models of explanation, yet not of repentance. Religion as oppression is not the type of spirituality that we seek. Rather, the hope is for the religiously bound to arrive at a new conclusion: the abandonment of religion as bondage, embracing a free-spirited, spiritual life.

# CHAPTER 7

# Searching for Paradise

*The belief that human life is subordinate to God, that we are responsible for our own actions and will be judged by the Creator, is simply an unbearable thought for the non-believer.*

## Theodicy – Suffering and Justice in the Afterlife

IN THE FILM VERSION OF J. R. R. Tolkien's trilogy, *The Lord of the Rings*, directed by Peter Jackson, two of the main characters have the following conversation just prior to a dramatic battle:

– "I didn't think that life would end like this."

– "End? The journey doesn't end here. Death is just a new path. One everyone must travel ... towards the white beaches below. There lies a fertile country and a new sunrise."

St Paisios of Mount Athos sums the Christian doctrine up in *Spiritual Awakening*, saying that "the meaning of this life is to be prepared for our homeland, for Heaven, for Paradise. The most important thing is for man to grasp this most profound meaning of life, which is the salvation of the soul. When man believes in God and in the future life, then he understands the vanity of this present life and prepares his passing to the next."

Literature is full of statements that illustrate how critical the question of life after death is to the living. To reflect on the meaning of life and how man, if possible, may live as content as possible in this life and after that in the next, is a major concern of religion that also touches moral philosophy.

And in European civilization, religion is intertwined with philosophy, arts, literature, architecture, music, the social sciences and other disciplines.

Jürgen Habermas interestingly points out that when post-metaphysical thought reflects on its own history, it refers not only to Western philosophy's metaphysical heritage but also to the origin of classical Greek philosophy, about 500 years BC. According to Habermas, religions that have their roots in this particular period of time have managed the leap from a structure of mythical tales to a discourse that distinguishes between essence and form in a manner similar to Greek philosophy. Since the Church Council of Nicaea in 325, philosophy has followed and assimilated many religious motives and concepts of redemption, especially those from the story of salvation.

Sociologist Max Weber has identified quite a number of common characteristics between religions. They all deal with the problem of evil, suffering and the righteousness of God, which he calls theodicy. Religion attempts to create a basis for moral actions that will profit man, as man's actions are interlinked with consequences in the afterlife. If there is a life after death, it becomes important to avoid its punishment and receive its rewards. This transpires a basic need to understand how God's justice functions, since He, according to the Christian religion, provides compensation for the injustice experienced in this life with rewards in the next. He sees the evil done to the innocent. Moreover, He will, on the last day, place His judgment upon those who trespass against others. The concept of Judgment Day involves a belief in the apocalypse where the world as we know it will be destroyed and the dead will be resurrected in order to face the Almighty on a final day of judgment. Each person's life will be shown to him, rolled out like a scroll, or a film in review.

Man should, therefore, use his freedom of choice not to only do what he *wants* to, but what he *ought* to. Ultimately, to do what gives selfish pleasure and well-being is not the goal, but rather to do that which benefits the betterment of human kind, – "love thy God and love thy neighbor."

Weber believed that the problem of suffering is an element that every religion seeks to explain. Morality spills into this – if there is a God watching us if man is to live on after death, the need to do *the right thing* while alive becomes vital. Both to avoid pain in the next life, as well as minimize it in this life. Religions suggest remedies to the ills of this world and seek to show a way out of pain and suffering. Since faith in the supernatural explains how people should deal with suffering and how to avoid it, religion may provide one of the keys to understanding people's actions.

According to Weber, the human psyche has inherent needs that extend beyond the observable. Man is driven to think deeply about ethical and religious questions, not just because he searches for the golden mean to achieve a satisfactory life, but also because he has an inner desire to understand the world as a meaningful place. He needs to know why he is here.

Weber was inspired by one of the philosophers of the 1700s, Gottfried Leibniz, who suggested when trying to solve the riddle of why we suffer, that our world is the best of all worlds. Despite the evil, our world is the least painful there is. In such a perspective, it becomes even more reasonable to think rationally about how one wants to spend eternity.

Evolutionists and nonbelievers, such as Steve Pinker and Richard Dawkins, have made a point out of the suffering in the world, claiming it proves there is no God behind creation. Leif A. Jensen points out in *Rethinking Darwin: A Vedic study of Darwinism and Intelligent Design* that Dawkins sees the world almost like Nietzsche: no design, no purpose, no evil and no good - nothing but indifference. This world view implies that man may do whatever he wishes, as there is no serious consequence awaiting him behind the eternal veil. Pinker goes as far as to call God a twisted sadist engineer since the world is imperfect and man has to live in it.

In a sense, aggressive atheism implies man trying to take God's place, reflecting "envy of God as the supreme ruler," wishing to be omnipotent like Him. Man wishes to rule the world, with nobody to thank but himself. From a religious standpoint, this would be the ultimate rebellion, wishing to take God's place as the master of the universe. Yet, the aggressive atheism's aim is for man to get all the glory, all the power, and the wealth, and not to in any way thank God for the gift of life. This is done by simply refusing to acknowledge God's existence.

The religious approach involves an active implementation of gratitude to the Creator and submission towards His eternal advice on how to live life. This world is viewed as entangled in the battle between good and evil. Religion points out that man is merely on a journey to the afterlife, that the purpose of the human life is to get free from the miseries of this world, by reviving our relationship with God, who will teach us how to avoid as many as possible of the sufferings of life.

A personal choice is involved, man has the power to decide his own destiny, and where he is to spend eternity. He cannot control every circumstance or every aspect of what happens to him in life, nor is that the point. Leibniz strongly believed that the sum of all good is always greater than the sum of all evil. Therefore there is always hope. This is a consolation to those who suffer from evil and injustice done to them by others.

Hanne Nabintu Herland

\*\*\*

# Judgment Day and the Justice of God

Observing the leading world religions and their understanding of paradise awaiting man in the future is refreshingly exciting, especially because finding the path to eternal bliss is a conditional question. Man does not automatically end up in a state of peace in the next world. Personal choices are existentially important because new realities are waiting, some of them quite horrifying. The Bible spells out quite an Armageddon before the doom, is not exactly comforting to read about, it brings a fear of God as it spells out what will happen to the unjust, the liars, the adulterers, the religious hypocrites and so on. If even some of the messages brought to us by religion are true, there is more than one reason why we should take heed and listen.

God will avenge all evil, and no one will be able to hide from His wrath on Judgment Day, states the Holy Scriptures. This is why man should fear and love God and not grow complacent. He should be very careful as to how he lives his life and how he treats his fellow man, as his own deeds will judge him. Christianity, Judaism and Islam alike tell approximately the same story, as well as other religions with similar predicaments entangled in their cultural and historical heritage. Based on an evaluation of how life is lived and choices made, either towards evil and thereby more suffering or towards good and less suffering, man will go to eternal rest or be exposed to new, ultimate challenges. This is because God is just. He sees that we are all inherently poisoned by the evil seed, tempted to selfishness rather than loving one another.

As with Christians; Islam, Judaism, Buddhism, Hinduism and other paths to spiritual light, also believe that this life is only a trial and a time of preparation for the next realm of existence. Earth is viewed as a perfect test environment. This life is a mere test. God wants to see what kind of choices we make, whether willing to forgive, to be humble, giving, slow to anger, work hard in order to learn how to show perseverance, grace, mercy and pursue justice.

# The Culture War

✱✱✱

# Conditions for Paradise

To take the time to log off computers, shut down the TV and social media, and simply sit still in the serenity of a silent room and reflect on one's life, can bring more mental health than most think. It is most rewarding to engage in philosophical experiments of the spiritual kind as well as self-reflection on the patterns of existence. After all, religion answers important questions. How does one get to paradise after death? How should one live in order to experience an amount of harmony and a kind of inner paradise in this life? Is it possible to find inner peace, or is this merely an unobtainable, unsustainable ideal? Is there a connection between the spiritual world and the material one, if so, how do they interconnect?

Moral philosophy from the ancient Greeks has an important point. In the *Nicomachean Ethics*, Aristotle recommended the golden mean or the middle way as the road to harmony. This is a state halfway between asceticism – a lifestyle that rejects the values of the physical world – and hedonism, the moral philosophy emphasizing physical enjoyment alone as the objective that leads to a good life. Aristotle believed that both these extremes were in error and recommended balance and moderation. He spoke of courage as a virtue, but if taken to excess, it could imply recklessness. On the other end of the scale, a lack of courage becomes cowardice. Philosopher Thomas Aquinas also argued that Christian morality is consistent with the golden mean. It attempts to provide constructive guidance that results in an accomplished, spiritually satisfied and balanced life.

According to traditional Islam, man receives a place in paradise as a result of good behavior and submission to God. The Quran discusses, as we know, both the internal and the external *jihad*, holy war. The struggle against man's inner tendencies towards evil is regarded by most Muslims as the most important form of *jihad*.[14] One is to work diligently to become a good person that has much to give to others in need. The inner, evil tendencies are to be fought and overcome by the help of God, and thus better one's life in preparing for the heavenly rewards. Man should dedicate his life to be pure of heart, to care for the family, to protect the women, the elderly and the poor. These are essential criteria for reaching

---

[14] For a detailed discussion of this, see *IS THE QURAN THE WORD OF GOD? Is Islam the One True Faith?* By Edward D. Andrews (978-1-945757-49-5)

the Islamic paradise, *Jannah*, described as a beautiful garden with indescribable fruit and other pleasures awaiting.

Buddha also taught of the middle way, a path between the extremes of religious asceticism and on the other level of extremity, hedonistic self-indulgence. In Confucianism, the doctrine of the mean has similar meaning and institutes a general guidance to perfecting oneself in life, for the benefit of acquiring balance and equilibrium in life. The ideal is for a person to follow a path of duty and obligation. The doctrine of the mean implies that a person works to perfect virtues such as moderation, objectivity, sincerity, honesty, propriety.

This is, again, of vital importance. The guiding principle is that he should not act in excess in any way; this will lead to a good life. Confucianism speaks of metaphysical realities by expressing that the heavens have disposed man with an inborn nature that he must realize in a process during his life. This process leads him towards a clarification, which implies an educational process towards greater understanding and a deeper equilibrium.

From the viewpoint of religions, the aspect of eternity is important because it motivates people to good actions in the hope of future rewards. The search for paradise concerns us all. Most of the old languages in the Middle East have a word for the phenomenon of paradise. In Sanskrit, for example, it means a distant foreign country. This place is described in the world's oldest legend, the *Epic of Gilgamesh*, as a closed garden (of Eden), a harmonious place. It is puzzling to see how much man actually may understand about the things of God, if he really puts his mind to it, considering the Christian belief that man has God's breath within him, and is made in His own image.

In essence, it becomes clear that in different cultures and across the ages, man has been able to reflect spiritually on the connection between this life and the next, as well as understand how much humans determine by their own use of the will and corresponding good deeds as they seek the "middle way"; their own spiritual destiny in the afterlife.

# The Culture War

\*\*\*

## Critical Choices in Life

In Western culture, it becomes even more important to reflect on the metaphysics of the afterlife, since contemporary society seems devoid of spiritual contemplation regarding inner values and their correspondence to rewards in life after death.

In *Daily Advice from the Heart*, His Holiness the Dalai Lama points out that it's not necessary to ponder for long hours in order to recognize that all living creatures naturally wish to avoid suffering. Harmony is, to him, associated with senses and an inner satisfaction. It has its source in generosity, honesty, and respect for others. Buddhism as a non-theistic religion striving for the right way of living tries to provide advice in order to help people find a state of cosmic balance.

The paradise of Buddhism, the ultimate goal, is known as *nirvana*, which means "the great awakening." It is achievable as the result of the extinction of cravings, ignorance and thus, suffering. Based on self-reflection, the human is advised to allow his actions to move on an ethically fruitful track. A life without spirituality is considered to lead unsatisfactorily to actions that poison the mind – such as envy, greed and a lack of compassion towards living things. Suffering may be avoided by emphasizing a spiritual path that cultivates love, friendship, encouragement, mindfulness, spiritual knowledge, and concentration.

Buddha also explains that craving sexual pleasure is a cause of suffering. Man should avoid engaging in the excesses of sexual desires. One should avoid sexual misconduct, which means one should generally follow accepted norms of sexual morality and behavior. For ordained monks and nuns, there is strict celibacy in Buddhism as well as in the Christian Catholic and Eastern Orthodox churches.

The goal of the Buddhist religion is that man should find a state of mental stability of the mind, not unlike the concept of the golden mean. Because everything is constantly changing in cyclical reincarnation, *nirvana* is an awakening – a final enlightenment that can be reached if one finds the way to the upper state of equality and balance.

Buddhism's guidelines for an ethical lifestyle indicate that when you remedy the causes of suffering in your own mind – causes like lies, hate and greed – harmony is a natural result. Therefore, people must remove the so-called toxins of the mind: greed, envy, hate, theft, violence, intoxication, arrogance, and being dominated by sexual desire. There is a sharp divide between right and wrong.

The Dalai Lama summarizes this philosophy in a noteworthy manner by stating that man can't help himself if he can't help others. We are all tied to one another. The way to *nirvana* thus comes through an ethical lifestyle.

Regarding the role of money and wealth, the Dalai Lama states that when meeting wealthy people, he usually tells them that prosperity is a good sign according to the teachings of Buddhism. Wealth is the fruit of good deeds, proof that one has been generous in a previous point in time, but wealth does not give a lasting feeling of happiness. To achieve this, a deep spiritual focus is needed.

Many recall how the apostle Paul once said: "All things are lawful for me, but all things are not expedient."[15] (1 Cor. 10:23) And Christ, considered both radical, controversial and remarkably truthful in his time, explained when meeting a wealthy man that the problem was not the wealth, but the dependence on it. Wealth is good for him that uses it wisely. There are many examples from the Judeo-Christian religious literature both of men of God living in poverty – like John the Baptist, the disciples, Jeremiah – and others who lived in wealth – Sarah, Esther, Joseph, and David.

Buddhism's focus on inner balance and harmony is tensely opposed to secular profanity and a materialistic culture that relentlessly focuses on the pleasures in the now. As one examines religions, it becomes increasingly clear that modern society needs a better balance between internal and external values. A culture that continually neglects the spiritual dimension and downgrades the role of religion as a motivation for good relationships between people is in danger of developing into a cold, non-cohesive place where cultural bonds wither.

The examples from world religions and creeds from different corners of the earth serve as elaborations of elements of morality that Christianity also addresses. The paradox, of course, is that Westerners these days seem to be quicker to accept the rationality of moral behavior when the advice comes from Confucius, Buddha or some other "exotic" religion, rather than the religion from their own cultural roots, Christianity.

---

[15] Paul's words can be rendered, "all things are not profitable" or "but not all things build up" or "all things are not beneficial." Paul was not saying that we can do evil and live selfishly as we please. We are all to submit to the advice of the Holy Spirit, as imprinted upon us in our hearts and according to the Word of God.

## The Culture War

\*\*\*

# Resolution with Toxins of the Mind

The value of Jewish ethics of the Ten Commandments as set out in the book of Exodus, chapter 20, clearly become evident, as they have been throughout history, ever since the time they were given to the prophet Moses on Mount Sinai several thousand years ago, and delivered to the Jewish people, founding the covenant with God.

The short version of these commandments, stated for the sake of clarity, are: You shall have no other God other than me; you shall not make for yourself an image in the form of anything in heaven above or on the earth beneath or in the waters below; you shall not misuse the name of the Lord your God; remember the Sabbath day by keeping it holy; honour your father and your mother, so that you may live long in the land the Lord your God is giving you; you shall not murder; you shall not commit adultery; you shall not steal; you shall not give false testimony against your neighbour; you shall not covet your neighbour's house, his wife or anything that belongs to your neighbour.

Many seem to agree about the ability of these values to form a more secure basis for the development of a better society based on more justice and a stronger degree of respect for others, where people actually are pushed to get their act together and behave more politely, more considerately and with respect towards one another.

It is something to consider: do you get a good self-esteem by lying, by stealing other people's personal belongings, by coveting after the neighbor's wife and setting up traps to deceive friends? Who feels good about themselves after spreading lies about those they envy, proving themselves to be untrustworthy and disloyal? Who gains respect from such behavior? How would society develop if it was acceptable to steal from businesses and workplaces? If the criminal would be treated with the same respect as the law-abiding citizen? If he wasn't punished when killing and raping the innocent, the bill for his crime sent to honest taxpayers with the requirement that they pay for his wrong doing?

The Holy Scriptures - The Bible - may be regarded as a description of the road to a balanced and more satisfactory life, one with less pain. In his Madison Square Garden crusade in 1957, Billy Graham also explained the central dogma of redemption and salvation in Christianity by saying that

God weighs the heart by the Ten Commandments, he weighs it by the Sermon on the Mount, he weighs it by the great Law, he weighs it by Christ and says that all have come short of the glory of God. The Bible says there is not a person that does good, not one. That is the reason Jesus said unless a man is born again, he cannot see the Kingdom of Heaven.

Man must become spiritually enlightened; he needs to step out of the cave of spiritual ignorance and see the light shine from the other dimension and understand how interlinked this world is to the Creator and the cosmos. Man is imprisoned by the fourth dimension – time – and cannot escape its control over his life. He cannot travel back to the past, or into the future, he remains caged in the now through his physical body. Man relies on information from a source outside of time and beyond the fourth dimension, in order to attain knowledge about that which is beyond his own, narrow scope. Confined to the concept of time, man's life becomes a journey which has a beginning and an end. Outside of time, the past does not exist, everything simply *is*. We know that one of God's names is "I am," signifying God's existence outside of the concept of time. What does this mean? Paul told the Roman Christians, "Do not be conformed to this world, but be transformed by the renewal of your mind ..." (Rom. 12:2) Through Adam, humans have inherited imperfection; we are subject to "sin and death." – Romans 8:2.

Therefore, we must be 'transformed by the renewal of our mind,' 'be renewed in the spirit of our minds, by drastically altering our mental dispositions. (Eph. 4:23) This change is brought about by the greatest enlightenment that man has ever known, the Spirit inspired, inerrant Word of God. (2 Tim. 3:16-17; 2 Pet. 1:21) This is not somehow miraculous infused into us by simply reading the Bible. It requires effort on our part by our using our power of reason. (Rom. 12:1) We need to choose to do that which God requires. Jesus clearly stated that: Why do you say Lord, Lord but do not what I ask of you? (Luke 6:46-49) Spiritual growth comes from understanding God's commandment and then, acting on them, regardless of the consequence for your own personal life, whether you will be "popular" or ridiculed, like the prophet Jeremiah. The sum of His commandment being, love thy God and love thy neighbor. We can use Romans 12:2 as our example. "And what offensive measure keeps the believer from being conformed to this present evil age? The consistent and deliberate renewing of the mind. To make new (Paul here uses the noun, renewal, *anakainosis*, instead of the verb *anakainoo*, to make new) is a combination of 'new' (*kainos*) and "again' (*ana*). Paul uses the verb form in 2 Corinthians 4:16 where he says 'we are being renewed day by day,' and in Colossians 3:10 where he says that the new self 'is being renewed in knowledge in the image of its Creator.'"[16] Kenneth Boa and William Kruidenier go on to aid us in understanding this renewing of the mind by getting at what the author mean, not what we feel, think, or believe he meant.

> Both of these uses of the verb shed light on his use of the noun here, especially the Colossians reference where he highlights a renewal of knowledge "in" (*kata*, according to) the image of God. In other words, believers are coming out of Satan's domain where lies and depravity are the language and currency and depraved minds (Rom. 1:28) are the norm. Therefore, our minds must be renewed in knowledge according to the image of God, not the age in which Satan rules.
>
> The ongoing, repetitive nature of the renewal is drawn from the present passive imperative of *metamorphoo*, to change form. It is from this Greek word that our "metamorphosis" derives—"a transformation; a marked change in appearance, character, condition, or function" (*American Heritage Dictionary*). The English definition describes perfectly the "metamorphosis" which took place before the disciples' eyes as Jesus was transfigured (*metamorphoo*) before them: "His face shone like the sun, and his clothes became as white as the light" (Matt. 17:2), "whiter than anyone in the world could bleach them" (Mark 9:3).
>
> These dramatic images are a picture of how different the believer is to become as, day after day, he or she is being transformed by the renewing of the mind. Instead of being *con*formed to the present evil age, believers are to be *trans*formed into the image of God insofar as knowledge and behavior are concerned. Paul has already stated that it is God's ultimate goal for believers "to be conformed to the likeness of [God's] Son" (Rom. 8:29). But in this verse, the "conformation" is of a different sort than the "conformation" to the world that we are warned against in our present verse. We are warned against being shaped into (*suschematizo*) the patterns and schemes of

---

[16] Kenneth Boa and William Kruidenier, *Romans*, vol. 6, Holman New Testament Commentary (Nashville, TN: Broadman & Holman Publishers, 2000), 365.

the world, system in which we live.[17]

Yes, it means that we do our utmost in taking in this life-saving knowledge, so that we are not "walking according to the course of this world" (Eph. 2:1-3), with its corrupt morals and values, debased entertainment, and distorted thinking. We are to be reborn into the mind of Christ by taking in the Spirit inspired Word of God, which "is living and active, sharper than any two-edged sword, piercing to the division of soul and of spirit, of joints and of marrow, and discerning the thoughts and intentions of the heart." (Heb 4:12) This is like experiencing a mental reincarnation and activate the seat of the soul, as Descartes described it. We are to open our inner eye towards the invisible spiritual power (namely, God's Word and the Holy Spirit) that has the ability to fuse spiritual light into our life and help us out of our darkness and human imperfection and weaknesses, i.e., our mental bent toward evil. (Gen. 6:5; 8:21; Jer. 17:9)

Graham continues by asking:

> Wouldn't you like to have a new heart, a new power, new strength and a new dynamic to your life? Wouldn't you like to have a new moral nature that would give you strength and power to face moral temptation? Wouldn't you like to have Christ who forgives the past? Are you willing to accept that your heart is sinful, that it is deceitful? Then, you will accept God's diagnosis of your heart. Are you willing to acknowledge it and renounce it and turn from your sin, come to Christ who died on the cross and rose again from the dead. Then, he will give you a new heart and a new life.

God's ability to intervene in time and give supernatural strength to those who ask for it, is an idea which stands at the core of Christian philosophy, motivating the individual to do good to others for the betterment of society.

---

[17] IBID, 365–366.

# CHAPTER 8

# The Rationality of Religion

*We ought to care for one another. We should not inflict terror on others, but treat each other with justice and respect. We are to do unto others what we wish they did unto us. It implies compassion and an obligation in the local community, on a national level as well as with regard to international justice, brought forth through a spiritual sense of love for humanity.*

## Religion Influences Morality

IN HIS AMBITIOUS WORK to establish a basis for communication, philosopher Jürgen Habermas has studied methods which show that normative questions – questions that address what people *should or ought to do* – can be answered in a rational manner. Moral questions are rational questions that discuss how we are to live the best possible life.

Ever since Habermas received his Ph.D. in 1954, he has attempted to shed critical light on the development of the industrialized society. His thinking has initially been considered neo-Marxist, following along the lines of the radical Frankfurt School that heavily criticized the bourgeoisie, traditional values in Europe. Yet, as mentioned earlier, Habermas came to a point where it seems that he departed from much of his previous Marxist views.

For decades, Habermas emphasized the need for social bonds between individuals and social, moral development. From a global perspective, this includes the relations between nations. In his later years – as also illustrated during his Holberg Price Award speech in Norway in 2005 – he has spoken of the need for a new respect for traditional Christian, European morality. This has dumbfounded many since Habermas for decades has been one of the architects of European secularism. He now has become an advocate for respecting Christian ethics in Europe, although himself being a well-known atheist.

Habermas explains his view in the Holberg speech by stating that there are weaknesses and shortcomings in modern science's inability to comprehend the equally important metaphysical dimension of human relations. Traditional science distinguishes sharply between faith and knowledge and takes a naturalistic position that devalues all categories of knowledge that are not based on empiricism, natural laws and causal explanation.

This singular emphasis on physical science makes it difficult for us to understand the complexity of the human spirit, he says. A more practical understanding of what it means to be an individual with responsibility for one's actions is particularly essential. According to Habermas, if the only approach is science, such an understanding is difficult to achieve.

We need a deeper understanding of the metaphysical dimension of human relations, focusing on a morality that may motivate citizens to a solidarity and an empathy that we seem to be losing in secular Western societies today. Knowledge of the spiritual world is waning.

✯✯✯

# It Is Rational to Care

It is thought-provoking: A Parliament can neither regulate nor legally require certain moral actions. The law cannot enforce morality. No prescription can prescribe it. It comes from another source than legality, as a deep moral ideal within the mental fabric of the mind and its interconnectedness to the community. Morality speaks of the rationality of what we *should*. What we *ought to* in order to participate in the betterment of society.

The early Christian thinkers and saints wrote much about faith as a rational choice. The idea was that the human being needs to acquire moral strength from a coherent source of comprehensive beliefs, not often found within himself alone, in order to out root the seed of egoism. The whole point of faith in God is faith in His ability to help the human overcome their evil tendencies. The commandment is for man to "love his neighbor," advocating for a society based on as much justice as possible Empathy makes you *feel* for others, it makes you want to help. Indifference to other people's pain implies complacency, a lack of collective responsibility.

It is obviously rational to motivate individuals to do good to others and take care of the community. This is the goal of spiritually aware individuals. The idea is that the metaphysical dimension goes hand in hand with the physical. Man does not consist of the body alone but has a soul and a mind with deep psychological and metaphysical needs. Religion does not preclude science; they work together for the betterment of mankind. This also concerns, the field of moral philosophy. Normative ethics tries to provide a framework from which man may assess which actions are right or wrong, then suggesting and recommending a certain conduct.

The nihilistic approach to understanding the world in relativistic terms and not morally pre-dispositioned, has become the predominant liberal moral philosophy in the West. If it is socially acceptable to be egocentric, with no authoritative ideals that demand solidarity as values are regarded as relative, citizens may easily lose the bonds of solidarity. There will be little room for empathy with those in minority, those who suffer injustice, who lack representation, those who are misunderstood, bullied and harassed.

Motives of compassion encompass a deep respect for fellow human beings. The seed of forgiveness and choice not to hate is cemented by virtue of compassion. It describes the deeper meaning of solidarity. We are to care for those who suffer, and leave the judgment to God.

Pope Benedict XVI states in *Christianity and the Crisis of Cultures* that the approach to reason, defined in the so-called Age of Enlightenment – the 1600s philosophical trend that centered around reason as the source of authority – was the starting point that led to a growing distance to the historical roots of European culture.

Philosopher and professor, Charles Taylor criticizes the common theories of secularization in *A Secular Age*. He shows that the Protestant Reformation provided precisely the basis for a reason-based belief in God, a faith that confirmed science. As we have seen, the relationship between faith and science has not been as diametrically opposed throughout history, as many hardcore secularists, today would like to have us believe.

Testing in laboratories cannot verify many philosophical and metaphysical aspects of life. This is because science explains the "how" rarely the "why." Taylor disagrees with those that assume that religion is incompatible with reason. The assumption that believers are automatically "unscientific and irrational," must today be regarded as one of the myths of secular society. It stems from the lack of knowledge about, not only human nature, our own history. Precisely, the Protestant reformers' emphasis on moral energy was critical for the growth of modern states founded on justice for all, free institutions and stability among its citizens. The struggle against poverty, unemployment, and lack of responsibility was an essential fertilizer for national growth that initially grew out of religious conviction.

Rational belief established itself as the ethical directive in society as a result of the cooperation between science and theology. Taylor states that precisely during this historical phase, the first interest in human rights was formed. Investigating the natural laws for which God set the premises was a source of thrilling wonder to many a scientist.

The plurality of dimensions speaks for the need of a multidimensional rationality. Secular society needs both belief in God and the spiritual realm, as well as sensible science that examines His creation and gains knowledge about the God-given laws of nature. The spiritual and ethical contribution of believers is an asset to secular society and not to be rejected in public debates. As Thomas Aquinas said, "Faith builds on nature and complements it." In that light, the attempt to label religious believers as superstitious and outdated individuals emerge as the truly irrational.

*In the Dialectics of Secularization: On Reason and Religion*, Pope Benedict XVI and his co-author, Jürgen Habermas, assert the importance of religion not being isolated in the private sphere. Instead, respect for historical European norms should be reinstated to curtail the trend of weakening solidarity and empathy. Europe needs to gather moral strength from its historic origins. It is an urgently needed ideological shift. Religious ethics have a role, a moral role, to play as the ethical foundation of society. Religious perspectives represent valuable contributions to strengthening the social community with a new sense of solidarity, kindness, unselfish acts and care for those who need it most.

Both Habermas and Pope Benedict XVI seem to share a deep concern over the moral decay in Europe. Habermas doubts that a state that denies religion social influence can sufficiently motivate its citizens to empathy and solidarity.

# The Culture War

\*\*\*

# Religion and Its Ethics Should Play a Role in Politics

It seems that Jürgen Habermas remedy the lack of solidarity that permeates current day Western thinking. He calls for a new type of reflection that does not exclude the relevant moral contribution of religious ethics. Again, these are revolutionizing thoughts from one of the leading atheist voices of our time. He states that this new type of thinking should continue to distinguish between faith and science – which is important – but it will reject the narrow scientific definition of reason that lacks respect for religious doctrines. In other words, Habermas feels that it is necessary to increase respect for the ethical considerations of religious citizens.

He states that religious citizens should be allowed to publicly express and justify their convictions, even in a religious language that needs to be translated into a more secular public language in order to be properly understood. Other citizens may learn something valuable, he says, from these statements. The ability of religious traditions to formulate moral perceptions is important to the fabric of society, and should not be underestimated. Religious convictions can have an absolute core of truth and offer valuable moral considerations to relevant political questions. In this way, useful ethical principles from the religious basis of the traditional European culture can be communicated to the society of today.

Habermas further says that the liberal state should have an interest in allowing religious voices to participate in the public sphere of politics. Otherwise, society runs the danger of becoming severed from sources important to the formation of opinion and identity. There is no good reason for reducing the complexity and variety of expressed opinions, in his view. Thus, diversity requires that not just the current-day popular minorities such as gays, immigrants or single mothers are to be given a voice, but also groups such as conservative Christians and those who fight for the traditional family structure should have the right to speak and be respected for what they say, even if in a strongly religious language.

Citizens in a democratic society owe each other the opportunity to justify their public engagement in society as a whole. People who speak up do so because they feel that their arguments may add something constructive to the debate. Habermas says that this civil duty can be defined much more tolerantly so that debate inputs are permitted in a religious as well as a secular language. Both paradigms belong to the European context and heritage.

This is, again, quite a revolutionary thought and far from the anti-religious and anti-traditionalist sentiment permeating the Western public debate today. If citing Bible verses is to be accepted as part of an intellectual argument, much would really have to change. Someone who quotes the Bible on national TV would definitely be ridiculed and quickly omitted from the public discourse, deemed unfit to participate. One can but imagine the public ridiculing he would have to endure in newspapers by columnists eager to belittle him.

Christian voices are brutally silenced in today's European public debates, exemplified by the harsh reaction against journalists, politicians or public speakers who wear crosses or religious signs. To speak openly about one's faith and refer to religious dogma almost instantly raises eyebrows. The extreme-liberal, atheist politically correct discourse almost instantly deem religious arguments as irrational, while secular atheists' arguments instantly are labeled "sound reason" or "pure logic." The intolerance against people of faith is appalling, especially considering how many of the vital Western values and freedoms precisely derive from a religious, philosophical pool.

Habermas nonetheless states that if religious participants in public debate observe the requirements of relevance and reason, their arguments should, none the less, be assigned value equal to those of non-believing participants. There is no good normative reason to exclude spiritual people's opinions from a pluralistic society. The introduction of religious freedom is the correct political answer to issues of religious pluralism, he states.

Habermas makes another point: the state's secular separation between politics and religion is a necessary, but insufficient condition for guaranteeing the religious freedom of citizens. It is not adequate to depend on the goodwill of a secular authority because if this authority goes extreme liberal, hostility for religion will soon follow.

He goes further than most and states that even the language of the religious should not be suppressed, but rather society should be able to translate its significance into a more secular language that is comprehensible to all. In other words, Christians and other religious people should be able to speak publicly and participate in the public discourse, using the religious language that they do in Churches, and secular society should view it as its responsibility to translate what is said into understandable secular language.

This way, he states, many may profit from the wisdom coming from the inherently religious person, even if his language may be somewhat foreign to some. What respect this would provide for the religious subgroups of society, legitimizing the contributions presented by precisely those that seem to be so hated and ridiculed in the heathen Europe of today.

One of our times' most influential moral philosophers, John Rawls, is well-known for his analysis of the importance of an institutional separation between politics and religion. In one of his early works, *A Brief Inquiry into the Meaning of Sin and Faith* he nonetheless states that religious arguments can be completely consistent with secular arguments. The difference is that these arguments often employ a different language than the secular. Both these forms of expression can be translated into a public language that everyone understands. The principle of tolerance allows religiously minded people an equal right to present arguments, as long as both parties treat each other with respect.

Rawls points out that the history of both religion and philosophy shows that there are many reasonable ways to understand the full breadth of essential social values. In fact, religion has an important contribution to make, as one of the influential forces of the science of moral, philosophical thinking.

Hanne Nabintu Herland

# CHAPTER 9

# Modern Science is Not Neutral, Nor Objective

*Humanist theories of science acknowledge the challenge of "objectivity" and "neutrality," as it is apparent that most of what we call objective, seldom is so. Especially research in social science tends to be filled with assumptions that are coloured by the ruling paradigm and whatever is currently deemed "popular thinking." History books, for example, often do not retell history as it actually happened, but rather present the past according to our current day politically correct agenda.*

## Is Research Ever Objective?

HISTORIAN AND PHILOSOPHER of science, Thomas S. Kuhn garnered attention in the 1960s when he showed how subjective much of the research at universities really is. The historical development of scientific theories illustrates how the dominant epistemology built atop politically correct ideologies strongly influences the opinions and writings of professors and students alike. The individual scientist is often much more influenced by the political ideologies of his time and subjected to a peer-pressure to reach the politically correct conclusions that he very well knows will be applauded. He, therefore, tends to end up interpreting his subject-matter in line with ideological trends. Sometimes he is aware of this; sometimes it is unintentional.

# The Culture War

In *The Structure of Scientific Revolutions,* Kuhn explains that in science, the dominant understanding of reality builds on a series of assumptions. It becomes the intellectual's role to produce evidence that supports the dominant academic consensus, which Kuhn calls the dominant paradigm. A paradigm, the theoretical framework of a scientific school, may work wonderfully and enable scientists to provide a framework within which the scientist may map the pieces of his findings into a system of understanding. Yet, if paradigms are inadequate, they end up making wrong assumptions, and its conclusions, in turn, fail.

In other words, research easily becomes biased and tendentious, based on the professor's personal convictions or ideological lens. Kuhn points out that the role of the oppositional intellectual is to challenge the ruling paradigm and break the logjam of politically correct assumptions. If no one dares break out of the deadlock, and nobody poses critical questions in order to examine whether the current hypothesis' actually hold water, the quality of intellectual thinking is steadily reduced.

Indeed, others before Kuhn had studied the problem of twisting history in order to make it better fit the ruling paradigms. In the 1600s, Francis Bacon complained in *Novum Organum* of the medieval scientist, that he did not sufficiently incorporate a sufficient range of experience in framing his decisions. The scientist first determined the question and then sought for the answers he wished for, Bacon said, those answers that fit his assumptions, to begin with. He stated that a scientist's method too often ended up bending the evidence to suit his own ideology or preference. Every age needs critical thinking, so to speak.

It is, for instance, a historical fact that the Early Middle Ages was a time when monasteries were the leading intellectual learning sites, educating the elite and providing for the poor and needy. Yet, modern-day professors have often referred to this age "The Dark Ages." It is true that the term also refers to the period after the fall of the Roman Empire onward, yet many regularly use the term when referring to the Early Middle Ages, negatively focusing on the religious world-view at the time. On the other hand, the 1600s is described as the "Age of Enlightenment," implying that as scientists were questioning God, increasingly critical of traditional religion, looking for other explanations of nature, that would somehow make them more "enlightened" than the previous generations.

There seems to be an underlying need, a hidden agenda, to insinuate that an age of strong religious beliefs automatically was "a dark phase" in European history. Yet, it was the early Christian medieval thinkers who first enhanced rationality on a large-scale, placing the ability to reason on the same level as faith, stating that both of these qualities lead to knowledge. The scholastics during the Middle Ages studied nature and the cosmos in order to understand God better, and strongly emphasized the need for rationality. They laid the foundation for the later study of modern science and order in nature.

If academic debates are to remain free and open, inquisitive questions must be posed in order to look for flaws in the current paradigm, and thereby find better solutions to unresolved problems. Reflections on how the professor or researcher taints his own research with a subjective approach has long been debated. How is it possible to attain research that is as little as possible colored by the views or opinions of the researcher? How do we know that the scientific papers that we read are not simply reflections of the professor presenting the politically correct narrative or paradigm? In other words, how exactly is he trying to influence me?

After all, empirical facts are interpreted by a researcher, who himself is part of a particular paradigm or academic world view. It is not only the facts that speak but the voice of the interpreter. He is the one that in qualitative research poses questions to informants, for example, in a particular way. He knows that if he asks the question in a certain way, it is likely that he gets more negative answers. If he, on the contrary, asks the same informants about the same issue but poses the question from another angle, he is likely to get many more to answer yes. Positively, the question "Are you sure that you, as a modern intelligent person, believe in an old-fashioned religion that is outdated in so many ways?" will probably give different replies than: "Do you believe in meaningful, spiritual values that create solidarity, empathy, and love between people?"

In social sciences and humanism, research thus implies that the professor is aware of the fact that he is determining how the informant's answers turn out, depending on the way he poses the question. If a professor is strongly influenced by Social Darwinism – that is the application of biological Darwinian evolution to social fields and cultures – it is quite easy for the same professor to make anyone from Borneo, Congo, Peru or somewhere else that sounds very "foreign" seem "backward" or a "less developed" human. For example, Borneo animism may be described with an underlying, condescending tone. A Congolese's belief in God will be depicted as relics from a dying world, something that "a rational modern person" understands to be "outdated religion and indigenous belief."

Professors and intellectuals who should have defended fearless speech, instead become puppets of an academic elite, rather than being critical voices, posing questions to those in power. If critical voices are silenced, and open discussions cease, scientific research itself glides into an apathetic self-confirming state.

In such a society, being an academic means taking the role of someone whose job is to confirm the ideas of the political establishment – to uphold the current narrative. To many professors, it becomes a question of complying in order to receive the necessary research funds, the right promotions, his job depends on it. After all, he has a career and needs to earn a living. Posing unpopular questions may easily result in his career coming to an abrupt halt, and he knows it. This is a subtle form of tyranny, a soft despotism.

It is ironic. We used to pity the intellectuals of the Soviet Union and speak of how they lacked freedom of thought. We said that living under such Communist propaganda and suppressive conditions, far from a free-spirited critical intellectual debate, must have been excruciatingly hard. We felt sorry for the many who had to flee the country and move to the West.

Now it is we who have university systems with much of the same kind of wide spread fear and censorship. This is happening in the heart of the Western culture. Some even move to Russia now, in order to escape Western repression – whistle-blowers, journalists, and scientists. Many are careful not to publish articles that contain material that deviate from what is politically correct, fully aware that if they do, the repercussions will be too hard to handle on a personal level. Just as many citizens in the Soviet Union could not see clearly to what extent they were being subdued to propaganda in the press, we also do not comprehend how stifled our freedom of speech really is.

For example, a professor stuck in a conformist structure, will be completely furious after reading just a few pages of this book, since he disagrees with my world-view. He will find it horrifying that someone believes that we have lost something by throwing away traditional European values. He will criticize the research; say that the list of references was too short; the authors cited were incompetent; that Habermas lacks knowledge about what a secular society really is; Chomsky lacks a proper understanding of the world; the Pope is religious, so he should not even be cited; Peter Berger is not reliable and so on. The professor's attitude and personal feelings would permeate that which he wrote to me. In essence, all research in the humanities is always at some level subjective. It is not neutral. This is probably also why, social science is an excellent field to penetrate if you want to dominate a generation, by imposing tools of propaganda to manipulate the way they think and thereby control how they act and, for example, whom they would vote for in an election.

Hanne Nabintu Herland

\*\*\*

# The Flaws of Empiricism and Positivism

Today many views "modern science" and "empiricism" – the practice of basing theories on testing of data derived from human experiences – as if these are infallible entities. Yet, one hardly remembers that for example lobotomy – drilling holes into a patient's skull - was considered "scientific" only a few years ago. In the 1940s and 50s, based on what was felt to be observable evidence at the time, drilling into the skull was thought to cure various mental illnesses. This "scientific practice" was kept until new theories emerged that suggested other methods.

This is but one example of how science is not always accurate although it professes to be, being dependent on current trends regarding what may be considered appropriate or not. Empiricism is based on experience and experiences are in constant change, also dependent on which elements that the scientist is willing to examine. As human experience tends to be flawed, empirical studies often end up reflecting that same bias.

In social sciences, new ideas and approaches have regularly overturned old paradigms. It has not happened without ongoing intellectual battles that often lasted for decades before new world-views won the fight. For example, as when the philosopher and early sociologist, Auguste Comte developed positivism early in the 1800s – the philosophical method that only recognized that which can be empirically verified through human experience or mathematical logic, therefore rejecting metaphysics and the supernatural.

Comte declared that the only matter we may know as "facts" are those derived from human experience. All authoritative knowledge had to be based on the experiences of human senses, interpreted through "reason" and "logic," denying any metaphysical reality that was not observable in the physical world. Knowledge was only attainable through empirical, testable hypothesis, which through the gathering of measurable evidence than could be called a "fact." Everything else should be denied as "non-fact." His thesis followed along the lines of empiricism, which may be defined as the theory that all knowledge *should* be based on experience derived from the senses.

In the 1800s, empiricism became a popular way of examining the observable evidence. It spread like wildfire. Now, everything was to be explained empirically, according to the observable by the human eye. It was a good method in natural science, mathematics and within other disciplines, helping the scientist to determine, with mathematical certainty, the probability of this or that. The original idea was to establish methods by which testable hypothesis may examine the evidence in order to determine how the world works – the object of science itself.

Yet, when applied to philosophy and religion, empiricism seemed unable to describe the metaphysical reality and the subtle inner rooms of the human mind. Comte's positivism ruled out the metaphysical dimension in a new and starkly atheist way. His definition of "fact" denied every other reality outside the purely observable. If empiricism is to be based on human experience and knowledge, and knowledge is subjective, empiricism is actually subjectively tainted.

"Positivism" – hoping to represent that which was "positively" certain – clearly should have been renamed "negativism", taking into account how it incorporates only one part of the driving forces in man, - the observable by the naked eye - explaining only approximately half of the evidence, and omitting the complex inner psychological and metaphysical elements in the human.

Positivism nonetheless became a major philosophical fashion in the West – it dominated the intellectuals, formed the basis for debates. It became the politically correct paradigm. "Everybody" agreed. Melanie Phillips states in *The World Turned Upside Down* that scientific materialism, the ideology that aims at destroying religion by claiming to be able to explain everything scientifically leaves no role for any other kind of inquiry of the universe. None whatsoever.

Comte became the popular founder of this kind of "materialist dictatorship," with the doctrine of positivism which hoped to replace Christianity with science. The idea was that "irrational religion" was to be replaced by "rational science," making the scientifically provable the only truth. If it was not empirically provable, it did not exist. Comte actually went very far in presenting empiricism as a religion and scientists as its new clergy – he boasted of this, as Phillips points out, saying he would preach positivism in Notre Dame as the only real and complete religion.

As we see, positivism was not as scientifically objective as it professed to be. Human experience is terribly subjective. Two people may be at the same gathering, yet later refer to it totally differently. Even time itself fluctuates depending on where you position yourself, as stated by Einstein's theory of relativity. Even what you hear is not an objective observable fact, neither what you observe, for example a kilometer away from where you are standing. The attempt to understand reality, solely in terms of material law, has ended up failing us as a comprehensive method of understanding the complexity of reality.

Let us take an example: A glass. It clearly exists, as it stands on the table. We may scientifically measure the amount of sand the glass was made from, what kind of liquids it may contain, its weight, the weight of the liquid and so on. We may state, or assume, that the glass was produced in a factory; we may study which factories make such glasses and the production process.

The problem with empiricism is that it only gives us information about the product itself and its production process. It is not able to access and prove the mind of its maker, his ideas, his intentions, his emotions. It is unable to measure the mental link between intention and its product, only its effects. Empiricism only reflects the materialistic realities and may only test hypothesis from the narrow scope of the tangible, touchable world.

The glass is actually the product of its maker. There was an industrialist somewhere who decided to make glasses and sell them, with, we may assume based on experience, the idea of earning money by producing things that people needed. The glass is actually the result of a thought – the thought of its producer, as it first came as an idea into his head. That particular glass would never have ended up on the table, if it were not for the thought process and then, creational process of its maker. The glass and its maker are interlinked.

What we see when looking at the glass, is only the glass itself. We do not see its creator, we only view the results of his thought process. The weakness of empiricism is its lack of access into the non-materialistic dimension. We may not empirically prove the initial thought process of its maker, neither how his ideas influenced its creation. We may only study the result of the production process and the glass itself, and *assume or believe* that we understand the mind of the producer.

Empiricism does not have the ability to access the creator's mind and prove by testable hypothesis the insight into his intentions, as it is confined to the purely observable. Empiricism does not even measure intentions, ideas, thoughts, feelings, spiritual matter. One may, of course, look at the effects of the ideas of the creator, and thus profess to have proven his intentions. Yet even here, there are myriads of variables that empiricism does not access.

Thus, even a small example like this, illustrates the many limitations of testable hypothesis, since many of them simply are not testable from a materialistic viewpoint alone. A whole array of disciplines was affected by Auguste Comte's narrow sense of defining reality, by rejecting man's spirituality and acknowledging only the physical part of the body. The study of religion, anthropology, psychology, as well as that of the human body and its medical needs, have been strongly marked by positivism's rejection of the non-empirically provable.

✳✳✳

# The Limits of Darwinian Evolution

The English naturalist and geologist, Charles Darwin, outlined in *The Origin of Species*, first published in 1859, the theories regarding the development of the species from the lower and simple to the higher and more complex, through the process of natural selection and the survival of the fittest. He called the process of creation "evolution." His theories of biological evolution quickly became immensely popular. Yet, this theory remains flawed as much of it still is not scientifically proven, it relies on a number of assumptions. Darwin's evolution has to be accepted by faith – as verifiable proof still is missing. Yet, the theory of evolution has remained at the forefront of Western atheist thought and strongly asserts that nature developed by itself.

Over the years, Darwinian theory has demonstrated its flaws. For one, scientists seem unable to prove development from one species to another. The only element that has been proven is that all species derive from one common ancestor. As pointed out by professor of biological science at Lehigh University, Michael J. Behe in the ground-breaking work, *Darwin's Black Box. The Biochemical Challenge to Evolution*, we still do not know how the development occurred. The forming of new species – "macroevolution" has never been observed, only variations within each species – "microevolution," such as birds getting longer or shorter wings and so forth.

Evolution beyond variation is still a hypothetical assumption. Those who believe in it, do so based on faith – they believe in it, regardless of whether it has been empirically proven or not. Darwin, as we know, could not even explain the complexity of a human cell. As Behe states, the universe as a whole is extremely fine-tuned for life, suggesting nature exhibits evidence of intelligent design rather than Darwin's randomness.

Another intelligent-design theorist, Michael A. Cremo points out in *Rethinking Darwin: A Vedic Study of Darwinism and Intelligent Design and Forbidden Archaeology*, that not only did the Neanderthals live on earth in the same time period as Homo sapiens, as modern science now reluctantly acknowledges, but human remains have been found in the Earth's layers millions of years ago.

Revealing such evidence would cause the Darwinian theory to collapse, and previous human-like creatures could not be called "human ancestors," as they lived on the earth, side by side for a very long time. Until this day, biology school books still show the illustration starting with a monkey, then the slow "development" towards Neanderthals and finally the upright *Homo sapiens*, a Darwinian illustration outdated long ago. Children's biology books continue propagating for the outdated view on the development of *Homo sapiens*, yet another illustration of how candid academic authors are to repeat the current paradigm, even if it has been proven to be wrong.

Cremo suggests that the current paradigm or the established worldview functions in such a way that data is suppressed if it does not coincide with current academic consent and belief in evolutionary theory. New revelations and findings are simply silenced, in order not to challenge the current understanding of evolution. There is little willingness to humbly admit: "We do not understand the complexities of creation."

Trusting Darwin's theory, requires a high amount of faith, just like any religion and its explanations of the complexities of the world. Still, Darwin is widely used as an example of how "modern empiricism and science" demonstrates how wrong believers in God have been in history. As it turns out, Darwinian theory is as dependent on pure faith as any religious explanation of creation.

As we see, modern science constantly changes its hypothesis, depending on the current "academic experience or belief." What was "scientific" yesterday, is not "scientific" today, as new "evidence" steadily arrives. One example. The doctors that used to operate ulcers and remove half of the stomach a few decades ago, now know that ulcer is bacteria. If someone said that ulcer is curable with a few pills back then, they would deem him "unscientific" or "delusional" for opposing status quo. And in the 1920s, most scientists believed that the world was static. Whoever contradicted the prevailing view, would be viewed with skepticism and called "unscientific." Then the American astronomer, Edwin Hubble studied the universe and found evidence of its expansion.[18] The debate was settled, and a new paradigm introduced: the universe as we know it expands.

---

[18] *Hubble, Edwin (1929). "A relation between distance and radial velocity among extra-galactic nebulae".* PNAS. *15 (3): 168–173. Bibcode:1929PNAS...15..168H. doi:10.1073/pnas.15.3.168. PMC 522427. PMID 16577160.*

Whoever now said that it was static, was suddenly the one deemed to be irrational.

Even Albert Einstein spent almost fifteen years denying that the universe was expanding, trying to rework the equations to prove that the universe is static. In his final memoirs, *The World as I see it,* he calls this the biggest mistake of his career, and complains that it caused him not to make any major discoveries during those fifteen years, stuck as he was in his old-fashioned thinking, even if science kept proving him wrong.[19]

As we see, even a genius such as Einstein struggled to accept new, scientific facts. Man's subjectivity when deciding what to believe in, whether it is scientific belief in new findings or rational belief in God, is quite remarkably able to make individuals stuck in a limiting way of thinking. The scientist will easily use his ability to rationalize and come to whatever conclusion he wants to.

Faith is not easily proven empirically. You cannot prove, according to Auguste Comte's philosophical empiricism – or positivism – that angels or demons were engaged in a particular situation, causing this or that. Empirical methods may analyze many elements of reality, but certainly not all. Love. How is love to be proven empirically? Hatred, jealousy, qualities such as perseverance. How to measure the long-term effects of hatred on the human body? The effects of infidelity on the quality of life? One may, of course, analyze the actions that tend to follow somebody that hates or loves. Still, somebody's actions of resentment may have an array of other reasons than hatred.

There are scientists who profess to be able to prove God's existence through science – the existence of a metaphysical force. The whole field of intelligent design aims at proving God's existence through the observable, stating that science itself *has discovered God.* The condensed knowledge of the universe today, represented by the sum of NASA findings, confirm that the universe is expanding from one particular point in time.

Physicist Gerald Schroeder, who worked many years at MIT, states in *Has Science discovered God* that even saying the universe expands would have been called deeply unscientific in the 1920s and even later. [20] He states that at that time, most scientists agreed that the Bible was completely wrong from its very beginning, in assuming that there was a beginning of time

---

[19] Einstein's 'Biggest Blunder' Turns Out to Be Right (Thursday, August 17, 2017) http://www.space.com/9593-einstein-biggest-blunder-turns.html
5 things Albert Einstein got totally wrong Thursday, August 17, 2017) http://tiny.cc/b5z6my
[20] Scientific Proof of God (Thursday, August 17, 2017) https://www.youtube.com/watch?v=LzetqYev_AI

from which the world developed. Ever since the theory of Big Bang entered the scene, the Bible didn't seem so wrong after all.

The Big Bang theory asserts that the universe began from an initial burst of immense amounts of energy at the beginning of what we would call time. That is, since we, as part of the product of Big Bang, are situated within time, are unable to fully comprehend or have insight into that which was before our kind of "time," so to speak.

We do not even comprehend much of what is going on within our own timeline, confined as we are to thinking within diagrams of time, space, and matter. Let's say if we look back three million years ago. The limits of the human mind are quite evident, as there is not that much we truly know about that time period. How do we examine this period? Due to our obvious lack of understanding of the universe, science tries to use the empirical data available and define that which was both before the Big Bang and after, through analyzing the forces of nature.

The big outburst of energy naturally posits that there was something prior to the Bang. Something, outside of our timeline, must have used the forces of nature at work within the universe and fused this into the Bang. We tend to define that which is outside the universe as nothing. Consequently, in the Big Bang, there must have been massive power at work.

The starting point of the Big Bang is often referred to as the point of quantum fluctuations, which states that the universe allows creation from the "nothingness" outside the universe, to "something," provided that you have the forces of nature – the laws of physics and relativity. Science has discovered that one may create something from "nothing," provided the laws of nature function, laws that are not physical but act on the physical. So, if they helped act to create the universe, that means that they predate the universe.

This leaves us with the following: We have a set of forces – the forces of nature that are not physical, but act on the physical, and are able to create something from nothing, thereby predating the universe and our understanding of time. Gerald Schroeder points out that precisely this is the Biblical definition of God. God – as manifest in the universe – predates time, he is outside of time, he is not a physical being, and he created the universe. As we can see, science, as we know it, may establish some facts, but not all.

\*\*\*

# The Limits of Empiricism

Let's return to the example of the glass. If we add for example a tree or a living creature such as a person – and compare these, empiricism – the practice of basing ideas and theories on testing and human experience – would instantly acknowledge that someone created the glass. It was obviously made in a factory. Yet, it would equally not be able to establish that the tree or a man, who is much more complex and advanced than the glass – was made by its maker or creator. Instantly, empiricism demonstrates its limits: it may not acknowledge that living matter has a maker, but readily acknowledges that a manufactured product has a creator.

The words of C.S. Lewis put the metaphysical into a physical context, philosophically stating in *The Case for Christianity*: "Supposing there was no intelligence behind the universe, no creative mind. In that case, nobody designed my brain for the purpose of thinking. It is merely that when the atoms inside my skull happen, for physical or chemical reasons, to arrange themselves in a certain way, this gives me, as a by-product, the sensation I call thought. But, if so, how can I trust my own thinking to be true? It is like upsetting a milk jug and hoping that the way it splashes itself will give you a map of London. But if I can't trust my own thinking, of course, I cannot trust the arguments leading to atheism, and therefore have no reason to be an atheist, or anything else. Unless I believe in God, I cannot believe in thought; so I can never use thought to disbelieve in God."

# CHAPTER 10

# Anti-Christian elites in a world of believers

*There are approximately 1.3 billion Muslims, and 2.3 billion Christians in the world, in addition to leading religions such as Buddhism and Hinduism. This statistical fact makes it clear that modern individuals continue to believe in God, a thought-provoking setback for the few atheists that actually exist. Just as reason and belief have been intertwined since the beginning of Christianity, it continues to work hand in hand in modern, secular societies.*

## A Surprising Focus on Religion

HISTORICALLY CHRISTIANITY HAS had a massive impact on Western civilization. Traditional religion influenced philosophy, art, music, social structures and institutions, architecture and science. Historical trends that stem directly from Christianity include the development of social welfare, economics and the Protestant work ethic, politics, literature and the traditional structures of Western family life, as we shall see. In *A Time of Transition*, Jürgen Habermas points out that universalistic egalitarianism, from which sprang the ideals of freedom and a collective life in solidarity, the individual morality of conscience, human rights and democracy, is the direct legacy of the Judaic ethic of justice and the Christian ethic of love. [21]

---

[21] Political Theory - Habermas and Rawls (Wednesday, August 23, 2017) http://habermas-rawls.blogspot.com/2009/06/misquote-about-habermas-and.html

An overwhelming international trend destroys the myth that there is an automatic conflict between rationalism and faith. Billions of people participate in the development of the rationally-based market Capitalistic society without any negative effect on their faith in a God.

Yet, as earlier stated, in the 1800s Nietzsche proclaimed that God is dead. He and many intellectuals of his time idealized nihilism – the belief that there is no higher meaning to anything in the world; and hedonism – a related moral philosophy that attempts to justify the individual's right to self-gratification and promiscuity.

Auguste Comte set out to destroy traditional faith by revolutionizing science through philosophical empiricism or positivism. As mentioned, empiricism stated that only that which was based on data of human experience was to be called "facts," thus excluding the *a priori* experiences of the metaphysical realm. He wished to replace Christianity and even called empiricism a new religion itself. Marx called faith in God opium for the masses. These were all revolutionary ideas at that time, advocates of atheism have been repeating it ever since. It was the Western elites' revolt against God, claiming man's right to do whatever he pleases. His conscience was viewed as a constraint to his personal freedom.

Scientific materialism claimed that everything in the material world could be explained scientifically. Therefore God may not exist. Here we find the seeds of the social legitimization of materialism and quest for money and fame as man's ultimate goal, attitudes that permeate Western society today. According to these theories, the only valuables were to be found in the tangible, physical world. If something does not fit into the "scientific model of empiricism," it does not exist.

For many years, this has been the prevailing view of Western intellectual elites. Professors and scholars alike agreed that religion would diminish and disappear entirely from the West. Even Habermas believed that secularization would eradicate spirituality and that society would flourish in the wake of this non-religious evolution in societies that focused on the values of materialism alone.

However, this has, as we all now know, not been the case. For quite some time, studies have opposed the strict theories of secularization that assumed that religion would disappear and instead confirmed that belief in God and the importance of spirituality has not diminished in modern society. Regardless of how "modern" they became, people still stayed religious. Even where traditional forms of religion and church membership lose their foothold, new religious movements and alternative beliefs continue to multiply outside the church, implying the human somehow need to believe *in something*. Put differently; one may say that belief in God did not diminish in the West; rather, it changed character.

One has to bear in mind that secularization is a difficult term. One of the challenges is the many definitions of the word, as also is the case with the term religion. How one understands religion gives way to different theories of secularization, as we shall see.

The term secularization involves discussions around empirical evidence on different levels. One may talk about the substantial impact of religion on the inner life – our consciousness and inner spirituality – or the functional, outer aspects of religion; our actions and societal structures, such as whether secularization has taken place in society, culture or in each individual.

Today, leading sociologists affirm that religion still stands firm in the general population. This is evident, even though the secularization of Western social institutions and cultural climate is a fact – inflaming strong anti-Christian sentiments. According to a 2012 study about Religiosity and Discrimination in the European Union, Christianity remains largely untouched in the local population, with 72% Christians, of which Catholics account for 48%, Protestants 12%, Orthodox around 8% and 4.1% other minority groups. This is happening despite the massive thrust from secular society to de-Christianize Europe.

Yet, other polls also show in parallel, the decline of institutionalized Christianity on the continent. In America, the Barna Group has conducted large surveys that seem to show that it actually is the strong Christians who often end up leaving today's Churches, as institutionalized religion is becoming more in line with secular society. It seems that many Churches in the West, both in the US and also in Europe, are becoming politically correct social clubs rather than places of spiritual enlightening. One may argue that as Churches become secularized, its strongest members lose interest as they did not sign up for a secular humanist cult.

It seems that the anti-religious political elites and academic establishment who so strongly are against reaffirming Europe's cultural identity, are the same pushing hard to devalue the role of Christianity. They are doing this against the will of the largely religious population. These elites are, still, after having worked diligently for so many years, trying to influence Europeans to reject the belief in the supernatural – but surprisingly high numbers believe in a God.

Unexpectedly, many now describe our age as the century of religion. Faith has turned out to play a surprisingly central role all over the world, and it influences political and social issues in an unexpectedly strong manner. The fact that religious beliefs maintain such a high degree of relevance in modern society has amazed and confounded many, especially those in the West who have fought so hard to quash the belief that man is interconnected with the metaphysical dimension.

*** 

## National Identity In a Globalized World

The renowned religious sociologist, Peter Berger, is also characterized by his dramatic shift in the view on religion. He had a mid-career transformation regarding how he perceives religion in modern societies and admits to a major mistake as a sociologist. In this sense, he is most extraordinary: Earlier in life, he indicated that modernization would cause religion to decline. He strongly advocated for it, assuming that a globalized society would gradually lead to religious alienation. He later found this to be erroneous and adjusted his hypothesis, convinced by overwhelming new research and statistics.

A society characterized by modern diversity does not at all need to mean breaking away from traditional religion. In *Peter Berger and the Study of Religion*, he gives evidence that modernization has proceeded hand in hand with persistent religious faith. However, the separation of church and state in secular societies has placed religion in a new and more deinstitutionalized position in the public sphere. Berger states that religion has a new role, but it is clearly not a diminished one.

The sociologists George Barna and David Kinnaman have addressed the issue of deinstitutionalized Christianity in the West and seem to find that churchless people are becoming the norm in the US. In *Churchless: Understanding Today's Unchurched and How to Connect with Them*, they reveal the results of a five-year study based on interviews with thousands of previous church goers, pointing out that churchless adults in the US have grown by one-third, only the past decade. Many people state that they are leaving the churches to look for a "genuine encounter" with God, something the traditional churches somehow seem unable to provide to the same extent as before.

In his research, Berger also found that spirituality appears to play an equally important role today as before. People tend to find new ways to approach the cultural values derived from religion. They find modern expressions for worship appealing in their search for spiritual awakening.

Berger also states that the American melting pot, a part of the religious and ethnic fabric ever since the beginning in the US, provide overwhelming evidence that diversity of beliefs does not necessitate the need to relegate religion to the private sphere.

One major point comes across strongly: Diversity and pluralism do not need to be in opposition to preserving one's own cultural identity and its values. The US has, traditionally, been closely linked to a Western form of Christianity and its values, yet it has still been a diverse and pluralistic society that respects both believers and non-believers. Immigrants have been highly welcome, but it has been expected that they join the American way of thinking, connecting to American ideals and principles.

Contrary to what many progressives state, national identity and a strong cultural foundation do not contradict having a positive attitude towards globalization. Respecting oneself does not mean disrespecting others. It is only natural that, for example, China determines which values are to be prevalent in China and that Russia determines Russian values and political preferences. In the same way, Europe should, of course, be able to dictate which rules and regulations apply to all who wish to move to its lands. This is not chauvinism, but justice.

Each nation has, according to international law, the right to determine, within its own borders, the values that should prevail there. This is at the basis of the UN charter and defines national sovereignty. To be securely rooted in one's own national values and culture is vital in order to be able to meet the challenges of internationalization. A strong national identity helps an individual to respect others and their differences, recognizing their right to self-determination in their country just as you determine the values in your own country. Diversity does not need to conflict with nationalism and a secure cultural foundation in one's own values as long as immigrants, foreign workers and citizens alike abide by the national laws and regulations, and respect the culture indigenous to that nation.

***

# Religious Belief: Remarkably Resilient

To sum up the academic debate, one may say that until the 1980s, hardcore secularization theories dominated the academic circles, arguing that the more worldly and secular society became – the more religion was removed to the private sphere – the less important the role of religion would become, both as an institution as well as in the private lives of citizens.

The German sociologist Max Weber argued that modernism's definition of rationality was considered to be incompatible with traditional religion. According to Weber, a demystification of reality occurred in society that greatly debilitated religion and all forms of spiritualism.

Sociologist of religions and professor, Steve Bruce, is a representative for this hardcore view, as explained in *God is Dead: Secularization in the West*, which claims that following industrialization and the Renaissance, religion has permanently been forced to retreat and disappear from society. He viewed secularization as a social condition manifesting the declining importance of religion in the state and institutions, a decline of its social standing and a decline in the extent to which people engage in institutionalized religious practices.

Sociologist of religion, Linda Whitehead points out in *Peter Berger: The Sociology of Religion* that modern researchers all over the world now consider the so-called strong theory of secularization out-of-date. Scientific research has largely proven the theory invalid, as far too much evidence shows that people who live in secular societies largely remain religious. The theory tended to ignore the fact that people still seek relationships and cling to social bonding found in religious groups. Religion also satisfies emotional and spiritual needs and meets desires for social belonging, as well as providing valid explanations of the meaning of life.

A softer theory of secularization states that the conditions for the growth of religion may actually be better in modern society than many have thought. Given certain conditions, religion may even become stronger. While institutionalized religion and religious expression in the public realm may decline, religious expressions can find new and unexpected forms in the private sphere.

This may, for one, be interpreted as the people's revolt against strict state rule over the Church and its dogma, which has been the case in several Northern European countries. In societies where religious people are harassed, belittled and persecuted, believers may also "go underground," meeting discretely in homes instead of the institutionalized Churches. In addition, when religious beliefs are considered socially unacceptable, many avoid admitting or openly speak about their beliefs, and so on.

Berger noticed how people in Europe are not publicly as religious as before, and therefore calls Europe an exception in regard to observations made in the rest of the world. Yet, the high number of Christians and believers in God in Europe, over 80%, in one study as we have seen, seems to contradict, on some level, his conclusion. Modern diversity has not caused religion to lose its importance elsewhere, Berger states. Religion endures both as a cultural phenomenon and as an inner force of conscience in the private sphere. This puzzling trend seems to reflect the Western culture as a whole.

In the US, the non-church-going populations are increasing, and the number of Americans who answer "no religious preference" in polls is skyrocketing, states Timothy Keller in *The Reason for God: Belief in an Age of Skepticism*. Still, religious faith is growing outside the Church buildings, and even in academia, pointing to trends that identify the growing number of spiritually aware Christians who simply do not visit the traditional Churches as actively as before. He cites surveys showing that up to 25% of philosophy professors in the US are what one may label as "orthodox" Christians, or firm believers, – only 1% being so thirty years ago. A number of Churches are also growing in America, pointing to a somewhat strange fact. Religion is both growing and diminishing in the USA.

Religious belief has proven to be truly resilient. Even in the Far East, Christianity is exploding. According to studies from Center of Religion and Chinese Society at Purdue University, China may have 255 million Christians by 2025, making it the largest Christian nation in the East – and maybe worldwide. If such trends continue, there may soon be more Christians in China than in the US – of course defining who is Christian in America is in itself not all that easy anymore. We shall later discuss Russia, where Christianity is expanding as the majority of Russians now attend Church regularly.

This points in a direction that may show that religion may not be said to be in decline. It is, on the contrary, on the rise in many parts of the world. This should not come as a surprise, as religion has always been woven into the very fabric of human society.

The so-called dialectic theory of secularization, as explained by Professor Otto Krogseth of the University of Oslo, tries to solve the riddle of public decline in religious attendance, yet its private sustainability and growth. He states that even though religion no longer plays an important institutional role, religion still appears in cultural and private spheres in society which is difficult to register in statistics.

Since research itself is tainted with subjectivity, often reflecting the current politically correct academic narrative, science may have, for one, "tried to prove decline," overlooking other trends. As we have seen, depending on how you ask the question in a public survey, the researcher knows he will get very different answers.

## The Culture War

Social conservatism has furthered this dialectic view, and have been an active force in Western society especially from the 1980s onward. The movement calls for strengthening traditional values rather than tearing them down, upholding national values when facing mass immigration, and recognizes the need for respecting religious people and their contribution to society.

New forms of religiosity have gained a foothold in the West, against the odds. Professor of Sociology, Robert Bellah argues in *The Robert Bellah Reader* that today, religion turns up in forms that are much more obscure, due to the "privatization" of faith. He discusses a new form of religion that consists of a mixture of faith and strong nationalism, a phenomenon that he calls "American civil religion." Bellah also speaks about the swift growth of charismatic Christianity, New Age, and other new religious movements that are happening at the heart of modern Western society, and yet outside the framework of religion as a political institution. Consequently, secular society practices a renewed and continued relationship to the sacred – often taking unexpected and unpredictable forms.

Some scholars say that the culture has become re-enchanted with a New Age set of thinking. The so-called New Age-trend has its origin in theosophy and spiritualism but has later been influenced by the counter-culture of the 1960s, as well as by Indian religions. At first, an expectation of a new age was in focus, a belief that people would reach a higher spiritual level, which would, in turn, bring social change on a global scale – correlating, as a matter of fact, with the beliefs of Social Darwinism. Hence, people would live in peace, love and in ecological balance with nature.

Maybe it is quite understandable why precisely many of the Western progressives and internationalists have chosen New Age and its "beliefs," eager as many have been to prove that man will rise above traditional religions and create a utopian society based on a non-traditionalist, Western liberal democracy. New Age is often referred to as a fellowship of people with a strong focus on self-development and may be seen as a religion that draws attention toward the self. It may be argued that it has a problematic tendency to create individuals who are preoccupied with "themselves," not "others," in direct opposition to the focus of Christianity – "loving God and your fellow man."

The goal is for the individual to reach inner peace in order to further his own personal development. Spirituality seems to be a tool in order to achieve something better "for me." Thus, it embraces the precise egocentric focus that traditional religion seeks to avoid – as religion suggests that man's happiness is closely linked to his ability to do something for others and function as a caring person in society. A critique against New Age may be that the movement has become synonymous with "solidarity to myself," rather than solidarity to others.

In a peculiar sense, these new religions – Hinduism, Buddhism, New Age - that have in common the revolt against traditional Western faith – have been quite accepted by the extreme secular society. It was, in essence, the traditional beliefs in the West that the scientific materialists sought to quash, and finish off the traditional religious values connected to Christianity and its Judaic roots. New Age has not been an enemy, so to speak, rather an ally in the attempt to remove Christianity. The same goes for Islam, paradoxically. Many an extreme secularist has fought quite hard for the respect of Islam as a new religion in the West, deeming whoever objected to parts of its cultural heritage or religious content a "racist," "Islamophobic," "illiberal" or "backward."

It is quite remarkable to observe how the film industry and culture of fame in Hollywood with its extensive influence on the population, uncritically idealizes the religion of New Age, witchcraft and sorcery, reintroducing the role of "witches", occult mediums and "spiritualist readings," while at the same time reflecting sharp anti-Christian and anti-Judaism values. One readily embraces that which historically was "foreign" to our culture, and despises the traditional values and religions that in history stood at the core of our civilization.

Much of the same critique may be directed at the institutionalized Church-systems in the West, where the focus on secular and materialistic values causes many Christians to complacently accept the politically correct status quo, endlessly focusing on "myself and my blessings from God, what God can do for me", rather than a spiritual awakening which would cause Christians to deeply begin to engage in society, solidarity, and the public discourse again. It becomes apparent that Europe has been plagued, especially since the 1960s with increasingly vague, secularized Church leaders who tend to go along with the politically correct establishment, instead of standing up for the foundational values of Christianity.

Protestantism seems to have been extra vulnerable to atheist attacks in the West, but Catholicism is affected too. This weakness and its corresponding hypocrisy which may be found within the Church itself, also strengthens the rise of atheism, as many complain that Christians do not live as they should, but choose cowardice. This will be addressed in-depth later as one of the causes of the rise of anti-Christianism in the West. The narcissism is hard to hide.

# The Culture War

✲✲✲

# The Need for Unity

Historically, there have been strong divisions between different denominations within Christianity, but today many speak about the need for more cooperation and even unification of the Church of Christ. The recent meetings in Cuba between the head of the Russian Orthodox Church, Patriarch Kirill and the Catholic Church and Pope Francis, illustrates this noticeable shift. The meetings addressed the dire need to help Christians in the Middle East as well as the worrisome development in the West as Christians are in a dangerous, critical situation with marginalized communities.

There seems to be a growing tendency within institutionalized Christendom itself towards greater respect for the cultural and minor differences of theology that characterize the Church in different parts of the world. The Orthodox Church has long worked for a stronger unification and respect between Christian groups. Pope Francis has become a strong and inspiring voice advocating a greater focus on loving one another, solidarity with the weak and respect for international justice.

The early division between Catholics and Protestants erupted, as we know, in 1517, when Martin Luther started a popular uprising delivering the 95 theses in Wittenberg, which criticized the Catholic clergy at the time for the implementation of the idea that putting a monetary price on forgiveness and the road to heaven was in concordance with the message of The Holy Scriptures. He was banned by the Church as a heretic and had to flee to the mountains. Sadly, one of the side effects of Protestantism was that it effectively caused a deep division within the Church, which later was used politically to instigate a major division in Western Christianity. Many have since lamented the divide that took place and wish that the Church should have been reformed, yet remained united. The deep rift almost instantly led to war in Europe.

The religious divisions grew into intricate systems of belief that differed, often only, in views such as how to baptize, or who was to receive Holy Communion, how to practice the liturgy and so on. The Protestant Church lost, in many ways, touch with the Orthodox and Catholic Church history and the early Church fathers, and thus its own heritage before Luther's 1517.

The old saying "divide and conquer" seems to have plagued the Protestant Church ever since, fuelling strife and regrouping, splitting churches and steadily forging new denominations. The lack of united leadership in the Church has been quite convenient for its atheist opponents. It is not too hard to conquer a Church that is already divided. If you drive through any city in Northern Europe, you will pass church after church, all Protestant and all divided into small groups with many not even talking to each other or visiting each other's churches.

Martin Luther's protest against practices within the clergy at that time was legitimate, yet his legacy somehow also contributed to the disconnect to early Church history. Protestants increasingly lost the knowledge about the early saints, the holy men, and women who lived in the early centuries after Christ. Yet, the knowledge about this part of history is, until this day, vividly kept alive both in the Catholic and as well in the Eastern Orthodox Church, where the traditions of icons remind the many of the holy people in history and their acts of humility and greatness.

Yet, Protestantism also brought constructive elements such as a strong belief in the individual and his personal link to God. Man was to work hard and prove his abilities; he was to care for the community and show his love for God this way. Author Rodney Stark describes in *Victory of Reason* how the rational elements of Protestant Christianity were a prerequisite for Capitalism's focus on individual freedom, thus forming the initial success of Western Christianity and culture as a whole.

The work of John Calvin in Switzerland focused on hard work and a strong morality as the main service to God. At the time, the city of Geneva was rife with prostitution, crime, chaos, and destitution. Calvin worked hard to strengthen the morale in Switzerland and reform society to the better. Calvin believed that the actions of believers should correspond to ethics that produced stability in society, peace, and order. In turn, this would lead to a constructive development built on the respect for God's commandments as a set of regulations that would provide justice to all – and form the basis for the elimination of poverty.

It is remarkable how focused the early Protestants were on helping the poor and laying a foundation for a society based on a strong work ethic, dignity, and self-respect. Until this day, Switzerland is marked by the values that once made John Calvin such a noteworthy reformer.

Today it is worth mentioning that the current head of the Catholic Church, Pope Francis, steadily reforms the Vatican and uproots corruption and lack of spiritualism from its ranks, unites Christians across denominations more than any other. Seldom does one see a spiritual leader receive such attention in mainstream media, speaking as he does about the suffering of the poor, the need for compassion and kindness, as well as reminding Christians from all faiths of the importance of love. The Catholic Church remains, as we know, the largest Christian group in the world with around 1.1 billion followers. The unifying force of the Catholic Church has proved to be a distinct strength in the modern world, despite its setbacks in the West.

As Victor Hugo, the author of *Les Misérables* said, "To love another person is to see the face of God." The renowned Protestant preacher and maybe the most famous Christian preacher in US history, Billy Graham, often spoke about the Catholic Church and other denominations within the Christian community in a positive way. To *San Francisco News*, in 1957, a period where Graham held crusades throughout the US that attracted millions of followers as well as had widespread influence all over the world, he said: "I felt that God had called me to love all people, whatever church they went to, Catholics or Protestants or whoever, because there is so much that we have in common."

One of the most important writers of the 1900s, C.S. Lewis, seems to concur in searching for the common ground upon which the different Christian denominations stand. In *Mere Christianity*, he states that the reader will not learn from him whether to become Anglican, a Methodist, a Presbyterian or a Roman Catholic. What he wanted to accomplish with the book, which has become such a classic, was to explain and defend the belief that has been common to all Christians in history, regardless of denominations.

Hanne Nabintu Herland

# CHAPTER 11

# Totalitarian Democracy

*Totalitarian democracies differ in structure from the original form of Western democracy. The aim is to form a radical system that produces better results in the West than its traditional culture. Just as Communism and fascism were totalitarian systems, another variation has also developed in the West: A totalitarian democracy based on a Socialist ideology and the enthusiasm of the propaganda controlled masses.*

## Freedom Defined As the Right to Participate in the Extreme Liberal Society

THE FRENCH PHILOSOPHER, Alexis de Tocqueville was worried about the development of democracy, fearing its decay under strong governments. He said that strict collectivist discipline is far worse than the most blatant stupidity of the traditional, pre-modern social structures. Modern democracies may become worse than previous forms of government if allowed to develop into an authoritarian system of conformity, where the institutions end up not tolerating dissent.

Tocqueville believed that when democracy sacrifices its historical ideals, it may easily be reduced to the opposite of freedom – as it turns into a culture of tyranny led by the popular mob. Democracy without the respect for different opinions is like Capitalism without the Protestant ethic. When trustworthiness and honesty no longer is an ideal, narcissism and lack of solidarity become legitimate ways of life. Under such conditions, democracy itself becomes a path towards the abuse of liberties.

In *The Origins of Totalitarian Democracy*, the Israeli professor T. J. Talmon notoriously argues that totalitarian democracies – defined as Socialist models that break with the originally liberal form of democracy – are characterized by an unusually low respect for the individual's right to free speech. Because the goal of politics becomes that citizens should unite and agree – work in groups, express themselves in unison and coordinate in groups – peer pressure becomes a method to keep people "in check." Control of citizen behavior becomes a goal. Control over the media too. Freedom is essentially manipulated to be "the right to participate in the extreme liberal society."

Talmon describes how those who disagree with the "politically correct norm" are regarded as an obstacle to development. They are "old-fashioned," "racist" and "illiberal."

A strong state is therefore needed to uphold consensus among its citizens and to motivate them to support a radical form of egalitarianism and "sameness," primarily through the control of what is published in literature, media, publishing, academia and political groups. This is what Harvard professor Harvey Mansfield in *Manliness* calls "soft despotism," claiming that the effects on the individual under a soft tyranny are just as hard to bear as the lack of freedom under any dictatorship.

Author and journalist Melanie Phillips speak about this in *The World Turned Upside Down*, stating that if religious totalitarianism meant Church domination with all its power structures, cultural totalitarianism means the rule by the subjective individual who is freed from morality, loyalty to society and any ethical constraints. Morality is privatized so that everyone becomes his own authority, and the laws and traditions rooted in Christianity and Jewish thinking, are under heavy attack.

Talmon states that in this type of totalitarian democracy, significant political pressure is placed upon society in order for its citizens to reach the wished-for collective agreement. A strong secular state led by an ideological and political elite becomes the source of morality. Those who disagreed and voice opposition, are regarded as "an enemy of the state."

The utopian, Marxist dream that humans would finally "become one" in an internationalist village, where national borders and religion disappeared, and globalization created total harmony between the races, was for many years the core dream of European thinking, Talmon writes.

Hanne Nabintu Herland

✸✸✸

# The Original Form of Liberalism – John Locke

In the 1600s, secularism adopted the conviction that political conditions should be discussed outside of the religious sphere, from a so-called "neutral" perspective. It was in this period that the Christian English philosopher John Locke defined liberalism and theories of human rights. The original concept of liberalism guarantees freedom of choice and is one of the main freedoms upon which democratic systems rest. Locke formulated the reasons for why religious tolerance is important, stating that enforcing uniformity would lead to more social disorder than allowing religious diversity.

Locke's understanding of liberalism stands in great contrast to the modern, hedonistic ideals in the West. Today, the meaning of the word "liberal" has almost turned into the very opposite of what Locke defined it to be, highly influenced by the social revolution and its rebellion against traditional morality and responsibility. Many now associate the term "liberalism" with its modern version - extreme liberalism - that advocates for free sex, the legalization of drugs in a hedonistic social climate that legitimizes selfishness in disregard of the obligation towards others. One feels that it is the responsibility of the state to provide care for those in need, there is not an individual obligation to solidarity.

Liberalism and freedom for Locke were not the individual's right to live selfishly. He did not advocate a hedonistic lifestyle in which man is to free himself from concepts of conscience, sin and the law of nature. The right to liberty did not imply the right to exploit others in pursuit of self-satisfaction. Freedom was defined as the individual's right to behave responsibly in the community, yet still, pursue personal liberties. For Locke, liberalism was not devoid of morality. Obligations and a strong sense of responsibility were closely knit to his definition of rights.

Jeremy Waldron shows in *God, Locke, and Equality. Christian Foundations in Locke's Political Thought* how Locke's belief in God permeates his very thinking. Locke saw man as sent into the world by God's order, to go about and do His business as His property and workmanship. He derived his fundamental political theory from biblical texts, insisting that people could not understand the law of nature without the assistance of the teachings of Jesus.

Locke further states that the concept of freedom as well as equality is originally derived from Genesis, the first book of the Bible. Consequently, to him, all men were created as free, rational beings and therefore democratic governments needed to acquire approval for the political decisions of its people. His thoughts are clearly reflected in the American Declaration of Independence.

✳✳✳

# The Origins of Totalitarianism

Individual liberty may easily suffocate in a democracy when peer pressure and a culture of consensus takes over in such a way that the masses are controlled by the state. The philosopher Hannah Arendt points out in *The Origins of Totalitarianism* that a totalitarian government then becomes even worse than a dictatorship. In a dictatorship, the elite strive to gather political power while simultaneously persecuting dissidents openly. People are killed and ruthlessly bullied in order to silence opposition.

She states that the elites in totalitarian regimes strive to gather not only political power but also to dominate every aspect of human life ideologically and to control every thought process to the smallest detail – what to think about family, sex, relationships, religion, school, church, law, ethics and morals and so on. Arendt finds this to be a terrifying system, that even your personal opinions, intellectual beliefs and even what you do inside your house are to be controlled by the state. This brings to memory the society described in English novelist, George Orwell's *1984*. The purpose of the elite in such a society is to gain control overall social developments, with a universal desire that the whole world should evolve into a unified system where religions no longer exist.

Arendt spent her entire life trying to understand how man's cruelty could be systematized and institutionalized to such an extent during World War II. This was an intolerant time in history when unwanted minorities and groups that represented other values than those of the establishment were openly terrorized in a society reeking with fear.

She analyzed the rise of Nazism in the democratic Germany of the 1930s and discovered that the people who carried out bestial actions, were not *per se* extremely evil. In fact, most actions of this nature were performed by common men and women who simply followed state orders. They neglected to reflect on the morality of their own actions, feared repercussions from the authorities and hid behind those bureaucrats who gave the orders.

When attending the Eichmann trial in Jerusalem, Arendt suggested that one of the effects of a strong state is the de-responsibilization of its citizens. She used Eichmann as an example, noting he steadily hid behind precisely this idea – that he followed orders and chose not to disobey them, considering the harsh times of war. Of course, it was beyond evident that Eichmann was one of the chief architects of the Holocaust. His excuses, nonetheless, point to the grave dangers of lack of individual responsibility in institutionalized societies where citizens become desensitized regarding personal morality, as they hide behind "only following orders."

Arendt concluded that in systems where the state demand for consensus thoroughly controls its people to the point that opposition is completely silenced, fear of the authorities is greater than individual sense of justice. Complacency, a passive attitude and lack of personal morals permeate those who should have stood up against injustice, but did not. "People become silent about things that matter," to quote Martin Luther King – that is if the fear of unbearable repercussions is perceived to be imminent. If it does not bear a cost to speaking up, one speaks the truth. If it implies a cost that is considered heavy to bear, one avoids doing that which is right, and silently follows the crowd. Consequently, Arendt argued that it was not hate that motivated brutality, but indifference and apathy. And a lack of empathy. People felt that "the system" was so authoritarian that there was no way a single person could make a difference.

The famous and maybe notoriously radical linguist and author, Noam Chomsky steadily maintains that there is a strong social responsibility inherent in exposing abuse of power and conscious distortion of the truth. He argues that the US is no longer a democracy, but a one-party state, similar to an oligarchy, where elites from both the left and the right often govern contrary to the interest of the general population. The least democratic institution may be the judiciary where judges and justices are above the electorates and appointed for life. A recent study from Princeton University arrives at the same conclusion. An example, a 2014 Public Policy Polling indicates that 74% of Americans are against a new war in the Middle East. Nevertheless, the American establishment currently remains deeply embedded in military conflict on foreign soil - Afghanistan, Iraq, Yemen, Pakistan, Somalia, Libya, Syria and so on. As stated, over 90% of the American media is now owned by only six companies, according to Business Insider. Back in 1983, over fifty companies did the same job. Media has never before been owned by this few. It is as close to a media monopoly as one possibly may get.

Chomsky seems to care little whether he is named left-wing or right-wing thinker, as the distinctions between the right and the left have long been outdated. For example, in Europe, the conservatives have largely embraced extreme liberalism, the same tendency is permeating the so-called progressive Democratic party in the US. Many conservatives even deny the value of national sovereignty and respect for historical traditions. Furthermore, the left hardly hails values such as solidarity with the worker who used to be intricate in their historical fabric, but rather relies on a neo-conservative Capitalist ideology, implying that the few should rule the many.

Americans are now at the mercy of powerful figures in business and government who are almost completely unaccountable to the public and its own citizens. Investigative journalist Sharyl Attkisson remarks in *Stonewalled: My Fight for Truth Against the Forces of Obstruction, Intimidation, and Harassment in Obama's Washington* that the Obama Administration was exceptionally controlling in its monitoring of journalists, intimidation and false accusations of opposition groups, as well as the massive surveillance of private citizens. The post-Obama era seems to confirm a continuation of the exact same trend. Attkisson's story speaks painfully of the decline of investigative journalism and unbiased truth-telling in America today.

If the political elite are closely connected to large multinational corporations, interlinked through business deals, judges ruling according to the will of the political elite, editors in the leading newspapers carefully adhering to the politically correct, corporations paying lavishly for politician's lectures and so forth, justice for the common man and the common good is often delayed.

Author Peter Jones says in *Vote for Caesar* that modern Western governments scarcely would be recognized as democracies in antiquity because the concentration of power bear too much similarity to an oligarchy – a form of government where a small elite decides on behalf of the people. The democratic quality of the system is steadily diminished if political parties consist of oligarchic cliques that increasingly act as cartels.

Hanne Nabintu Herland

\*\*\*

# The Faltering Welfare State

During the years following World War II, the establishment of a political system that emphasized a fairer distribution of wealth in Europe – the welfare state – came into being. Politicians sought to help ordinary Europeans out of poverty after the war. The objective was more equality. Cities like London lay partly in ashes, Germany was shattered, there had been immense amounts of damage, not to mention the lives lost.

The US, the Marshall Plan, was implemented, and Europe slowly began its rebuilding process. Throughout the 1950s, the standard of living increased in most European countries. Europe steadily repaid its debt to America, the US grew into an economic superpower, greatly profiting from not having had the war destroy its own territory.

Author Pat Buchanan points out in *Suicide of a Superpower* that around 1905, Western empires controlled almost the entire world. After two World Wars in which approximately 80 million, mostly Western people were killed, one of the consequences was that Western nations lost the empires as other nations grew stronger. The West lost much of its army and navy – but most of all we gradually lost the Western eagerness for excellence. Today, the birth rate is rapidly slowing down, especially since the legalization of abortion in the 1970s and the implementation of the radical ideas of extreme feminism, as shall be discussed later. The West and its people are shrinking. Of this, many have spoken in the past decennials and warned of the dangers of Western disintegration, moral decay, and growing civil unrest.

Since the late 1970s, many Western countries and especially the European started evolving from a work- and responsibility-oriented society, to a bureaucratic society with a strong welfare state based on benefits to all. The lavish systems of benefits naturally began attracting recipients, some exploiting these social safety nets.

In the 1980s, concepts like solidarity, values that first characterized the labor movements, began deteriorating. The old working-class slogan: "Do your duty, demand your right" now increasingly omitted the part about "duty." People now increasingly spoke solely about human rights, not of its duties and obligations. The culture of entitlement without responsibilities slowly began breaking down the ethics of the welfare state.

# The Culture War

The American writer Ayn Rand spoke with an almost prophetic voice, analyzing how the social-democratic welfare state would crumble over time and overly large government structures would end up failing to meet the intended goals. In *Capitalism. The Unknown Ideal* she says that the welfare state is nothing more than a mechanism by which governments confiscate the wealth of the productive members of a society to support a wide variety of welfare schemes. The financial policy of such an arrangement requires that there be no way for the owners of wealth to protect themselves, and the "welfare policy" will gradually deteriorate. [22]

The now faltering welfare models would not even be possible if it was not for private capital, company owners, and workforce contributions to the state funds to begin with. The task of political leaders is only to manage these funds and redistribute these fairly back into society.

The point is that in the welfare-state model, the government has thoroughly assumed the role of the caretaker. If the individual is divested of any responsibility for his own life, citizens end up passively waiting for the welfare state to solve problems.

The system was not set up for fraud and took it for granted that people would not misuse the benefits given, but only apply for these if they really needed them. The system relied on trustworthiness and honesty, culturally embedded in a Protestant culture where man's conscience was viewed as his compass to a good life. Many thought it impossible that the welfare system could be exploited. The whole idea of the welfare state was to create a social democratic system in which a citizen had to contribute to society, *then* he received his benefit in case he lost his job, became sick or experienced tragedy of some sort. The original philosophy was that those in despair, who had come into some misfortune, would have some help until they quickly got back on their feet.

As the system was implemented, the traditional focus on the personal responsibility to take care of your own – your neighbor, family members, the elderly, the poor and the community – was increasingly replaced by dependency on the welfare state. The growing demands towards the state gradually produced new attitudes. One of the welfare state's unintentional effects was that it ended up providing state funds drizzling onto citizens in the form of lavish benefits that essentially encouraged people to take it easy.

It may be argued that whatever is free, tends to be regarded as of little value. In Northern European countries, where education is free, the new generation is the first with lower educational standards than their parents.

---

[22] http://aynrandlexicon.com/lexicon/welfare_state/3.html

Young men and women in countries like Norway are now reportedly "taking a year off on welfare" in order to play *World of Warcraft* or watch *The Kardashians*. The singular focus on rights has been galvanized by gigantic, Scandinavian bureaucratic systems, characterized by large state institutions employing as many as possible, taking the role of "Big Brother."

Asle Toje, scholar at the Nobel Institute in Oslo, Norway has pointed out in *The Iron Cage. Liberalism in Crisis* that hat today Europe has 80% of all asylum-seeker applications in the world. Yet, Europe has 7% of the world population, 25% of the gross domestic product, with expenses rating as high as 50% of the benefits paid worldwide. No wonder the welfare state's expenses have become too heavy to bear.

The 1960s generation and its raging rebellion against authorities – be it the teacher, the priest, the father in the family or the law itself – has ended up almost completely stripping those in authority for their ability to sanction undesired behavior. Even the politicians who watch how the welfare system is abused, hardly dare stop it. The slogan of the day has become: "I deserve it because I am me." The system hardly differentiates between the rights of value of law-abiding citizens and criminals. Everyone is considered equally eligible for benefits, whether he or she arrived in the country yesterday or have spent a life time paying taxes. In countries like Norway, criminals on the run from the police or have been expelled from the country due to criminal offenses, still, receive their benefits from the welfare system.[23]

*\*\*\**

## The Fear of Setting Boundaries - Education

In today's nihilistic climate, it becomes close to impossible to say anything in general about "the truth" or "what is right and what is wrong." The lack of normative advice, rules and firm cultural ideals creates a society without a strong sense of order.

The educational system is a sad example. Seemingly, endless radical reforms have ended up reducing the quality of schools, rendering a nation such as the US with clearly worsening results since the late 1960s. Failing a

---

[23] Does not stop NAV payment to expelled criminal (Thursday, August 17, 2017) http://www.nettavisen.no/nyheter/--stopper-ikke-nav-utbetaling-til-utviste-kriminelle/3423252430.html

class or a test at that time meant scoring below 70% in the American system in the 1980s. What used to be a "B" back then, is grade "A" today.

*Forbes* recently referred to a Council on Foreign Relations report that only 31% of fourth graders are proficient in reading on the National Assessment of Educational Progress ratings, more than 25% fail to graduate high school in four years. For Hispanics and African-Americans, 40%, – only eight in ten – speak English, only 22% of high school students met college standards in their core subjects. It is utterly depressing to read about the educational decline in a nation that used to be a role model.

Social criticism is massive as public schools are "expiated as retirement parks for lazy, unionized teachers to indulge their habit of force-feeding the innocent on Marxist propaganda," writes Niall McLaren in *Truthout*, calling American public schools "mind-deadening[24] factories designed to propel working class white students into brain-dead jobs and minority students straight into the arms of the prison-industrial complex."[25]

Looking at Forbes cited 2012 numbers, US now rates lower than Mexico and Brazil in world rankings such as PISA 2009 yet spends more than any other country per school age student. The record level of student debt shows that while it took students only three years to payback loans back in the 1960s, they are now stuck with twenty years of payments, sending many straight into poverty when finishing their studies. Student debt in the US amounts to $1 trillion dollars. An average degree in medicine may cost as much as US$400,000.[26] There are almost as many children living under the poverty line in the US as in Brazil.

The US used to have some of the best public schools in the world with high respect for the teacher. In the US, many now are illiterate and cannot even read or write after twelve years in public schools. *Business Insider* even states that half of the Detroit population, cannot read, Detroit once being the symbol of American wealth and industrial capacity.[27] In the

---

[24] The Perils of Zombie Education (Thursday, August 17, 2017) http://www.truth-out.org/opinion/item/17103-the-perils-of-zombie-education

[25] What Do You Do When You No Longer Need Your Slaves? (Thursday, August 17, 2017) http://www.truth-out.org/opinion/item/18168-what-do-you-do-when-you-no-longer-need-your-slaves-or-your-workers

[26] Medical School at $278,000 Means Even Bernanke Son Has Debt (Thursday, August 17, 2017) https://www.bloomberg.com/news/articles/2013-04-11/medical-school-at-278-000-means-even-bernanke-son-carries-debt

Med Student Gives Sober Assessment Of Future With $500K In Student Debt (Thursday, August 17, 2017) https://www.forbes.com/sites/danmunro/2014/01/30/med-student-gives-sober-assessment-of-future-with-500k-in-student-debt/#694ef86b5b30

[27] Nearly Half Of Detroiters Can't Read (Thursday, August 17, 2017) http://www.businessinsider.com/nearly-half-of-detroiters-cant-read-2011-5?r=US&IR=T&IR=T

extreme liberal system, teachers are hardly even allowed to tell obnoxious students to be silent in class without instant complaints about "lack of tolerance." The attitude implies that bad behavior should be accepted. The result is disharmony, lack of structure, lack of discipline, frustrated teachers, and non-achieving students. According to Forbes, 75 % of US citizens ages 17-24 cannot pass the military entry exams due to criminal record or being physically unfit or unable to, for example, read maps properly.[28]

In Italy, there has been quite an uproar because of the lack of discipline, as the European Union is implementing what Cardinal Angelo Bagnasco called indoctrination and a true dictatorship that aims to devalue the role of parents. *The Local* reports him saying that schools are turning into re-education camps where hedonist, anti-Christian new ideologies are being implemented. "In reality, they seek to instill in children preconceived ideas against the family, parenting, religious faith, the difference between father and mother," he said. Bagnasco pointed to the weakening of the authority of the Catholic Church in Italy's school systems, where priests and nuns have for centuries played a role in educating the country's children.

In Scandinavia, the educational reforms have been seemingly even more endless than the US. A few years back, even the concept of the classroom was abolished. Parents protested all over the countries but in vain. Walls between classrooms were torn down, memorizing was substituted by active use of computers during class, – resulting in the active use of Facebook and social media during class hours. In Norway, one-third of the teachers now consider quitting the job,[29] in a country where women use sick leave 70 % more than men.[30] It is not strange that countries like Sweden, Norway and even the UK, rank remarkably low in recent years on the OECD Program for International Student Assessment (PISA) surveys. The classroom has turned into a hellhole, teachers' salaries steadily sinking and the requirement to become a teacher dropping to a "D" in many colleges.

Finland is a remarkable exception. Year after year, Finland has been rated number one in the world in public education, now only beaten by China, Korean, Singapore and the "Asian Tigers." Finland has followed the opposite path as the rest of Europe regarding education. One of the Finish Ministers explained that due to Finland's lack of sufficient finances, they

---

[28] 7 Signs That U.S. Education Decline Is Jeopardizing Its National Security (Thursday, August 17, 2017) https://www.forbes.com/sites/jamesmarshallcrotty/2012/03/26/7-signs-that-americas-educational-decline-is-jeopardizing-its-national-security/#3de2ea5659b6

[29] MANY TEACHERS WILL QUIT (Thursday, August 17, 2017) https://www.arbeidsmiljo.no/mange-laerere-vil-slutte/

[30] Therefore, women are more often ill-treated (Thursday, August 17, 2017) http://www.kk.no/livstil/derfor-blir-kvinner-oftere-sykmeldt/67876229

had had no money to implement reforms in the school system. The explanation is noteworthy.

When the UK, Scandinavia, France and other areas pushed for liberal reforms, Finland kept its school system from the 1950s. The teacher is as highly regarded and well-paid, on the same level as doctors and dentists. The requirement for teaching in high school implies at least a master degree. The class focusing on hard work, memorizing, much homework and self-discipline. In the classroom, order and silence are required, so that students are able to work efficiently with the goal of accomplishing excellent academic results.

The American author Christopher Lasch speaks at length about the cultural challenges associated with a cultivation of benefit-oriented individualism in *The Narcissistic Culture*. When the carousel is spinning rapidly towards the legitimization of selfishness and lack of order, one slowly approaches the state of moral anarchy – the condition previous to the fall of a civilization. History is filled with examples of how great cultures began faltering when they lost their sense of morality, obligation, and justice.

In *The Evolution of Civilizations*, historian Carroll Quigley associates the expansion and development of civilizations with the existence of a permanent military, religious, politic and economic, organizational structure to maintain growth and prosperity. Decline begins when a civilization ceases to emphasize the very ideals that initially resulted in expansion and productivity. These are commonly replaced by alternative values that focus more on enjoyment, rest, and leisure.

The Russian author Alexander Solzhenitsyn, renowned for his active dissent to the Soviet dictatorship, died in 2008. In an editorial the following week, *The Economist* asked: Who will follow in his footsteps and pose the perilous and important questions of the day, not just in totalitarian states, but also in the West? Solzhenitsyn's warnings to the West resound loud and clear: if it were to follow the same path of the Soviets, it would soon get the same results.

Hanne Nabintu Herland

# CHAPTER 12

# Financial Greed and Economic Crisis

*Christianity speaks of capital and finances as a means to build society and do good to others. One is to earn money in order to have something to give to society for the betterment of all. The initial form of Protestant Capitalism had solidarity at its core. Yet, in the West today, a Capitalism devoid of morality has become the means to justify greed, injustice, and selfishness.*

## The Protestant Ethic and the Spirit of Capitalism

IN *THE PROTESTANT ETHIC AND THE SPIRIT OF CAPITALISM*, sociologist Max Weber states that when modern Capitalism took form in Protestant countries such as Switzerland and Germany about two hundred years ago, the ideal was to earn money and increase wealth – not to squander one's income away on status, luxury and consumerism. The duty of the believer was to use their abilities to achieve success in all aspects of life, in order to honor God and help their fellow man.

This thought is also deeply embedded in Jewish thinking, from which Christianity derives its roots. The created world is viewed as imperfect, and it is the duty of the human being to use his life to make it better. Some become musicians, some intellectuals, some scientists, some skilled workers, some excellent teachers, and nannies. Jewish tradition keeps this ideal very alive; each man is to strive to become the best version of himself, to "help God" make the world a better place with whichever abilities he has.

In the early Protestant countries, the point was to reinvest capital into the economic system and make sure the whole society prospered. The contingent culture of sincerity that Protestantism represented at that time emphasized pietistic, frugal attitudes combined with income-producing hard work. Solidarity was front and center, at the very core of the early Capitalists.

One of the economic model's brilliant principles was the association between saving and innovation. The possibilities that lie in the individualistic approach of owning the fruit of one's own labor contributed to the break with pre-industrial society and its fixed focus on hereditary titles and vocations. New opportunities were abundant. In the USA, immigrants from Britain who were farmers and fishermen increased their status by harnessing their own expertise, willingness to work side by side in the fellowship of men, founded on virtues and ethical qualities.

By virtue of hard work and industry, many who came from the lower classes in England became wealthy landowners in the New World. Poor Puritans from Germany, became the large landowners of Brazil, creating industries, plantations and stimulating trade that to this day fuel the economy of South America's largest country.

In *Fixing Fragile States*, author Seth Kaplan underlines how decisive the elements of Christian thought have been for the growth of stability in the West. These are the precise cultural roots that now are ignored as Western culture has undergone a cultural revolution that rejects Judeo-Christian values and looks to the extreme liberal, non-religious society to bring sustainable solutions.

Kaplan states that both humanism and the idea of equality have their origin in Christian ideology. Man is to not only think about himself and acquire wealth "only to his own benefit," but he is to work for the betterment of society as a whole – he is to "love his neighbor." The social ethic that formed the foundation of the Capitalist economic model aimed to develop society through a structure that encouraged individualism and the right of the worker to own the profit of his own labor. In addition, Protestantism attached great weight on education. People were to learn to read and write so that they could read the Holy Scriptures. This served to increase literacy, book publishing, and printing, as well as the growth of active journalism. People became much more knowledge-oriented – which again is an idealized necessity in democracies.

Pope John Paul II once said that one of the fundamental principles of modern Capitalism is dissatisfaction, not being satisfied with what you already have. This dissatisfaction is a two-edged sword: if used correctly to the betterment of society, it becomes constructive. If used to legitimize egoism, it produces a negation of its original intent.

Max Weber also demonstrated in his work the close relationship between religious ethic and the growth of constructive Capitalism. Its ability to motivate people to work hard leading to the growth of a disciplined working class, where the ideal was to use the stream of capital to re-invest in new businesses which again created new jobs for even more people. The result was a remarkable creation of a value-added system that differed completely with the previous generation's economic system. The religious influence of the Protestant Pietists and their attitudes fuelled a holistic approach to money that ended upbringing prosperity to millions and millions in the West.

To achieve success was considered a sign of God's favor, a means through which one should do even more good. Early Protestants, such as Calvinists, Quakers, and other independent denominations, all urged an individualization of faith that made the individual responsible for their own moral; wealth and spiritual growth. It was not the "relativistic individualization" we see today, where individualism is used to legitimize a person's right to selfish behavior and disentanglement from the fellowship of men.

These Christians had strict moral standards – they were harsh – and demanded honesty and integrity of their political leaders. Kaplan claims that especially the above-mentioned strict Christian attitudes produced closely knit groups with high moral standards that demanded an ethical lifestyle based on the Ten Commandments. You could trust a man to keep his promise. If he failed to keep his word, the punishment was severe. Fear of these consequences kept many within prescribed limits. It is hard to build well-functioning societies without well-functioning institutions based on a justice system that works to the benefit of the citizens. The advantage of a society centered on consequences was that cooperation and trust also formed the basis for trade, business, and investment.

As mentioned earlier, in the ancient Greek democracies, political leaders who failed to serve the people also experienced dire consequences. This kept "the elite" on their guard. Some faced capital punishment, others sent into permanent exile. Those who wanted the privileges of political leadership were also forced to take the responsibility. To become a political leader in the ancient city states, meant putting your life on the line in case you failed.

A number of countries outside the Western hemisphere today successfully implement a well-functioning Capitalism that continues to stress the strict moral significance of hard work, individualism, personal property rights. Today, millions of people embark on the same journey out of poverty, especially in Southeast Asian states. Ironically, they seem to want the technological advancement in order to grow economically and become prosperous nations based on a strong work ethic and discipline, yet do not want to implement Western values and ideologies such as the current hedonism, anti-religious culture, and nihilist morality. South Korea now sports one of the world's most expansive economies, with a substantial increase in prosperity over the last fifty years, 67% of the population rated as middle class, according to Hyundai Economic Research Institute.[31]

The Asian nations implement the industrial, technological, educational advancements that historically stem from the Western achievements. Take Communist China, which has implemented a strong market Capitalism, yet still been very cautious to avoid following what they perceive to be decadent Western values. China regularly bans certain songs from the Western music industry and shuts down pornographic internet pages with unwanted and violent content, as seen massively in 2016.[32] They emphasize marriage and family values, modesty and a culture of politeness in accordance with traditional Asian ideals.

According to a study by McKinsey & Company over 550 million Chinese will be rated middle class in China alone by 2022, according to *Business Insider*. This is more than the total European population.[33] According to OECD numbers, Asia will in 2030 represent 66% of the global middle-class population and 59% of middle-class consumption, compared to 28% and 23%, respectively in 2009.[34]

Where would the West be without the Christian ethic and its respect for hard work, honesty, reliability, trustworthiness, saving and not only spending money? How would the traditionalist West have looked if individuals did not invest capital into new projects in order to create jobs for even more people, engaged in paying one's taxes for the benefit of society? When political leaders become selfishly preoccupied with tending to their own benefits alone, solidarity crumbles.

---

[31] South Korea's middle class is shrinking, according to recent report (Thursday, August 17, 2017) http://english.hani.co.kr/arti/english_edition/e_business/678354.html

Hanne Nabintu Herland

***

# The Problem of Greed and Lack of Trust

It may be argued that the deterioration of traditional values in the West is contributing to the economic decline. A quick glance at the recent 2007 financial crisis may serve an example. Leading financial acrobats and insurance giants, real estate agents and other individuals had over time developed structured financial products that ended up exploiting the forces of Capitalism in order to maximize personal gain. They disregarded the basic rules on how value is created and acted solely with their own personal profit in mind. It became all too obvious that bubbles had been allowed to grow – bubbles of greed and lack of a moral code, which resulted in the coming lack of trust within the system.

Satyajit Das explains the background to this development by reminding us that since the early 1980s, economic growth has increasingly been driven by financialization – the replacement of industrial activity by financial trading. People like financial mogul and hedge-fund investor, George Soros, who has been called the world's most famous investor, have greatly benefitted from financialization. Soros explains in his infamous *60 Minutes* interview from 1999, how he advises more regulation of the system, yet he himself has the main part of his hedge fund companies registered outside the US, precisely in order to, as he states, not to have them regulated.

In the same interview, when asked about his engagement in hedge funds and the financial market, often causing a nation's downfall or sending nations into economic crisis, Soros says: "I don't feel guilty, because I am engaged in an amoral activity which is not meant to have anything to do with guilt". Soros states that he solely acts based on monetary gain and do not look at the social consequences of his actions. Soros is, of course, famous for funding Hillary Clinton, The Clinton Foundation and a number of other politically ideological initiatives, and is well known for funding civil activities and "philanthropic" policies that in mysterious ways end up supporting and funding extreme-liberal initiatives and radical political change in many nations.

In the same interview, Soros, notorious remorselessly addresses his past, when he as a young Jewish boy collaborated with the Nazi's in expropriating Jewish properties from those who had been sent to the concentration camps in Hungary. He recalls his collaboration with the

Nazi's with no regret, stating that World War II under occupation was his happiest moments in life. "I was fourteen years old, and I would say that that was when my character was made." It seems to be the tendency among some to view financial steering as acts disconnected to morality, as an amoral act – thus, of course, a justified act. The attitude seems to be, "If I do not do it, someone else will, so I might as well go ahead."

Satyajit Das points out that forty years back, America used to have its own industries, carpenters, electricians, factory workers. Then, most of this was outsourced to China and the Far East, leaving regular Americans without the manual skills that they used to have, the skills that once built America. The financialization has increased the level of borrowing to finance consumption, investment and consumerism. There is a slower increase in innovation and productivity, as the West struggles with a lower and aging population and growing inequality.

By 2007, the debt level had risen beyond the repayment capacity of borrowers, causing the financial meltdown. He points out that the weight of debt eventually acts as a brake on growth. Capitalism is, after all, an economic system in which the means of production are privately owned – that is, individuals are to own the fruits of their own labor. The art of competition provides incentives for this particular individual to produce and excel.

When the individuals involved no longer work according to a certain standard, the system malfunctions and breaks down. The result of twisting the system was that the market's circulation, the finance sector, was seriously injured. When the horrible result became known to everyone, it proved that Capitalism actually does work according to one of the fundamental Capitalist norms: the market will react to bad deals.

Regardless, it became clear that the economic sector desperately needs to strengthen its ethics. If the quest for wealth becomes a personalized project, "a financialization game" devoid of social responsibility and devoid of its initial focus on "the betterment of society," it becomes a counterproductive catalyst for limitless greed. There needs to be, as Adam Smith pointed out, a dissatisfaction to stimulate economic activity and growth – a constructive deconstruction, but one that does not overwhelm it all and cause a lack of balance which ends up causing both cultural and financial crisis.

Many have put the blame for the financial crisis on the bankers and real estate agents. However, the hunt for-profit by using loaned money – not your own – the race for consumerism and shopping only on overloaded credit cards, is something that was done by "almost everyone". The blame cannot only be pinned on financial agents. They offered houses that many were more than willing to move into, knowing that they would not be able to pay the mortgage.

Steve Sailer claims in the article "The Diversity Recession" that previous to the financial crisis, American banks loaned money to low-income families based on a multicultural mindset. Families, often with Hispanic and African-American backgrounds, who really did not have the economic qualifications to buy homes, were still given loans. When the house bubble popped in the USA – the crisis of millions of Americans not being able to pay the mortgage – 75% of the bad loans were these same "multi-culti" loans.

The over-heated house market in the US was one of the problems, but individuals who knew of their economic limitations still succumbed to the temptation to borrow more than they could afford. People wanted to *seem richer* than they actually were, not thinking of the consequences. It is a general challenge: too many want to *seem richer* than they are, *seem* higher on the social ladder than what they are, *seem* to be wealthier than they actually are.

One of the human challenges is that people tend not to be sufficiently sensible or rational. When we borrow more than we are able to pay back, and when banks issue larger loans than they know that the borrower can handle, both parties are not thinking clearly. We live in a loan addicted culture where the main goal is to *seem to be rich*.

The reason for the 2007 financial crisis is remarkably simple: too many were too greedy. The Capitalist system will not work without a certain sense of moral codex. If you disrespect the required ethics, you will get a Capitalism that acknowledges greed and cheating, as long as it benefits the individual involved. In the wake of this type of nihilist Capitalism – which acts as though there is no tomorrow – morality is no longer in the equation. In addition, due to the transnational character of international banking, the mal-regulated system ended up – and is in 2017 still causing – serious economic downturns both in Europe and all over the world.

A study of requirements for the optimal functioning of Capitalism quickly uncovers the need for a strong focus on trust. This applies to economics on the micro/individual level as well as the macro/societal level. *Trust* is one of the ethical principles that make the difference between constructive and self-destructive operation in profit-driven financial businesses. In cultures where social development does not place sufficient weight on ethical norms and the reliability of its institutions, trust gradually dissipates. This has profound implications both on the national level and on the individual level.

Former central bank director of USA, Alan Greenspan – who was part of the problem as the Federal Reserve failed to recognize the pre-crisis housing bubble – makes a vital confession in his memoirs, *The Age of Turbulence*, when he states that we cannot build an economic society without an ethical foundation. He admitted that the structured products were so advanced that the system's ability to self-regulate in case something went wrong, started too late. The challenge was the human factor. The assumption that the financial agents would show ethical reservations when it was necessary and act rationally, completely failed. The moral foundation failed completely. Mutual trust disappeared as people ceased to be trustworthy.

Greenspan claims that economic theories are based on assumptions of how people react and choose to act. It is critical for the survival of the system that an individual makes good choices and operates with economic integrity and rationality. Something went off the rails. What we need are more sober financial institutions, new structures, better monitoring, humbler bankers, and agents. That may, alas, be exactly what we shall not get, as the aftermath of the crisis seems to show that bailouts from the US establishment and helping hands have so far not faced any major judgement.

Peter D. Schiff points out in *The Real Crash: America's Coming Bankruptcy – How to Save Yourself and Your Country* that the US is enjoying a government-inflated bubble that will explode with horrifying consequences for the economy. Since 2007, the situation has become worse, as the chosen solution to nearly defaulting the national debt was to further raise the debt limit. Schiff predicts this ride will lead to an abrupt devaluation of the US dollar and a crash that will end US power, its political system, and its way of life. Whether he is right, remains to be seen. Schiff states that entitlements, debt service, and other spending programs consumed over 100% of federal revenues in 2012. The rest of the government is paid for by borrowing. So, what's to come is probably way worse than what we have experienced up to now – and all of it the end result of limitless greed, lack of self-restraint and self-discipline, lack of honesty and modesty, lack of trustworthiness and accountability, lack of precisely the kind of morality which religion points at as the way out of deep trouble. We have gone in the opposite direction of modesty and are suffering the consequences.

It is an unavoidable fact that an individual's moral foundation plays a central role in order for market Capitalism to work properly. It is of utmost importance to be rendered trustworthy in the eyes of others. Alan Greenspan points out that people cannot function together unless definite values regulate daily choices. However, the content of values is culturally contingent. Thus, the question arises: which values are we pushing for in the West today? Certainly, not the traditional foundational ethics that defined the age in which Capitalism first originated, as an economic model strongly tied to the Protestant Ethic.

Lack of trust in governmental structures or banks, end up encouraging financial actors to think only in terms of selfish profit. This very same problem permeates many African countries. When this happens in African or Asian countries, we call it corruption. There is little trust in the political institutions or the banking system; the rich enrich their own clan and family alone. When selfishness begins to permeate central positions, trust slowly begins to disappear, and each man takes care only of himself and his own family – which is the curse of Africa.

Some correctly assert that there is a tendency within the Capitalist structure to produce some wealthy individuals. Such individuals bear a significantly larger responsibility to use their wealth not only to their own benefit but again, "to the betterment of all." If a country has responsible, rich individuals, the country will prosper due to the wisdom and trustworthiness of these individuals. If a country has wealthy elites which only spend their earnings on their own families, the country will suffer poverty, corruption, and lack of justice.

Pope John Paul II said that the problem is that the current style of Western Capitalism is wrenched off its original moral foundation. If Capitalism is equivalent to individual profit without moral responsibilities, the economic system becomes self-destructive, placing wealth into the hands of some, not searching for ways of more just distribution. Some will become steadily richer, while the rest of the world population remain even poorer than before.

In 2015, 1% of the population in the world had more wealth than the rest 99% combined, according to Oxfam numbers. One of the results of globalism is that 56 individuals now own more than 50 % of world assets, again Oxfam. [ii]A 2013 Pew Research Centre survey that asked people in a number of countries whether they believed that their children would have better-living standards showed that only 33% of Americans believed so, 17% of British and as low as 9% among the French. The depressing mood is all-encompassing. It shall be most interesting to follow the US economy in years to come, now soaring unbelievable 20 trillion US dollars in debt.

The Culture War

\*\*\*

# Western Cultural Decline

Since the end of the Cold War in the early 1990s, the Western hegemony has been largely unchallenged. Yet, more recently the superpower façade of the West has begun cracking. Ill-advised foreign policy choices such as the war in Afghanistan, Iraq, Libya, and engagement in Syria has cost the US billions of dollars as well as having led to a remarkably negative shift of opinion on the US worldwide. Deep felt financial crises have crippled the Western economy and its institutions and displayed an amount of greed and dishonesty that has left millions in shock. Serious socio-political unrest now rocks the entire Western world, with deep-rooted financial issues in a system that lacks sufficient self-regulation. Millions in the US have lost their homes and jobs, scrambling for the leftovers. Pensioners are now working at McDonald's; living standards are plummeting in the country that used to be the richest in the world. Some say we are slowly returning to the serfdom of the Middle Ages, where the rich controlled almost everything, holding ordinary people captive in a pseudo-feudal system - people would never be able to fully pay their debt to the "lord of the lands."

Historian Niall Ferguson points out in *The Great Degeneration. How Institutions Decay and Economies Die* that unemployment is concealed in the US, in ways too familiar to Europeans – who have lived with Socialist structures for decades – now facing the result of mismanagement by political elites with ideological aspirations and dreams, yet not rooted in reality. Ferguson refers to Adam Smith's quote "the stationary state," which defines the condition of wealthy states that have ceased to grow.

Wages for the majority had to be horribly low with an elite that was corrupt and monopolistic, exploiting the system, its laws, and regulations to their own benefit. He calls it an "inglorious revolution." While Adam Smith had China in mind when stating the above, China is now ahead of the US. In 1978, Americans were twenty times richer than the average Chinese; he is just five times richer today, writes Ferguson. The US is declining, while the Rest is rising.

Peter J. Schiff states in *How an Economy Grows and Why it Crashes* that very few economists had any idea that trouble was lurking on the horizon prior to the 2007 financial meltdown. Years into the mess, the problem is still not solved, economists basing their hope on the theories of

John M. Keynes that became popular in the 1920s, pointing out that the remedy is to spend even more and thus going deeper into debt based on larger loans, both in the public and private sector.

At the core of Keynes' ideas is the notion that governments should play a much stronger role, and smooth out the volatility of the free markets by expanding the supply of money and running large budget deficits when times are tough. Schiff explains that when the Keynes' theory first became popular, it came into deep conflict with existing economic theories, such as those of the Austrian School who followed economists Ludwig von Mises. They felt that recessions are necessary to compensate for unwise decisions made during the booms that precede the busts. It could, of course, on another level be argued that what really solved the American economic problems was the World War II. After it ended, Europe lay in ruins, the untouched USA benefitting on every level, rising to superpower status.

Satyajit Das, who predicted the 2007 financial meltdown, states in *In The Age of Stagnation: Why Perpetual Growth is Unattainable, and the Global Economy is in Peril,* that the official response to the financial crisis was a policy of "extend and pretend," as authorities ignored the underlying problem, covered it up and "kicked the can further down the road". The assumption is that of Keynes, to increase government spending, lower interest rates and supply cash to money markets. Increasing inflation was meant to help reduce the level of debt, by decreasing its value. Yet, the market has not responded sufficiently to these measures; global debt has increased, large banks controlling the financial assets in the US even more in 2016 than back in 2007. The real economy has not yet returned to normal.

The economist Milton Friedman wrote in *Capitalism and Freedom* that during a financial crisis it is essential that those that have behaved irresponsibly and avariciously, and thereby ended up in financial straits, should be made responsible for their reckless actions. "Let them play with their own money instead of others," he said. "Only then will they act responsibly." Professor Jeffery Miron at Harvard University states that the responsibility of the individual remains the key concept to success. He points out the dangers in state interference and economic aid packages because they prevent the natural realignment of the system. Historically, additional regulations eventually cause new problems.

Individual accountability is the moral prerequisite for constructive, sustainable profit. If the individual does not behave in a manner that inspires trust, then the glue in the economic model fails. Where egoism is permitted, arrogance and pride are short to follow. This is the very core of what Protestant Calvinism attempts to combat through values like boundary setting, self-discipline, and a certain level of asceticism.

Here lies the challenge. Capitalism, in its purely theoretical form, is not perfect but has proven to be the best system for wealth distribution so far. Those who work the most, get paid the most, and thus, the incentive to work even harder motivates those involved. In Communist societies or bureaucratic Socialist societies, it does not matter how hard you work, everyone is paid the same, whether the person is lazy or strives for excellence, the state gives out the same amount of money to all.

Many argue that the recent financial crisis is another nail in the coffin the global American hegemony. Kishore Mahbubani, from the University of Singapore, has said that the greatest failing in modern Western thought is the lack of a basic common moral understanding. This great cultural divide will sap and divide the West in the years ahead. Mahbubani argues that as a result of the Western ethical decline, the West has developed structural faults in its moral foundations. In *Clash of Civilizations: The Debate*, he asserts that Western countries fail to recognize that democratic values, like individualism, also carry destructive tendencies. The fall of the West comes from within, from the culture's own moral decline. Mahbubani points to a dwindling work ethic, lack of care for elderly, and expectations for free handouts.

What we observe today has happened before. The English historian Edward Gibbon's *The History of the Decline and Fall of the Roman Empire* highlights these historical phenomena. When a civilization is at its zenith, with power and influence over many other cultures, it often develops the notion that it represents the noblest and most advanced civilization thus far known in history. In these moments of self-exaltation, a blind sense of invincibility prevails. No matter if the civilization abandons its original values – the precise values that led to its greatness – no matter how it deals with its minority groups, how much injustice goes unattended, no matter how many wars it initiates in foreign territories, somehow its elites still believe that its civilization will always remain superior.

For instance, the Romans had a firm belief that they were superior human beings, composed of a greater rationality and intelligence compared to others. Romans, therefore, felt that their civilization was the best ever seen; they did other people "a favor" by imposing Roman culture on them. One civilization was to rule them all, one culture to take world dominion. This arrogance was particularly dominant in the later phase of the history of the Western Roman Empire, angering other ethnic groups and eventually leading to the bitter resentment from Germanic and other groups, which resulted in the sacking and final fall of Rome in AD 410. Centuries before, the Roman orator and politician, Marcus Cicero had already warned against this behavior. "The arrogance of political leaders should be tempered and controlled," he wrote, later stating: "the higher we are placed, the humbler we should walk."

The economist Mancur Olson points out in *The Rise and Decline of Nations* that it was precisely Great Britain's high status before World War II - and even higher status before World War I - that contributed to an initial state of arrogance that obstructed the need for progress and growth. There was an ongoing optimism after the war that all the economic and social problems of the Western world would be solved, since "Great Britain always is the greatest." The belief was that economic growth was limitless, with no end to the rise of living standards. Complacent self-satisfaction and cultural indifference gradually permeated British society, with the result that industrial growth and expansion received little or no attention. The British increasingly emphasized strong labor organizations and the development of a welfare society with extensive rights to social aid and welfare. Protectionist policies excluded other countries from the British market, in spite of their better-priced and higher quality products. The British borrowed money and incurred debt.

Great Britain blithely ignored increasingly competitive economies in other countries. Self-confident winners of the war, they still lost the leading role as a Western world power. Germany, in contrast, lost the war and humbly endeavored to meet the challenges of the future. They formed a society based on hard work, the re-establishment of German institutions, and limited debt. Post-war modesty, self-discipline, and hard work have worked well for them. Today Germany is again the strongest state in Europe, with the strongest economy of them all.

Satyajit Das now states that we are entering a new era of protracted stagnation. In *In The Age of Stagnation,* he questions the ability of the current Western political leaders to impose the structural changes needed. He maintains that the idea of growth being perpetual is not sustainable, pointing at the dangers of excessive debt and the current fundamental imbalances in the economic system. Das views with concern the way Western governments "solved" the 2007 crisis, by "not solving it at all," just postponing the full weight of the consequences, by fuelling "easy money" into the system. He fears that the lack of rationally structured solutions will end up causing effects that will affect the lifestyles and prosperity of citizens today and also future generations.

Alternatively, as Niall Ferguson puts it, the present system is completely fraudulent. Huge liabilities are simply hidden from view, with hardly any accountability regarding accurate official balance sheets. No legitimate business can continue this way. If the course is not altered, it will end in a big, black crunch of hopelessness and utter despair, yet this outcome predicted and foreseen by so many.

# CHAPTER 13

# Christophobia in the West

*"We see that many Western states have taken the way where they deny or reject their own roots, including the Christian roots which form the basis for Western civilization. In these countries, the moral basis and any national identity are being denied, national, religious, cultural and even gender identities are being denied or relativized." Vladimir Putin, Valdai Summit 2013.*

## The Russian Defence of Christianity

Russian-Orthodox bishop, Metropolit Hilarion stated a strikingly valid point, as cited by *Observatory of Intolerance Against Christians*: "We often hear about antisemitism and Islamophobia, and very little is said about Christianophobia, which is gaining strength in many European countries." The Organization for Security and Co-operation in Europe (OSCE) Reports have commented on recent attacks on Christian communities in Europe and have highlighted the necessity to address the problem of intolerance against Christians with a specific focus on hate crimes. It seems that the Catholic Archbishop of Chicago, Charles Chaput is correct in painting quite a bleak future for Christianity in the West when he, according to *Observatory of Intolerance Against Christians* says that Christianity will become a faith that can speak in the public square less and less freely.

The growing tendency to persecute Christians in the West worries many. In an interview after the 2016 meetings between the head of the

Russian Orthodox Church, Patriarch Kirill and Pope Francis in Cuba, the Patriarch stated:

> I strongly believe that we should work together in order to save our society from de-Christianization – because, facing increasing atheistic pressure, which has become quite aggressive in some countries, Christians are being squeezed out of public life. In a sense, we may say that Christians are uncomfortable in many developed countries today. Christians are under pressure. Specifically, attempts are made to limit religious manifestations in public space. All this indicates that we are dealing with a dangerous, critical situation, with regard to Christian reality and Christian presence. I think our meeting with Pope Francis came at the right time.

According to the International Society for Human Rights, 80% of all acts of religious discrimination in the world today are directed at Christians. The Pew Forum states that between 2006 and 2010, Christians faced some form of discrimination in 139 nations, which is almost three-quarters of all the countries on earth – constituting an unreported catastrophe of our time.

Furthermore, one hundred years ago, 80% of the world's Christians lived in the West, while today the number has dropped to around 40%, according to *Freedom Outpost*.

Patriarch Kirill is among those who seem deeply worried about the growing Christophobia in Europe. He highlights that the rise of euthanasia and self-killing, the cult of sensual pleasures, the rise of non-Christian values and the development of a sense of permissiveness is a serious step away from the original values of Europe, according to *Pravmir*.

The speech of Russian Foreign Minister, Sergey Lavrov, held at the 28th session of the UN Human Rights Council in Geneva, 2015, stands out as a relevant illustration. Lavrov is among the non-Western leaders who steadily address the growing issue of persecution against Christians in Europe. He voices, on a regular basis, concern about the aggressive secularism in the West and the persecution of Christians, as morality and traditional national, cultural and religious identity is eroding in Europe. At the Council, he noted that: "Christianity is the world's largest religion in terms of both the number of its supporters and its worldwide presence. After all, every country has at least one Christian community. Today, increasingly more Christians – in fact, millions of them – are being subjected to persecution, false accusations and discrimination, or are even falling victim to atrocities."

Many would be amazed, reading his words. It is indeed, to a Westerner, surprising to see that a country such as Russia, which before used to be purely atheist, now is leading the fight for the Christian faith internationally. It illustrates that at least some of the information given to the public through mainstream media is not balanced. We hardly ever hear about Russia's defense of Christianity, in fact, it is hard to find any positive comments about this large nation that borders on Europe. Yet, as mentioned, it is noticeable that six companies now own over 90% of the American media, according to *Business Insider*. Back in 1983, over fifty companies did the same job. Media is owned by the very few and easy to control. It is, so to speak, in the hands of the few to paint different foreign countries are either good or bad, in order to fit geopolitical or ideological goals.

History may explain part of the reason for this new Russian approach. After the fall of the Soviet Union, most Russians were weary of the anti-traditionalist, atheist Communist society that they felt had limited them for so long. Many welcomed the new freedoms of religion and today, around 70% of the Russian people are Christians. This implies massive movements within society to return to the old, cultural greatness of the Russian state.

As mentioned, the Russian Foreign minister, Sergey Lavrov addressed the same issue of persecution in Europe against Christians at the UN Human Rights Council. He voiced deep concern about the aggressive secularism in the West and the persecution of Christians in Europe, as morality and traditional national, cultural and religious identity is eroding. After speaking about the terrible situation that Christians and other minorities are experiencing in the Middle East, he said, as stated by *The Ministry of Foreign Affairs of the Russian Federation*:

> I also have to mention the problems experienced by Christians in a number of Western European states, where for some reason it has become politically incorrect to identify oneself as a Christian, and where people are even starting to become uncomfortable with Christian values that form the foundation of the European civilization. Aggressive secularism is gaining momentum. The notions of morality and traditional national, cultural and religious identity are being eroded. Incidences of vandalism and desecration of churches, temples, holy places, cemeteries and Christian symbols are growing fast. It is increasingly difficult for believers to uphold their convictions.

He added:

> Lessons of history show that a civilization that has

> abandoned its moral ideals loses its spiritual strength. All of us must remember this, especially this year, when we are marking the 70th anniversary of the Great Victory in World War II, in which tens of millions of people of all ethnicities and religions perished. Our common duty is not to betray the feat of the victors, and to counter uncompromisingly any attempts to fan up hostility and hatred. The efforts to defend the values of all world religions – the vehicles of the common heritage of humanity – are called upon to play a tremendous role in this respect.

How strange it is to see a Russian speak like this, while our own progressive political leaders, steadily make the point of omitting references to our religious heritage when they speak. The world is truly changing when one has to look to Russia in order to find support for Christianity in the West.

An address by the President of Russia, Vladimir Putin at the Valdai. Summit in September 2013, illustrates the point. He stated:

> The people in many European states are actually ashamed of their religious affiliations and are indeed frightened to speak about them. Christian holidays and celebrations are abolished or "neutrally" renamed, as if one were ashamed of Christian holidays. With this method, one hides away the deeper moral values of these celebrations. And these countries try to force this model unto other countries, globally. I am deeply convinced that this is the direct way to the degradation and primitivization. This leads to deeper demographic and moral crisis in the West. What can be a better evidence for the moral crisis in human society than the loss of its reproductive function? Without the moral values that are rooted in Christianity and other world religions, without rules and moral values which have formed and been developed over millennia, people will inevitably lose their human dignity. And we think it is right and natural to defend and preserve these moral values."

## "Christophobia"

Europe has arguably become the most secularized and spiritually antagonistic region in the world, marked by "Christophobia" to such an extent that even wearing a Christian cross or any sign of religious affiliation may easily be labeled offensive. As noted by columnist and former lead singer in the notorious death punk band, *Turbonegro*, Hans-Erik Dyvik Husby, the same politically correct elites who constantly complain about Islamophobia and homophobia, have nothing against practising what he labels by the term "Christophobia" - a widespread tendency in popular culture and the mainstream media to disrespect and ridicule Christians.

Little is said about the gross persecutions against Christians in the Middle East, where according to Italian CESNUR Centre for Studies of New Religions, 600 million Christians now are under the threat of persecution. Around 90 000 were killed in 2016 for their Christian faith, one-third by ISIS Salafi jihadists.

Yet we hear little from the media on these issues, fearful as they are of being perceived as "Islamophobic" or "racist," Husby stated in a recent article. Christophobic editors and columnists want to please their liberal friends and not write about the crucifixions, the beheadings and how Christians are burned alive in the Middle East, out of fear of being perceived as "anti-gay" or "anti-abortion" – the usual stigmas quickly given those who defend Christianity.

So, when bands such as Norwegian Troll sing "Kill the Christians," experts say that such statements are within the limits of free speech. Christians are told to expect nothing if they complain. One could only imagine if Troll chanted: "Kill the Muslims" or "Kill the Jews," writes Husby, yet Christophobia is so rampant in Europe that "kill the Christians" is a completely acceptable song title. We have reached a stage where it is considered the high mark of Western civilization to accept the slandering of our own religion and cultural heritage in the name of progress. It is regarded as a proof of how civilized our rational, scientific society has become: Christophobia is to be given all possible free space to develop.

As political radio and TV show host, Alex Jones of *Infowars* notes: "There is a war on Christians worldwide, coming out of Washington DC as well. This should concern you even if you are not a Christian, it should concern you because of the way that this is being done because it is another example of how the rule of law is being shunned in favor of dictatorship. The dictatorship of a president, the dictatorship of a bureaucracy, the dictatorship of political correctness."

A good illustration is the steadily ongoing debates regarding the public use of crucifixes in Europe. Schools in Italy have faced this issue as the Catholic faith is increasingly met with hostility by EU regulations which profess to speak up against discrimination, but end up instead fighting traditional European values and cultural ideals that are at the core of historical European identity.

In 2009, a ruling from the European Court of Human Rights banned crucifixes in Italian classrooms, on the grounds that they "breach religious rights of children." Politicians all over Italy reacted, and Italy's then foreign minister Franco Frattini said that regressive moves such as this are a death blow for European values and historical rights. Europe's roots lie in its Christian identity, he stated. At a time when Italy is trying to bring religion back as an important stabilizing factor in its disintegrating society, its very enemies turn out to the extreme liberal EU elites, who are supposed to make the European identity stronger in a time of upheaval, rather than tearing it further apart.

In the search for a better Europe, the ideological and political elites have chosen to diminish precisely the values that once made Europe a strong civilization. The anti-Christian hostility is quite notable. Many speak with shame of the original religious and philosophical values that formed the basis for the growth of a strong Western civilization, ideals that have lifted millions out of poverty and brought prosperity to nations all over the globe. They - progressive in name, but highly regressive in reality - seem to wish to destroy the very core of the common European geopolitical and cultural identity.

In Italy, rage engulfed many when the Court of Human Rights in Strasbourg in 2009 issued a judgment defining the cross as an improper influence on European youth. Following the rulings, it finally became obvious to many that this institution is the long-term ally with the extreme liberals who seem bent on destroying the historic cultural fabric of Europe. The court has long been commonly hostile to traditional European values, its elites issuing numerous judgments that comply with the ideologies that gradually have weakened European culture the past decennials. It could easily have ended up becoming illegal to bear the cross in Europe if the Court of Appeals in Strasbourg had arrived at the same conclusion as the first judgment issued in the case.

As expected, citizens all over Italy, and particularly in public offices, responded by exhibiting the cross. The judgment was understood as a clear attack on Italian culture and its religious affiliations. The attitudes expressed by this kind of judgment will, over time, succeed in marginalizing central elements of our culture.

The European Court even rejected that the crucifix was a national symbol of culture, history and identity, tolerance and secularism, according to the *Telegraph*. Countries like Denmark, Iceland, Norway, Greece and Great Britain could probably have to remove the cross from their national flags. A number of European nations have the cross in their national flag. The flag issue is still on the discussion table. In Switzerland, an immigrant group recently called for the abolishing of the cross in the Swiss flag, according to Gatestone Institute. The EU itself has voiced concern over religious symbols, suggesting that several of the European countries should change their flags and remove the cross.[iii] Many argue that it is "offensive to Muslims" for Europe to have national flags that incorporate the Christian cross and that the flag should be multiculturally neutral.

The hostility towards religious faith within the EU has been obvious for decades. In the ideological approach of trying to diminish the Christian faith, one hides behind leniencies towards Muslims, saying that the new immigrants are offended by the European Christian identity and that we, therefore, need to let go of it. The rationale is questionable, as Jesus, or Isa, is a highly regarded prophet in Islam. On the contrary, it is in the extreme-liberal, anti-Christian European establishment, Jesus Christ seem neither revered nor respected – thus the acceptance for "Christophobia." It can be argued that Christianity as a system of morality is incompatible with the secular extremist, hedonist establishment – with its strong aversions against moral regulation – that Europe today seems consumed by.

In a 2008 prize-winning editorial in Aftenposten the Norwegian physician, columnist, and author, Mohammad Usman Rana stated that modern society is increasingly marked by a secular extremism and uniformity. He claimed that in order for plurality to be maintained, the degrading views of religious believers must stop. Christians who claim that the Bible contains truths to be followed are bashed harshly in public debate – while the politically correct, and liberal theologians who hail the current progressive trends in society receive no criticism at all. The challenge is to find an identity of faith: will this European nation be a moderate secular state that respects freedom of religion or will society be extremely secular, where the state and the politically correct establishment dominates and dictates what Norwegian citizens are allowed to believe?

Rana, who also defended Christian bishops, claimed that a moderate secular state implies that even if faith is relegated to the private sphere, the individual's right to practice his faith in public should still be respected. In public debate, there is an accelerating tendency to marginalize religious people who wish to live according to their faith. They are quickly described as brainwashed and narrow-minded fundamentalists. The growing secular uniformity is characterized by a striking willingness to stop conservative arguments coming from believers, ironically claiming that they are the ones lacking tolerance.

Religious traditions that have existed in Europe for a thousand years are now considered unimportant. This includes both Catholic and Protestant countries. Pope Benedict XVI commented on the brutality of this development in his Good Friday sermon of 2009, stating that religious sentiments now seem to be regarded as unwelcome leftovers of antiquity, held up to scorn and ridicule. He compared the harsh secularism in Europe and the aggressive attempts to remove religion from public life to the mockery by the mob that Jesus was faced with when going to the cross. Christmas, the celebration of the birth of Christ, has undergone quite an immense scrutiny by those pushing for the de-Christianization of the West. Outright public mention of the Easter message, Pentecost, or the Christian origins of Christmas traditions is frowned upon by the politically correct establishment.

The debate about the offensiveness of saying "Merry Christmas" to someone at Christmas – as it supposedly offends the non-religious and non-Christian – and the need to replace it with "Happy Holidays" - defined as a non-offensive word, illustrates the problem quite well. The trend is that Westerners are no longer allowed to celebrate their own national, traditional holidays. Europe is ashamed of its own historical values. How can a culture survive in such a self-hating climate?

✳✳✳

## Social Disorder and Christian Decline

There are a number of perplexing developments few wish to discuss in the West. Beneath the glossy wrapping of materialism and technological advancement, there is undeniably growing social disorder, growing social unrest, lack of discipline and order in schools, lack of respect for teachers, a rampant denigration of the religious, be it Muslims, Christians or others, combined with high divorce and suicide rates, destructive drug abuse and faltering economies. We have soaring numbers of abortions, gigantic abuse of prescription pills especially among women and serious issues with mental disabilities. Remarkably little is done to stop it. How can we be so plagued by mental and social disorders, and yet be rich and prosperous?

According to *US Forum on Child and Family* statistics, rates of births born outside of marriage have rocketed from 5% in 1960 to 41% today. In 2006, only 21% of families were married-couples with children under 18, according to the Labour Information Centre 2007. Suicide rates among teenagers tripled between 1960 and 1990, according to the National Institute of Mental Health, and in the same time span William Bennett points out in *The Index of Leading Cultural Indicators*, violent crimes such as murder, rape and assault increased in the US by 550%. Today, there is less disposable income for a two-parent working family, than a single parent working family in the 1950s.

The 1950s are often depicted as a time where women were deprived of their rights, locked in the kitchen with men who demanded her services at all hours, without freedom of any kind. She was a slave to his wishes. Were women really refused education in the US in the 1950s? Was life really that horrible?

Looking at the statistics above, the quite the opposite seems to be closer to the truth: we have never been worse off socially than after accepting the extreme-liberal restructuring of society that culminated in the 1960s rebellion against traditional values.

The negligent attitude regarding the massive social challenge of, for example, legal and illegal drug abuse is deeply problematic. In terms of numbers, legal drug prescriptions far exceed the number of people commonly associated with the use of illegal drugs. This has turned us into a culture of drug dependency. The careless way in which physician's write prescriptions for calming medications socially legitimizes drug abuse among inflicted and hurting individuals.

Political analyst Pat Buchanan says in *Suicide of a Superpower* that American culture has undergone a cultural, moral and religious revolution that spells out the end of Christian America. In the 1960s, also known as the "age of permissiveness," the militant secularism in the US which has always had a strong grip on the secular academic elites, grew into the universities and colleges across the country and captured the younger generations. The national cultural war began.

Since then, an extreme secularism and distorted version of its original form, characterized by a gross lack of respect for believers, has dominated the academic community, the entertainment industry, and the political scene, but not fundamentally across the nation as a whole. This is the basis of the great cultural war the US is undergoing. It is a militant anti-Christian, anti-God and anti-traditionalist revolution that has caused a deep split in the US, morally, socially, culturally and theologically.

What is worrying is how these trends coincide with the statistics of the decline of the institutionalized Church. Pat Buchanan points out that, according to the Religious Identification Survey conducted in 2008, 16% of all American adults have no religious affiliation, 30% of all married couples did not have a religious wedding and 27% of Americans do not want a religious funeral. One may add the Pew Forum survey that in 2007 found that 44% of Americans have lost their faith or changed religions. Compared with 99% who were Protestants at the time when the US was born as a nation, only 51% were so in 2007. The numbers vary and may be discussed from different angles.

Nonetheless, Catholicism is on the rise in America with the growing influx of Mexican and other immigrants from traditionally Catholic countries and may probably be the largest segment in the US in a few years. Yet, among "white Americans," Catholicism has faced major blows since the 1960s, only rivaled by the crisis of the Reformation in the 1500s. While 62% of those over seventy were Protestants now, only 43% of Americans below twenty-nine now call themselves Protestants.

The whole religious fabric of Evangelical Christianity in the US is undergoing dramatic change, yet surveys also show that the American religious fabric still states that around 80% believe in God. Even if this constitutes a fall from the well over 90% believers years back, the fall in the actual belief in God is still not as dramatic as one may get the impression of when studying the decline in institutionalized religion, as Buchanan analyses. If you compare these statistics to the ones on the previous pages, stating the exploding divorce rates and the break-up of the family, the numbers are startling. Many aspects could be discussed, for one if the decline in institutionalized religion equals the rise in social problems. This debate will probably continue for years to come.

The UK is in a similar situation with alarming social trends. Chronicles editor, Tom Piatak, states that British children have the earliest and highest consumption of cocaine among the young in Europe. They are ten times more likely to sniff solvents than Greek children; they are seven times more likely to smoke pot than Swedish children.

## Abortion – Millions of Unborn Lost

A substantial silence accompanies the maps of pregnancies aborted, millions of unborn children removed from their mother's womb since the West implemented self-determined abortion in the early 1970s. Abortion may sometimes be necessary, yet today the procedure is used in order to avoid pregnancies. We arguably live in a child-hostile culture that simply does not want its own offspring. The fertility rates have dropped dramatically in the West. Italy has the lowest birth rates in 150 years, according to The Guardian,[iv] with 1.4% fertility rate, Denmark 1.7%, Switzerland 1.5% and Portugal 1.2%, Germany 1.4%, according to 2016 numbers from World Bank.

According to World Health Organization (WHO) and other surveys, Eastern Europe and Russia have abortion rates of pregnancies as high as 30–50%, shockingly up to 80% in some areas. In Scandinavia, UK, and France the rates are as high as 20–30%, Germany, Finland and Benelux 11–14% and Poland, Switzerland and Portugal at the bottom end of the scale with only 1–2% abortions. Since abortion was first legalized in the early 1970s, Germany has had a rate of around 120,000 annually, France around 200,000 and growing, Netherlands 30,000, Norway 15,000, Sweden 35,000 and a sharp decline in abortions in countries like Russia with 3.4 million in 1992 to 1.3 million in 2008.

In the US, over 50 million have been lost to abortion since 1960, according to former Newsweek editor Meacham in what he calls "The end of Christian America."[35] When you add up these numbers, they are formidable. The question of abortion rights cover a range of difficult issues, from the aftermath of rape and pedophilia to social and financial reasons for women. The termination of a pregnancy may arguably be necessary in some cases. Yet, the silence regarding the "defence of the unborn" from Church leaders is remarkable, considering the Scripture's teachings about the value of a human life.

Church leaders seldom discuss these children's right to life, nor are there open debates about the ethical implications. A number of the measures instituted by health authorities to reduce abortions, such as free

---

[35] Meacham: "The end of Christian America." (Friday, August 18, 2017) http://www.newsweek.com/meacham-end-christian-america-77125

birth control pills to young girls, free condoms and information programs at schools and health clinics, have not worked as intended in reducing unwanted pregnancies.

The high numbers of teenage abortions should cause concern. The solution so far seems to be continual supply of free birth control pills and condoms, encouraging free sex. How does living in this society, which ruthlessly encourages sexual activity affect a young person's psyche? Does human sexuality function such that the more sexual partners you have, the healthier you are? Why is restraint not recommended to young women in the risk zone for unwanted pregnancies?

During fieldwork among Muslims in Kenya in 2004, while working on a thesis at the University of Oslo, I was confronted with the following paradox: a well-known Muslim leader asked me why Europeans call Saudi Arabia "barbarians" when they chop off the hands of thieves as punishment for stealing. He was amazed that this Arabic custom could be so harshly denounced, with reference to human rights and other Western statutes. Yet in the West, he said, a mother has the full right to take the life of her own child when inside her womb. He repeatedly pointed out: "She has the right to kill her own child," saying that, unlike thieves, these aborted children are innocent, and have committed no crime. He asked me: "Which culture is really barbarian? Which culture is most inhumane?"

One of the ironies of abortion is that Europe and the US now have to import millions of migrant workers, many of them from Muslims nations, as those young Westerners who should have filled the vacancies, were never born. The continent is now being populated by Muslims and other non-Westerners who have another view of children than liberal Westerners. They love children and see them as a gift from God, and wish to have as many as possible. Statistics show that Muslim families often have 6–8 children each. They simply love children, unlike Westerners who steadily try to reduce the number of children. When looking at demographics, it is only a question of time before the Caucasian European becomes a minority in Europe, if this trend continues.

✼✼✼

# Civilizations Die From Suicide

The American author Patrick J. Buchanan states in *Suicide of a Superpower* that the spiritualism within the true Christianity revived Europe and held us together as a community and as a civilization. The ethics of Christianity have been the basis of moral consensus, the moral code by which a community thrives. This deep sense of spiritual awareness which in history has shown itself to translate into solidarity with others immediately is now disintegrating, both in secular society as well as within many institutionalized churches. The historian Arnold Toynbee famously states that a civilization dies from suicide, not murder.

The Catholic Archbishop in Brussels, Cardinal Godfried Danneels, states that until the 1700s, mental illness and neuroses were quite unknown in Europe. In *Handing on the Faith in an Age of Disbelief,* he offers another explanation than the usual one – lack of awareness of the problem at that time. Prior to the so-called Age of Enlightenment, that began percolating into the population during the 1700s–1800s, people lived in a collective culture where traditional authorities were accepted.

Everyone tended to find their place in the community with larger ease than seems to be the case today. The individual was surrounded by a strict social network in which he had duties and responsibilities, religious ethics and faith providing a social adhesive. What Danneels points to is that from the 1800s onward, with the emergence of philosophical empiricism and its narrow-minded definitions of rationalism – definitions which only acknowledged the empirically observable and thus left out large scopes of what defines the completeness of a spiritual and physical human being, something slowly began to go wrong.

Danneels claims that psychoanalysis and some of the work of Sigmund Freud and Carl F. Jung had some constructive influence on the lives of many, leading to liberation and increased self-knowledge. However, he makes an essential point: sexual liberation has not resulted in less mental illness. In fact, psychological suffering is immensely more widespread than ever before. Western culture is today characterized by a vague melancholy and widespread depression.

There is a notable silence – laden with taboos – that today accompanies discussions about the metaphysical dimension in the West. Few find sufficient answers for the indefinable, existential sorrows and depressions that so many live with. The collective denial of essential aspects of being a human burdens us. We need to turn the tide of this ongoing cultural decadence, encourage a new sense of respect and solidarity and tend again to the betterment of society and the fellowship of men.

An underlying sorrow seems to permeate Western culture. Our civilization is blanketed with a melancholy fog consisting of financial crises, moral decay, a sense of helplessness, neuroses and mental pain. Man is nihilistically alone and unprotected in a godless, dark and dangerous world where no God above sees or cares for him, nobody watches his steps, he has no purpose beyond the here and now, beyond selfish pursuits, in a non-spiritual world in which the only strength that may help him succeed is his own. He has nowhere to turn, the bonds of fellowship and ethic solidarity quenched in an increasingly hedonistically, self-oriented culture where the only goal is to become rich and famous.

We are in yet another age of upheaval, cultural decline and limited freedom in a Western political structure where a small globalized economic and political elite with strong ideological links to neo-Marxism and in parallel neo-liberalism have tight control over the very few corporations that own the mainstream media, thus easily controlling public opinion and thereby democracy itself.

✻✻✻

# The Influence of Faith on Health

We live in a culture that almost completely denies the spiritual realm and its influence on the human. *Time* magazine recently referred to broad international studies that confirm that spirituality can be beneficial to your health. Since 2000, over 6,000 studies have been published that concern the constructive influence of religion on illness. The study on the influence of prayer on the psyche is especially persuasive.

In *How God Changes Your Brain*, psychiatrist Andrew Newberg explains how the parietal lobe, a structural area of the brain, is highly activated during prayer or meditation. Activity in this part of the brain has several positive effects on people, among other things increased memory. Fasting, as practiced by Muslims during Ramadan, and also by Jews, and by Christians before Christmas and Easter, has specific health benefits that can strengthen the brain's ability to think clearly. Fasting also causes pleasant, harmonious emotions.

Ninety-four percent of those interviewed in Newberg's study expressed a sincere wish for physicians to show more interest for their religious belonging, which the medical profession seldom does. Seldom do physicians recommend alternative medicine like acupuncture and zone therapy. Why not recommend both alternative methods as well as prayer and the laying on of hands for healing, many asked. Another study showed that regular church or prayer-house attendance increased lifespans by two to three years. The correlation between participating actively in a social community and mental health is much more real than many may think.

Psychiatrist Gail Ironson, also cited in the Time Magazine study, has studied the relationship between faith and health for many years. She says that in work with HIV patients, those that emphasize spirituality and prayer have better control over their illness than others. HIV patients who believed in God and the spiritual dimension produced on the average more CD4 cells which play a major role in protecting the body from infection. Even more importantly, prayer and meditation led to the production of fewer stress hormones, which again reduced patient's blood pressure, regulated blood sugar, and improved immunity.

It is peculiar that the relationship between religiosity and mental health doesn't receive more interest. A person with psychological problems should not be seen just as a patient, but as an individual who has a body, soul, and spirit – with physical and metaphysical dimensions. A holistic approach should be applied, looking into why we get sick in the first place. Alternative medicine could be used, homeopathic methods, acupuncture – disciplines that view the body as part of a larger system and seek to heal in accordance with the early methods of Hippocrates and others. Body and mind seem to be vastly more interlinked than many may assume. Research on cancer also shows how vulnerable someone might become if psychological problems become too many and the person must carry the load alone.

Sarah Lazar, a neuroscientist at Massachusetts General Hospital and Harvard Medical School, has studied the benefits of spiritual meditation and tested it in brain scans. One of the benefits of the MRI, which is able to take photographs of brain activity, is that it allows the scientist to look at the brain in a way that one could not do before, monitoring the changes in the brain if the person changes lifestyle. In the 1970–90s, most MRI scanning was done to animals, not humans, as the scanning technology was developing. Today neurobiological studies, which study how the brain works, look at humans, determining not only the effects of prayer and meditation but music, love and its effect on the physical brain, areas of study that were not possible to do before.

MRI scans which study how meditation and mindfulness affect the brain are new fields – traditional Western medicine has long denied the assumed beneficial links that now may be documented by MRI scans and ground-breaking neurobiological work. Little has so far been known about neural mechanisms associated with therapeutic interventions that incorporate meditation and prayer. Scientists have, for quite some time, studied the immune system or the endocrine system and the biochemical fluids that flow through the body. It has long been known that the brain controls movement. What is new with cutting edge research, like that of Sarah Lazar at the Harvard Medical School, is that one now realizes that there is a lot of two-way connections, that what goes on in the body also reflects in the brain and vice versa – and that the brain can also influence the body, even on the cellular level. In other words, what you think and how you live has direct influences on your physical body and the cellular level within it.

According to the *Washington Post*, Lazar found that meditation and spiritual thinking literally changes your brain, documenting how parts of the brain that are connected to memory and the ability to memorize, maintain emotional regulation and stability enlarges in individuals who are spiritually aware and meditate regularly.

The Lazar study, showed differences in brain volume after only eight weeks of meditating, documenting how meditation and prayer lead to increases in regional brain gray matter density, many experiencing a reduction of stress levels, anxiety, and depression. The prefrontal cortex shrinks as we get older, but in people who meditate and learn how to quiet the mind by praying or through mindfulness, fifty-year-olds have the same ability to memorize and remember as regular twenty-five-year-olds, the mentioned Harvard Medical School study found.

The study further showed that the individuals who participated in the eight-week program, none of them having meditated before, enlarged the part of the brain called the temporoparietal junction, which is connected to the ability to have empathy, compassion. It also affected the amygdala by making this part of the brain shrink, the part that is connected to anxiety, depression, and stress. The participants who meditated or prayed were, in essence, able to better handle depression – the well-known state of mind that has been labeled the illness that engulfs America today. Depression and mental pain are one of the most common mental disorders in the US, according to the US National Institute of Mental Health.

Yet, studies confirm that prayer and meditation have a remarkably positive effect. In Japan, at the National Institute for Physiological Sciences in Okazaki, similar studies have shown that meditation reduces pain-related neural activity in a number of areas in the brain. It seems to relieve pain perception in humans, and anatomical changes occur in the brain of those with long-term meditation training.

Another analysis also documented segments of the relationship between positive emotions and mortality. People that often use positively charged words like hope, gratitude, and love, lived longer than those that were negatively programmed. A study that was first published in *The*

*Journal for Psychosomatic Medicine* was based on a comparison of autobiographies written by young Parisian nuns in the 1930s. These autobiographies were penned prior to their final vows and were compared to their situations sixty years later. The results were dramatic. Those that used positively charged words in their autobiography lived nine years longer than those that used negatively charged words. Since then many studies have been performed along the same lines, all largely confirming the study of the nuns.

The *Norwegian Journal of Psychology* published a study sometime back that showed that even though most believe in God, faith is not at all emphasized in the education of for example nurses or psychologists. Ninety-three percent of those interviewed said that there was no focus on religious faith at all during their studies. A third indicated that the discipline employs negative stereotypes and shows a general lack of respect concerning religion, which they regretted. Ninety-two percent agreed that a focus on religion would improve the profession and 15% felt that believers in God were directly ridiculed in lectures.

Research shows that it is just as important to do good as it is to have a good life. Genuine positive emotions influence the body's biochemistry, enhancing, as Lazar's work showed, both compassion and empathy in humans. By being active, grateful, and forgiving, you strengthen your experience of social cohesion and have better health.

Auguste Comte's philosophical empiricism – or positivism – implies a denial of all which is incomprehensible to the human mind, – all that is outside of his limited knowledge. This kind of thinking heavily affects disciplines such as the study of psychology, which as of today hardly addresses spiritual matters or how to deal with believers or problems of spiritual origin. Medical students report the same. Even though it is common knowledge that doctors and nurses are the ones closest to old people, the sick and many with mental issues, there is still hardly any focus in the curriculum on how to deal with people who are believers or need spiritual help. It is quite remarkable how far we have come: spirituality is becoming a non-existing theme in the study of the human body. This is also the criticism that is often heard from alternative physicians, acupuncturists, experts on Chinese medicine and others with a more holistic approach.

Even though modern medicine is able to provide excellent remedy to many illnesses and scientific research has solved medical riddles, it is still unable to cure a whole range of issues that often are interlinked with deeper layers in the human. There is still little or no holistic approach to the human body, no wide definition of what it means to be human that incorporates the metaphysical level with understanding of its spiritual implications.

Many in the West end up resorting to "alternative methods" such as homeopathy, natural medicine, acupuncture and other Eastern holistic disciplines that have existed for thousands of years, rather than solely trusting modern medicine which has been around in its current form for only two hundred years.

How the body works is an intricate and complex question. Physical symptoms often develop as a result of mental or spiritual imbalance. Yet, many patients are treated with symptom-reducing medicine alone, as modern doctors are not able to correctly prescribe a cure, a patients' problems often brushed off as "psychological" or "instability issues." It is quite the easy fix to resort to prescribing painkillers and antidepressants. If the doctor's job is reduced to merely reducing symptoms chemically, but not cure the illness, we are not as advanced as we profess to be.

✻✻✻

# Revivalism Worldwide

One who lives in a society marked by an intolerant marginalization of believers can easily lose sight of the major religious revival that is actually occurring in the rest of the world. The Muslim belt girdles the world from Indonesia to Morocco, with powerful expressions of religious identity also occurring in the Islamic communities of Europe, while Christianity dominates a number of nations in the southern portion of the African continent. According to *Foreign Affairs*, the number of Catholics and Protestants in South America shows an explosive increase; in South Korea approximately 35% of the population is Christian; in Russia, Orthodox churches are rapidly reopening as critical elements of a national-religious-back-to-roots movement.

As Patriarch Kirill recently said in an interview with *Russia Today*:

> There is only one word to describe what happened in Russia in the 1990s and 2000s and what is happening today in terms of the revival of faith: it's a miracle. After decades under the atheistic regime, we see a genuine revival of religious faith. This revival involves all sorts of social classes: ordinary people, well-educated people, business people, politicians. All those people are involved with the Church today, one way or another, and very often we see people explaining their actions by citing Christian values.

The Christian priest, Alexander Dugin, one of the leading Russian ideologues who steadily works to restore the historical memory and traditional culture in Russia, recently said to *Time* magazine that "For us, Orthodox Christianity is the axis of the Russian world we seek to build. If you want to understand the Orthodox world as we see it, understanding Athos is the place to start."

Mount Athos is a peninsula in north-eastern Greece – the whole island is considered a monastery- may be said to have been the center of spiritual and intellectual thinking in the Eastern Christian world for more than a thousand years. The Holy Mount Athos is a place with numerous ancient monasteries and hundreds of monks, distant from the Greek mainland and considered to be one of the main places of pilgrimage for men in the Eastern Church.

The Eastern Orthodox Church is vastly larger than many in the West are aware of, counting 250–300 million followers in Greece, the Middle East, Russia, and Africa. Its break from the Catholic Church in year AD 1054 came about over the dispute on the papacy. The Orthodox Church does not acknowledge the Papacy. It teaches that all bishops are equal, and their priests marry and have families, each Church being overseen by an assembly of the clergy. Only monastics, monks and bishops practice celibacy. The Orthodox Church is preoccupied with participating actively on a social level, and its churches and clergy are regularly used for consultations, psychological sessions and as problem solvers in the lives of the average person.

The church is viewed as a motivational center for spiritual healing in a way that does not interfere with modern life. Church services may, in this part of the world, last for hours with heavy incense and singing, yet people are at liberty to come and go as they please. There is no requirement to sit still during the whole service, as is the tradition among Protestants. People come and go during the service, some stay ten minutes, some an hour, some the whole service which regularly lasts for hours. Orthodox Christians traditionally have a focus on practical Christianity, including donating to and aiding the poor, taking care of the old, advising the young and showing compassion when things go wrong – a Christianity that in many ways resemble the first years of the ancient churches when they first appeared in the Middle East.

Traditionally, the Orthodox Church has not been subject to the same type of decline as seen within Protestant and Catholic groups in the West. What characterizes the Orthodox faith may be the deep-felt focus on the practical life of a Christian and its connection to the metaphysical realm of existence. St Ignatius, one of the early Christian teachers who ended his life as a martyr, saw the Church as both hierarchical and sacramental, stating that the local community *is* the Church. The outward organization is second to its inner sacramental life, as stated by Timothy Ware in *The Orthodox Church: New Edition.* This mood seems to have penetrated the Orthodox Church in a strong way. The Church carries a central role in social society, practicing solidarity with the weak on a much broader basis than is usual in the West. The priest tends to function as a psychologist, social worker, helper of the elderly, organizer of social events, not afraid to have a beer from time to time, often attending marriage parties. He is visibly marked by black clothing and a long gown, head covered and with a long beard.

# CHAPTER 14

# The Rise of the anti-Christian West and Islam

*As we have seen, a startlingly high number, around 80%, of the American people believe in God, 75-80% call themselves Christians in Europe. Imagine the numbers. As few as 2–6% are atheists and little more than 1% belong to non-religious humanist associations. The vast majority of the Western population are discriminated against by the current anti-religious progressive elites, who control the media and state institutions. Is this democracy or a dictatorship?*

## Extreme Secular Tyranny

Religious traditions have a major impact on the large majority of individuals in the West. To repeat, in a country like the US, *Pew Research Centre* surveys shows that 80% of the citizens believe in God. Other surveys show that around 70% of the American people believe in God.

In Europe, the number of believers in God is about 75%, and as many as 70% in the UK and Germany call themselves Christian, according to Pew Research Center 2012.[36] That is definitely what you would call the vast majority of a population. If one adds millions of Muslims and numbers of other faiths in Europe, these numbers definitely represent a broad majority. Atheism and extreme secularism, on the other hand, which seems to be the

---

[36] Regional Distribution of Christians (Friday, August 18, 2017) http://www.pewforum.org/2011/12/19/global-christianity-regions/

leading force within mainstream media and the political establishment, may comprise as low as only 2% of the world's population; another poll showing 8%, according to Encyclopaedia Britannica. These are startlingly low numbers. In short, almost no one in the West are atheists, compared to the vast majority of believers.

Even in a secular country like France, about 90% of the population call themselves Christian, according to the *World Factbook*. Statistical numbers steadily vary depending on, for one, how the questions in the surveys are worded. Pew Research show that around 70% of the French population consider themselves Christian.

These, again, are remarkably high numbers given the fact that the European population has been subjected to fervent anti-Christian influences for decades, given the influential powers in proportion to their public support. As Kirsten Powers has pointed out in *The Silencing. How the Left is Killing Free Speech*, the more success the illiberal left – where one tends to find the highest numbers of atheists – has in terrorizing, demonizing and defaming people who express dissenting views, the fewer objections there may be. Most people understandably just want to do their jobs and support their families, which is hard in academia if you are not sufficiently politically correct. A quick glance at some of the debates where famous British atheists appear, is a show of bullying tactics, rude comments, lack of manners and respect for the broad majority view on religion. They speak as though they own the world, yet the statistics show this is not the case.

❋❋❋

# Islam Respects Jesus More Than We Do

Let me quote Patriarch Kirill once more, from a Russian Christmas 2016 interview:
> Well-to-do Europe has turned into a place where Christians are oppressed. Christianity is being pushed out of the public space. In many countries, the word 'Christmas' isn't used now. The plight of Christians in Syria, Iraq, and many other countries, has been driven to extremes. Christians are currently the most oppressed religious community in the world, and not only in the Middle East but also in well-off Europe, where a public display of faith, such as openly wearing a cross, can lead to dismissal at work.

Kirsten Powers, who herself is a liberal, still she fights to end the illiberal tendency within the American left, writes in *The Silencing. How the Left is Killing Free Speech* that she finds the current situation problematic. A 2007 study of faculty in college campuses, found that 53% of university professors had negative attitudes towards evangelicals. Powers states that this raises serious questions on how fair a treatment young Christians would get when entering college.

A 2012 study, showed that 82% of liberal social psychologists would feel uneasy and prejudice if a Christian Conservative was to be employed at their faculty. Christian groups have been denied university status by student government organizations on the count that they hold views that are not liberal enough. Powers points out that disagreement is fine, discrimination is not, finding that the current situation in the US involves a left-wing movement that is becoming increasingly radical, to the point that it today fights tolerance and free speech – when Conservatives and Christians speak. She calls this type of one-way tolerance "repressive tolerance." She states that the illiberal Left believes that people who have different ideological opinions than them should be completely silenced. Instead of using rhetoric or persuasion, they turn to delegitimize the person, using character assassination, demonization and dehumanization tactics.

According to EU lawyers, the increasing persecution of Christians in Europe is driven by groups whose ideological agendas counter Church teaching, both centrally placed in the EU and the UN. Let us take the case of Pope Benedict XVI. It was nearly impossible to read a positive sentence about him for several years, even though he was hailed as a fearless and uncompromising teacher of morality in other parts of the world.

After spending Christmas in Dubai a few years back, this injustice became even more evident. In the United Arab Emirates, a Muslim nation, the Pope's Christmas speech was cited in its entirety in the leading newspapers. There were large photos, front-page images, respectful articles on how Pope Benedict XVI had encouraged everyone to take better care of one another and show respect for others. It struck me with force. The pope would never have received the same type of respect in Western media outlets.

The Pope openly encouraged everyone to love one another. Muslims were the ones who appreciated it. Yet again, on Christmas Day, there was a two-page spread with photographs of Christians in prayer in Muslim newspapers, respectfully acknowledging their prayers. To honor the birth of Christ, Burj-al-Arab, one of the world's very seven-star hotel, was illuminated by particularly glittering colors. Dubai was sharply colored in vivid brightness, to honor the birth of Christ. The Quran regards, as we know, Jesus as the second most important prophet after Mohammed.

It is notable to remember the words of renowned evangelist, Billy Graham, who also showed respect for one of the world's most influential Christian leaders, the pope. He said in one of his TV interviews, as quoted by the Saturday Evening Post that the pope at that time, Pope John Paul II was the greatest religious leader of the modern world, and one of the greatest moral and spiritual leaders of the century.

Being astounded by the respectfulness of the Muslims, it was clearer than ever that the pope was on a serious collision course with the radically illiberal forces in the European debate. There seemed to be no end to the slander of Pope Benedict XVI's name. He was, at that time, almost consistently referred to in the Western press as arch-conservative, rigidly bound by old traditions, an opponent of modernization, narrow-minded, backward and old-fashioned. The Pontiff had to endure both unfair, scornful and overly generalized critiques from his opponents. This type of illiberal treatment illustrates the present willingness of the Western ruling elites to use totalitarian means to silence opposing religious viewpoints.

The West is turning into a desert of godlessness and pride. We have lost the sense of the sacred. The food you eat, the water you drink, the experience of life itself is a sacred gift. We ought to be grateful, filled with humility. Instead, we live in a culture that increasingly abuses both animals, humans and the environment, greedily craving for more.

Increasingly, one has to turn to non-Western nations to find leading political leaders who actually steadily address the need for sovereign nations to uphold religious and traditional cultural values as the cornerstone of society. Somehow, issues like the devastating atrocities committed against Christians in the Middle East, simply do not get mainstream media attention in the West.

✼✼✼

## Islam, Geopolitics and the Refusal of the Extreme Liberal

Pushing for Islam has, during the past decades been a convenient tool to many progressives, one may assume, in the attempt to diminish Westerners' trust in their own cultural heritage and Christianity. It has been quite a useful tool, though recently backfiring. In the age of mass immigration into Europe, tolerance has been described as the willingness of

Europeans to let go of their own heritage in order to accommodate foreigners and newcomers.

This approach has resulted in Islam now being one of Europe's strongest religions. Many of its believers have political ambition to influence society with values that contrast those of the same progressive, anti-religious elites who opened the way for Islam in the first place. Islam is the second largest religion both in France and Britain and other European countries. Christians and Muslims now often fight the same battle for the reimplementation of the respect for religious freedom in the West, as many of the "pro-Islam European atheists" now have realized that they may be outnumbered precisely by Muslims in just a few years.

Some say that it was the terror attacks in New York on September 11, 2001, that enthused new attention towards religion in general. The bombing of the Twin Towers came as a shock to most Westerners, although claims later have been made that the mostly Saudi Arabian hijackers were part of a larger geopolitical strategy. It remains uncertain whether the attack was done due to religious or political reasons. Nevertheless, shortly after the attacks, the US went to war in Afghanistan, then Iraq, Libya, Yemen, Somalia, Pakistan, Syria. Regardless of the driving forces behind the current geopolitical strategies, the Western secular elites revised their thoughts on the increasingly politicized role of religion in the modern world.

Jürgen Habermas also revised his position on the role of religion in liberal societies, as we have seen. Upon receiving the Holberg Prize in Bergen, Norway in 2005, he delivered a remarkable acceptance speech that deserves to be cited. Its unique message represents a stunningly strong abandonment of the academic theories that professed that faith in God is an attribute of an unenlightened, old-fashioned and archaic society. He stated that the historical European ethic has a role, a moral role, to play as the ethical foundation in a secularized Europe. The tendency for solidarity to decline in liberal society and for egoism to dominate is a worrisome development. Numerous moral philosophers have actively warned against this trend for quite some time.

Habermas is, as most know, a leading neo-Marxist philosopher and proclaimed atheist who has argued for a strong secularization his entire life. His dramatic change of view is therefore quite sensational. Habermas now seems to acknowledge some of the flaws in the neo-Marxist thinking that characterized post-war Europe. The speech reflects the new attitude, as Habermas acknowledged that religious traditions and denominations had taken a new and unexpected place in politics. He states that religion has ended up playing, in clear contrast to what many secularists predicted, an increasingly important role in the modern world. The essence of the speech focused on the necessity of a renewed focus on the value of religious ethics in order for secular society to rekindle the waning spirit of solidarity, empathy, and respect for one another.

Habermas provided a compelling example of how dramatically unexpected this change was by citing an article published in the *New York Times*, "The day that extinguished the enlightenment." It summed up the general feeling of many in the aftermath of the 9/11 terror attacks. The rushing wave of secular modernity did not succeed in wiping out religion, he said. At the very least, Islam's rise with its political and social clarity dictated that religion again assume a position on the political agenda that was surprisingly strong.

Even in the wake of the extensive *niqab* and *burka* debates, as well as the quest for implementing Sharia law in Europe, the influence of Muslim cultures – both in its traditional Islamic form as well as through its more political, ideological and jihadist wings – has become more and more apparent as a socio-political force that will dominate European debates in the years to come.

In addition to global religious trends, the much uncontrolled wave of mass immigration from non-Western countries has greatly changed the face of Europe, much in accordance with the will of the multiculturalist movement. They have succeeded in moving millions from their countries of origin and into Europe.

Ironically enough, Islam has gained a foothold in the West, precisely through the help of the non-believing liberals who fought for open borders and the multicultural implementation of other cultures and their values into the European fabric in the first place. The term multiculturalism is generally understood as the acceptance and promotion of multiple cultural traditions within one country so that the host culture does not require the assimilation of new coming immigrants into its own society. New immigrants are to keep their cultural traditions and not submit to the cultural regulations of the host culture. In other words, paradoxically one is not to criticize Muslims but may very well do so with Christians and other traditional Western denominations.

Millions of non-Westerners came to Europe in search for a better life than that of their cultures of origin. New arrivals looked for economic development and job opportunities, yet still kept their Islamic zeal for the worship of God and submission to Allah. One may be astounded by how thousands of European mosques are filled with hundreds of thousands of active worshippers, how Muslims take over church buildings and collectively refuse to succumb to the secular standards of "privatized religion" and still pray openly in the streets of Paris, London and Rome.

The entry of Islam into Europe has shocked secular atheists, as they finally thought to be on the doorstep of getting rid of religion altogether. They assumed our Muslim brothers would lose their religion once they entered into the Western liberal hemisphere, alas, the opposite happened. Precisely the extreme-secular that effectively silenced the Protestant bishops and other religious groups to such a degree that they almost seem invisible in the European political landscape is a failed tactic against the Muslims. Muslims in the West now raise their voices even higher and complain about the decadence among the cultural elites in their countries of origin as well as in the West. This type of critique has, as we know, also been an issue in Islam throughout the ages. Islam became the fastest-growing religion in the modern world.

One thing is certain: with the influx of millions of believing Muslims into Western societies, we are set to become more openly religious yet again. The question is which religion? Will the Christians rise to meet the challenge or will they leave the scene to Islam?

In his Holberg speech, Habermas pointed out that the political revitalization of religion occurs right in the heartland of Western society. Even though a wave of secularization has washed over most European countries since World War II, the significance of religion for political purposes has not decreased in the rest of the world. He stated that against this background, the secularized Europe is the exception from the rest of the world. Habermas stated, that precisely by the elimination of capital punishment, liberal abortion laws, the equality of homosexual partnership with heterosexual marriage, the unconditional rejection of torture, and generally giving priority to individual rights over the collective good such as national security, it seems that European countries have left USA behind on the road they once shared. In the light of world history, the European form of anti-religious rationalism is actually an exception to the rule: People in the rest of the world still believe in God and the spiritual realm.

The growing importance of religion indicates a dramatic change in civil society, where academic debates about religion increasingly re-enter the public sphere. Habermas further maintains that the ongoing process of religious renewal has reinforced the divide between Europe and America. In the US, spiritual faith has, so far, been met with more respect than in Europe. In *The Divided West* Habermas explores this theme more extensively. He herein states that the fact that religion has no place in the public sphere, becomes evidence of Europe's actual disconnect with the rest of the world.

## The Culture War

\*\*\*

# Humanist Movements – Exploiting Muslims and Harassing Christians

The aim of the atheist and humanist Associations in Europe has been to seek the end of religious privilege, promote a secular worldview and to bring an end to discrimination against the non-religious. The last point is excellent, as there should be no discrimination against those without a religion, atheist or agnostic alike. There should be no discrimination against those *with* a religion either. The Humanist Associations have dominated the public sphere, harassing bishops and dictating theologians, constantly on the watch if Christians speak out in the media to instantly there to bully them, portraying their own work as if it is all about "tolerance." Ironically, the Humanist Association's statutes are but a copy of original Christian values – only omitting any reference to God or spiritual search.

A quick glance at the humanist movements in Europe shows they have gained remarkable political influence despite their puzzlingly low number of members. An example is the Humanist Associations in countries such as Norway and Sweden, which represent as low numbers as 1.6% of the population, according to their own websites. A recent UK survey, 'The Profile of the Members of the British Humanist Association' by Glyndwr University, cited at *Science, Religion and Culture* showed that the UK Humanist Association has as few as around 12,000 members and only around 30,000 supporters.

In 2011, the first time the UK Census provided the opportunity to register as "humanist," only around 15,000 people from England and Wales did so. If one compares with the overwhelming number in Europe that call themselves Christians, the humanists have a remarkably strong political influence. Humanists should not be given the right to suppress the majority.

Yet, the humanist movements' often militantly hostile opinions on religion and the influence of the Church, have been at the centerfold of public debate for decades. They speak the loudest about tolerance, yet fight the right of the broad majority to freedom of conscience and respect for religious faith. Humanists are cited in the media as if they represent millions, and not only the one percent. They speak at all kinds of rallies, relentlessly fighting traditional values and portraying furious criticism in what seems to be a profound hatred towards Christians. They represent a tiny minority but still push with an extreme anti-Christian agenda as if they speak for all.

An analysis of the Humanist Association's public reactions shows an almost endless attempt to label Christians as irrational people who advocate for an old-fashioned superstition.

Puzzlingly, as previously mentioned, the same atheist groups tend to strongly defend Muslims' rights to practice their traditions, the claim being that Christianity represents a discrimination against Islam. This paradox has, for example, made the Humanist Association in Scandinavian countries into "defenders of Islam," even though their own statutes states that the aim is to quell religious privileges as a whole – obviously including those of Muslims in the long run. Can it be that some are cynically using the newly arrived Muslims in order to condemn traditional European values, and believe that bullying Christians would serve the cause? Once they finish off Christians, they would begin the same tactics with Muslims?

Among other issues, humanist protests have widely been held against church attendance for school children before Christmas. The point is that one should no longer celebrate the birth of Christ since it is offensive to the newly arrived minorities. Yet, Muslims repeatedly confirm that they do not see the point in this, Jesus being a major prophet in Islam. Many openly stating that they do not object to celebrating the Christian feast of Christmas. Many Muslims even state that it is obviously not "racist" when Europeans wish to adhere to their own holidays and religious celebrations, the same way Muslim countries celebrate Islamic holidays.

If it was to be the case that celebrating Christmas is "racist," where is the criticism of Saudi Arabia when it hails the pilgrimage to Mecca as Christians are not allowed to join?

# CHAPTER 15

# Hedonism, Feminism, the Breaking Up of the Family

*Hedonism states that pleasure, personal happiness and the avoidance of pain is the ultimate goal in life. In its nihilistic belief - we come from nothing, we are going to nothing – it asserts that values are relative. The issue that many philosophers, including Socrates, Aristotle and Plato had with permissive thinking, was that it tends to omit "the other" from the equation of human fellowship - serving only the self.*

## The Value Struggle in Europe

DURING THE HOLBERG PRIZE AWARD ceremony, Jürgen Habermas commented on the deep rift between values that characterize Western society. The far-reaching disagreement is fundamental. One of France's leading philosophers, anti-Marxist Andre Glucksmann, states in *Ouest contre Ouest* (*The West against The West*) that the conflict of values in Europe is a struggle between nihilism and conservatism. Atheist nihilism follows the path of Nietzsche – a hedonistic morality that pursues a promiscuous attitude in life.

The moral philosophy of "hedonism" defines that which is good in terms of pleasure and pain, and indicates a system of thought in which man's ultimate purpose is the enjoyment of pleasure and the avoidance of pain. Actions that increase pleasure are deemed right, and actions which increase pain are deemed wrong. Critically, it may be described as a moral philosophy that attempts to justify the individual's right to self-gratification and promiscuity. "Just enjoy" is the message, as there is no tomorrow.

The essential idea in nihilism – which literally means the belief in nothing – is that evil does not exist. The human conscience is perceived to be a socially constructed effect of negative historical dogmas that dictate what is wrong and right – especially religious dogmas, to which the preferable response is rebellion. The thought is that once we are liberated from the negative feeling of having a conscience that reacts with inner pain when one does something "wrong" towards others, the individual will be able to live a truly free life. To free oneself from the traditional concept of right and wrong is therefore essential to nihilism. Nietzsche eventually became insane and ended his life in an asylum.

The value struggle reflects widely different values. Nihilistic freedom is defined as the abandonment of the "constraint of conscience" and its traditional norms, also in regard to sexual ethics. On the other hand, Christian norms imply that a man's conscience is God's instrument to teach him the best way to handle life, for him to attain the end goal: to love his fellow man. Man is to develop attitudes over time, virtues such as compassion, perseverance, humility, generosity, respecting others, revering parents and the elderly, adhering to the Ten Commandments, self-restraint in a lifelong goal to do good to others. If he so does, Christianity teaches, he will be able to live a more fulfilled life and help to build a society to the betterment of all.

Philosophers like Nietzsche had completely other values than the above listed. He believed that Christianity and its philosophy inhibits man's natural predilection for cruelty. As Christianity tries to tame this need for cruelty, we become, instead, cruel to ourselves – we are tortured by our own conscience, he stated. The conscience, with its taming of one's "inner evils," was *per se* that which man ought to break free from.

Nietzsche idealized the so-called "free life," free from conscience, free of the burden of morality and having to abstain from sexual urges, free of the concept of solidarity and compassion. Later, these anti-Christian principles paved the way for Nazi atrocities – especially the notion of the Superman, the *Übermensch,* who transcends all morality and activates his own will as his only compass and the lust for power his ideal.

The rise of hedonism as a modern social trend gained its legitimization precisely here. Nihilism and hedonism are related moral philosophies that both attempt to justify the right to one's own pleasure without sufficiently contemplating consideration for others. Nihilism says there is no higher meaning to anything, while hedonism says that, like animals, the best we can hope for is temporary and transient material pleasures.

Whatever is pleasurable, is good. Consequently, those actions which increase the sum of pleasure are thereby right and what increases pain is wrong. Whatever feels "good for the body" is a desirable action. It may be argued that hedonism has been a strong force to legitimize selfishness as the search for personal pleasure overrides consideration towards others in the community.

It may be useful to read the Austrian neurologist and father of psychoanalysis who has had a significant influence on modern psychology, Sigmund Freud. In the late 1800s, he treated a number of disturbed women. In his consultations and later studies, he concluded that lack of sexual enjoyment and "good feelings" was the contributing factor to their mental imbalance and psychoses. He found that sexual trauma in childhood was the main reason for mental imbalance and neurosis in adults. *Freud: A Life for Our Time* by Peter Gay gives some insight into the way he perceived the world.

It seems that Freud helped many as he was able to penetrate some of the mysteries of human sexuality, yet suggested remedies that ended up legitimizing permissiveness to the degree that since greatly influenced Western culture. Freud did not work in an intellectual vacuum – just like other intellectuals at the time. He was influenced by Nietzsche and others and assumed that the solution to early sexual invasions was to submerge even deeper into sexual encounters.

He became – predictably enough – negative towards the traditional family structure, and argued that religion and science were enemy forces. In his analysis of the Oedipus complex, in which he certainly seems to come across as someone who finds the traditional family quite an inharmonious, sick and unnatural entity, he strongly reflects the tendency to sexualize almost every human interaction: mother-son, father-son and so on.

To him, polyamorous relationships were the ideal. The family was to him a repression of man's natural inclination to the polyamorous. Instead of resisting the temptation of engaging in sexual behavior, freedom to Freud was not faithfulness, loyalty or being honest with one's partner, but quite the opposite.

Consequently, in Freud's opinion, women who suffered neurosis had frustrations due to the denial of their need for sex. Again, freedom corresponded to the opportunity to be liberated from the guilt of having a bad conscience. Man's conscience was considered to be plagued by negative social constraints. More sensual enjoyment was an emancipating goal and the path to happiness.

These ideals were later further developed by among others, Herbert Marcuse, who ended up in a way becoming the father of the feminist movement in the 1960s. Radical feminism further developed, as we know, the ideal of breaking away from the "destructive family bonds between man – woman and their joint offspring," which we shall study in a later chapter. Freud thus ended up becoming one of the leading anti-Christian nihilist voices in his time, with massive influence on popular culture, calling religion an illusion and brutally breaking away from traditional morality and its view of human life. He died in 1939, from assisted suicide by a lethal injection of morphine.

✽✽✽

# When "feelings" Becomes Slavery

A number of ancient Greek philosophers, especially the Stoics, ferociously opposed hedonism and the pursuit of pleasure as the main goal of life. When permissiveness and a lenient attitude become prevalent, it legitimizes a cultural trend that allows excessive freedoms of behavior. Those who have any objection or dare to be critical, are openly harassed, as definitely is the case today. One is quickly labeled. "backward," "old-fashioned," "non-sexual," "ascetics" and so on. In such a relativistic setting, it becomes almost impossible to say no to anything. Whoever put up a boundary, especially within the field of ethics, is instantly called "a moralist," "illiberal," "intolerant." He is somehow perceived to be against freedom.

These cultural currents now permeate Western thinking, creating a political atmosphere in which one is to pity the criminal, not punish him for violating the lives of law-abiding citizens. The idea is that offenders should not be punished for breaking the law, as punishment itself is regarded a cruelty that will lead to more offenses. The modern nihilist denial of evil makes punishment problematic since he perceives evil not to exist. This worldview is found deeply embedded in disciplines such as criminology, among defense lawyers and judges, who are more influenced by philosophers like Nietzsche than many are aware of. We end up with societies that are permissive towards criminal offenders, rapists, illegal immigrants who deliberately break the law, thus arguably hostile towards law abiding citizen who are the ones suffering from increasing lawlessness and anarchy.

Sociologist Peter Berger asserts that modern liberal society creates a kind of homeless, an existence without access to the joys that lie in knowing one's own spirituality. He calls Western relativism and lack of morality a recipe for cultural self-annihilation. Where cultural stability disappears, the foundation for the individual's spiritual health is also threatened, as the culture is weakened. In *The Social Reality*, Berger points out that man dreads existential loneliness, he fears being ostracized and isolated from society and yearns for a meaningful existence. This drives him towards maintaining social relationships with others.

Where promiscuity and sexual selfishness becomes socially acceptable, it is increasingly hard to form any type of faithful marriage and family nucleus based on a partnership of trust, fidelity, loyalty, and patience. As the Eastern Orthodox monk, popular in the Greek world, Elder Paisios of Mount Athos, put it:

> It is not freedom when we say to people that everything is permitted. That is slavery. Freedom is good when the person can use it appropriately. Otherwise, it is a disaster. To improve one must have difficulties. Let's take an example. Look at the child. We limit his freedom from the beginning. When he is first conceived, the poor thing is limited in his mother's womb and remains there nine whole months. Later he is born, and immediately they swaddle him in a blanket, they tie him up, as soon as he begins to grow they set a railing, etc. All of this is necessary for him to grow. It appears to take away freedom, but without these protective measures, the child will die in the first moment.

Western hedonism greatest flaw rests on its failure to recognize that compassion for others is a fundamental component of civil solidarity and genuine happiness, without which the stability in society will crumble. Today, the chronic focus on "feelings" permeates contemporary culture. Whether a movie was good or bad, depends on how "inspired" or "excited" one felt when leaving the movie theatre. Hollywood culture and the modern term "happiness" is translated almost exclusively into the category of feelings. The news industry follows the same path. Watching CNN is like going to a concert, designed to give you either "good or bad feelings," arguably swaying a person negatively or positively towards the CNN desired view point. The persistent use of music during the evening news is a strong trait in American media, disturbingly manipulatively done, as felt by many.

The advertising industry has equally perfected this type of propaganda, insinuating that acquiring material wealth instantaneously implies instant happiness. A review of recent Coca Cola ads illustrates this to perfection. Someone is running on the beach, a beautiful girl gives him a Coke and instant bliss, surrounded as he suddenly is by gorgeously smiling people. The instant drinking of the Coke solves his problems as he now "feels good."

The modern definition of happiness often described solely in relation to feelings becomes the prevalent mainstream doctrine. Yet, our sense of "instant happiness" stands in stark contrast to the old Greeks whose moral philosophy defined happiness as a state of mind that develops over time. It was regarded as the result of attitudes and virtues acquired in a lifelong search for wisdom. They did not believe that "instant bliss" had much to do with the state of happiness.

Aristotle believed that the way to happiness was, over time, to develop a strong character – and use one's abilities to the betterment of society. The person who spent his time doing this, would, again over time, develop a balanced mind and a sense of satisfactory fulfillment as he engaged in the lives of his fellow-men and sought to use his abilities in the best possible way. Aristotle famously states in *Politics* that "Man is by nature a social animal; an individual who and not accidentally, is either beneath our notice or more than human. Society is something that precedes the individual. Anyone who either cannot participate in the common life or is so self-sufficient as not to need to and therefore does not partake of society is either a beast or a god".

Over the course of their lives, both Plato and Aristotle struggled against the trends of social dissolution in the Athenian democracy. Plato's *Republic* and his dialogues with Trasymakos provide examples of challenges in legitimatizing hedonism and its form of legalizing egoism. He speaks of the ongoing conflict in the human soul between reason and feelings, how it may be, for example, reasonable not to steal yet the feeling of greed may still tempt a person to do so. The role of reason is for it to steer the soul in the right direction so that feelings do not take negative dominion. Plato famously said on the origin of tyranny in the *Republic* that: "The probable outcome of too much freedom is only too much slavery in the individual and the state." He further describes the intolerable lack of boundaries that lead to tyranny, sentences that bear remarkable resemblance to contemporary culture, saying that:

> ... the father accustoms himself to become like his child and fears his sons, while the son likens himself to his father, and feels neither shame nor fear in front of his parents, so he may be free. The teacher, fears his pupils and fawns upon them, while pupils look down on their teachers as well as their overseers; and, overall, the young copy the elders and contend hotly with them in words and

in deeds, while the elders, lower themselves to the level of the young.

The quest for the Aristotelian "golden mean" has been discussed since ancient times. When and how should our physical needs for gratification be limited? To which degree should reason control feelings? How may we avoid hurting and harming others? How do we achieve true happiness? Such normative reflections touch upon deep philosophical questions about how to experience life as meaningful.

Many Greek philosophers believed that hedonism's legitimization of no authoritative ethics would cause social disintegration over time – and ultimately result in the fall of Athenian democracy. They were correct. In *Nicomachean Ethics,* Aristotle pointed out that those who live according to hedonism in search for self-gratification, eventually become disappointed and spiritually imbalanced. They become emotionally incapacitated by an addiction to stronger and stronger stimuli, always looking for an even greater "sensual kick of emotions."

Aristotle's ethic of virtue recommends moderation and indicates that the road to happiness is not unilaterally equivalent to the satisfaction of carnal desires. He felt that asceticism does not *per se* lead to a harmonious life, neither does hedonism. The desirable is the middle way.

\*\*\*

# "Feelings," Free Sex and Infidelity

When examining how nihilism has affected Western culture, the new ideal of "free sex" remains at the core of the debate. Contemporary culture is brutally sexualized, magazines directed towards young women are all about sexual intercourse and explicit matters. Hollywood portrays the culture of nudity as the new norm for women. Hardly a single article promote self-control or how to be faithful and a trusted partner. TV-series like *Paradise Hotel, Real Housewives, Big Brother, Glamour* and a variety of programs on entertainment channels, frankly promote betrayal, lack of loyalty, evil, gossip, lying, and deceitfulness. "Feelings" are front and center, people quarrel, women fight, almost kill each other, jealousy and hatred – go to jail and come back – and still, they are the stars of the reality show, invited to talk shows and portrayed as role models to the young girls watching.

The phenomenon of infidelity offers a salient example. It is simply astonishing how much support is offered to unfaithful women and men who suffer from guilt, the prevailing attitude being that it is natural and even "healthy" to have an affair. Why do so few discuss the tragic effect which infidelity has on a relationship, of the years of suffering ahead should the two attempts to repair the damage?

Few, if any, speak of the moral conditions for a healthy and lifelong sex life: trust, faithfulness, responsibility, and compassion. We have become a society that encourages betrayal of partners if it "feels good." Which social structures and healthy bonds will survive the strain as faithfulness and honesty no longer are the spoken ideal?

It is alarming to see how well some contemporary marital columnists boldly applaud disloyalty and promiscuous behavior with frivolous recommendation to enjoy casual sex with married or unmarried partners alike. How is trust in marriage going to survive these licentious, unscrupulous trends, not to mention the family? For a marital expert, educated in psychology, psychiatry or other fields, to gloss lightly over the mental consequences of engaging in sex outside of marriage displays a serious lack of insight into how human sexuality relates to the psyche, the desire to be appreciated and the hope to be loved.

Some experts even seem to insinuate that Christians "are against sex" altogether. The idealized lifestyle of trust and fidelity is ridiculed and deemed by some to be "old-fashioned." In the extreme liberal climate, the attempts to demonize those who fight for the family turn to bullying tactics on opponents that are quite shocking to watch. How could God be against sex? It was God himself who created intercourse and erotica and made us long for one another in a loving, lasting relationship. How would the Almighty be against that which He created?

It is true that sexuality arguably is one of life's greatest gifts. Christianity explains how God marvelously created sex for the unification of two individuals, as they share the commitment to love and make their way through the harsh landscapes of life. Sex satisfies the existential needs of humans to feel deeply valued psychologically, sexually gratified on the physical level and satisfies deep longings for recognition and love from another person. It is well-known that the Holy Scriptures abound with sensuality, joy of life, exciting epic tales of love and sex. The *Song of Songs* is but one example. Even the Church itself has been described as a love story between the believers and Jesus Christ.

# The Culture War

✳✳✳

# Pornography

In the West, generations now grow up believing that sexual expressionism with no regard for conscience, is the road to a fulfilled life. Sex is the new god. Sexual satisfaction, deviations – anything that leads up to an orgasm seems to be the ultimate goal of literature, Hollywood films, and contemporary music. Yet, without consideration of the damage inflicted on one's sexual partners, the individual is drawn into a lonely and mentally troubled state of mind where, in the end, the ability to love is lost.

The exploding growth of internet pornography is an issue that touches on these very matters. The concept of masturbation while watching other people's intercourse seems to suit the lonely Westerner well. There is no need for him to meet up with any girl, no need to take the time to flirt, or go to dinner and pay for it, no need to communicate, open up, share opinions or show understanding, let alone love. Romance and courting are out of the question. A quick glance at the iPhone app gives you access to whoever is physically nearby, for you to make the arrangement for casual sex, often right there and then. To know someone by name is not needed.

Statistics show that 83% of the porn addicts are men. He watches lustfully the mostly white, Western girls on screen, even if it is general knowledge that over 90% of those who end up in this kind of prostitution are scarred and abused women. Of course, there are also those who willfully participate and choose prostitution. My concern is the thousands and thousands who are in that business as a result of early violations and degradation, abuse and emotional chaos. Leading surveys show that 88% of the pornographic videos show physical aggression against women.

When confronted with this perspective – the abuse, the destroyed emotional life, which arguably made it easier to go into this business – all this does not concern the masturbating man. The only thing that matters to him is the sexual pleasure he gets from exploiting these women. Where are the feminists who were supposed to defend the honor of these Western women in the multi-billion dollar pornography industry? Why do we allow this to continue, undisturbed? Many feminists are actually supporting pornography, *cheering for* the legalization of prostitution, alongside the same males who gladly employ these abused women.

A few decades ago, the only pornography that was available consisted of pictures of naked women in magazines that had to be purchased at stores. Many had these hidden under beds or in some available space, out of reach from mothers or girlfriends. Ever since the problem has inflated to out of this world proportions. It is a revolution, a dramatic change, from the DVD-age when pornography was bought only during opening hours, to now, porn being available just a click away. Statistics cited in *Psychology Today* show that 56% of all divorces involve one party having an obsession with pornography.[37] People wake up at night and find their husbands masturbating wildly to horse-porn, watching gang rapes and so on.

This is a grossly heterosexual problem. There are actually very few homosexuals in the world, and yet they are wrongfully given much of the blame for the current hedonist trends. The 2013 National Health Interview Survey, in which 34,000 Americans participated, states that as few as 1.6% are homosexuals in the US and 0.7% bisexuals. Another 2011 survey showed that 1.5% define themselves as asexual and simply not interested in sex, while only 1% defined themselves as homosexual. So, there seem to be even more people who simply are not interested in sex than there are homosexuals – the non-sexual group being one that hardly anybody speaks about or whose challenges are hardly ever addressed.

The sexualization of the Western culture and its almost complete loss of modesty represents a serious development. Ten-year-olds grow up with hardcore porn, a click away. Things you had to go to hardcore sex clubs to watch a few years back are right there on your computer now. How does this affect the mind of the young? A National Union of Students Report shows that two-thirds of young people in Britain use porn to understand sex.[38] The extent of the use of pornography is illustrated by *The Telegraph* who referred to a study claiming they could not find one man who had not watched porn. 90% watched porn on the internet, only 10 % used magazines.[39]

Puzzlingly enough, hardly anyone reacts, Christians included. It seems almost impossible to get men, or women for that matter, to engage in this debate. To repeat, with *Time* magazine's survey report showing that approximately 70% of all internet clicks go towards porn, and knowing that an estimated 420 million adult web pages exist online, surveys have

---

[37] Inside Porn Addiction (Saturday, August 19, 2017) http://tiny.cc/epo8my

[38] UK teens turning to porn for sex education – study (Friday, August 18, 2017) https://www.rt.com/uk/227451-uk-teen-sex-education/

[39] All men watch porn, scientists find (Friday, August 18, 2017) http://www.telegraph.co.uk/women/sex/6709646/All-men-watch-porn-scientists-find.html

repeatedly shown and experts testified that this degree of hedonism is dangerously addictive.

The effects of pornography on the brain have been labeled as "toxic," analogous to drug addictions. Psychologists have long claimed that prolonged exposure to pornography causes the need for stronger stimuli in order to get sexually aroused. Such over-stimuli lead to what was formally called "perversions," including group sex and other excess sexual activities, sadomasochistic practices including the active use of pain and suffering as a stimuli for orgasm, or bestiality – sexual intercourse with animals. All readily accessible on the internet. Still, hardly anyone reacts. It is baffling apathy.

Maybe the lack of reaction is due to the degree of pornographic consumption amongst people in general. It is hard to stop it because too many love it. Surveys seem to point in that direction, and modern technology is a factor. 90 % of the women watch porn accessible on the internet – the rate according to *New York Times* being that one in three women watch porn weekly.[40] On a global scale, pornography is more than a $100-billion-industry; 66% of men under the age of thirty-four watch pornography monthly and 40% of women are involved in cyber-pornographic behavior.

Anne Layden, co-director of Sexual Trauma and Psychopathology at the University of Pennsylvania called "pornography the most concerning thing to psychological health that I know of existing today," according to *Wired.com*. It should be quite clear to most rational people that not all forms of sexual contact produce healthy marriages and good lives.

Recent British surveys have shown that extreme pornography causes criminals and weak-minded individuals to commit murder, rape and other forms of sexual assault.[41] A number of disturbing surveys over the past years have indicated that sexual propaganda aimed at minors, leads to unhealthy sexual development.

This led then prime minister, David Cameron to support the restriction of pornography in the UK. In recent years, the UK has made it illegal to show a whole range of sexual acts deemed to be unhealthy to the public. Considering that two-thirds of young people say they turn to pornography in order to learn about sex in the UK, according to the *Guardian*, the warning signals should cause major debates across Europe and in the US regarding the flow of porn into every home through the internet. Now,

---

[40] Study finds that 1 out of 3 women watch porn at least once a week (Friday, August 18, 2017) http://nytlive.nytimes.com/womenintheworld/2015/10/22/study-finds-that-1-out-of-3-women-watch-porn-at-least-once-a-week/

[41] Extreme porn the cause of rape and violence, claims top judge (Friday, August 18, 2017) https://www.rt.com/uk/227147-uk-porn-violence-judge/

Iceland is considering becoming the first country in the West to ban pornography on the internet altogether.

What effect does the idealization of promiscuous performance and a self-invasive lifestyle – the use-and-throw-away - mentality have on the psyche and self-esteem? Do hedonistic liberals really want a society where trust and sexual responsibility disappear completely?

Teenage girls are under massive pressure in the sexualized Western culture. Violations of personal integrity early in life, such as incest, rape or physical/mental violence, affect all levels of human existence. Replacing violated limits by no limits is not the way to heal a damaged personality. Studies show that especially vulnerable girls are those who entered puberty early, socialized with other youngsters who encouraged early sexual activity, placed little value on education and had a poor relationship with their parents, particularly their father.

A New Zealand study, in which one thousand young people in their mid-twenties were interviewed about their first sexual experiences, showed that on average the men were sexually active at seventeen, and women at sixteen. Looking back, more than half wished they had remained virgins longer; 70% of the women who started having sex before fifteen felt this way.[42] Rebuilding confidence and self-esteem often consist of re-establishing healthy limits in relation to other people, especially regarding sexuality. It is not true that the more limitless you are sexually and the more partners you have, men or women, the happier and more harmonious you will become in life.

In a UK report, "A generation under stress?" cited in *The Guardian* showed that 42% of the 10- to 14-year-olds surveyed knew someone who had harmed themselves; 32% had a friend who had suffered from an eating disorder, and half knew someone who had suffered from depression.

Numbers also show positive trends, which the Church should have enhanced with a loud voice in public debates. Even in the US, the rate of teenagers having sex in high school was reduced from 1991 to 2005 from 53% to 46%, according to Key National Indicators of Well-Being Federal Interagency Forum. In 2007, less than 48% of high school students reported ever having engaged in sexual intercourse, compared to 1991 when over 54% of students were no longer virgins. Yet, after many years of advocating free sex in the West, maybe the trend is beginning to see some pushback, as some seem to choose more conservatively than their parent and simply do not want to repeat their lifestyle.

---

[42] First sexual intercourse: age, coercion, and later regrets reported by a birth cohort (Friday, August 18, 2017) http://www.bmj.com/content/316/7124/29.full.print

In a volatile cultural climate like this, the rationality of religion and the reshaping force of its morality may be reintroduced into the Western culture. This happened in England at the end of the 1800s, when William Booth was moved by the despair of the English people and started raising his apologetic voice, speaking about the need for a social revolution that could set the nation on the right track. After being spat on and harassed by the angry mob for years, his message eventually took hold. His work thoroughly reformed England as he helped the poor, gave prostitutes another source of income, educated the deprived, helped the young and was able to address the merciless alcoholism amongst English fathers and motivate them to become responsible men once again. William Booth founded The Salvation Army, an institution that is highly regarded until this day.

\*\*\*

# The Dangers of Extreme Individualism

If man is no longer bound by the social contract or responsibilities towards society, individualism may develop and drift into a dangerous type of hedonism. The liberalist Friedrich Hayek criticizes this extreme form of relativism in *The Constitution of Liberty*. He points out that to be a liberal, in John Locke's sense, meant fighting for personal freedoms and performing one's duties and obligations to the community.

The German sociologist Ulrich Becks' term "the second modernity" also seeks to describe the loss of true freedom – which innately focuses on the needs of others, not only oneself – on the national scale. He uses the modern family as an example. The family has traditionally been considered to be a vital entity and cultural cornerstone that creates stability in societies. It consists of parents and children who care for one another and share the burdens of life. Children grow up with family dinners and active conversation, being taught politeness, order, and respect for the elderly, learning communication skills and kindness, how to deal with problems and so on.

The family entity has been smashed in the past decennials by skyrocketing divorce rates, a culture of loneliness and a club scene that seeks to provide sexual partners – which statistically now is about 50% in the US. Beck calls the modern family a "zombie-category" that is almost losing its meaning completely. What is a family nowadays? Your children, my children, the new role of the divorcee, the remarried and new grandparents, new grandparents, new partners and steadily new lovers, and their children from previous marriages. Every other year, or often sooner, new break-ups and it starts again: new step-children, new in-laws.

The renowned sociologist Zygmunt Bauman's term "liquid modernity" attempts to address this cultural uncertainty, confusion, and disintegration. In *Liquid Modernity*, he describes the hallmarks of modernity: the constant, unstoppable, obsessive search for new developments, an overwhelmingly insatiable desire for creative destruction – the destruction of all that which does not function optimally in order to produce reforms that give us better products, improved structures, smarter societies – all this is done with the hope of producing wealth and progress. To be modern is becoming equivalent to constantly being on the move, an eternal hunt for that which you do not have.

Another sociologist, Robert Bellah, talks in *Toward the Recovery of Wholeness* about "the empty self" in a time where love is considered to be something negative because it threatens individualism. We live in a fragmented cultural state where the constant ideal is to pass status quo, which, according to Max Weber, makes it impossible to be content in the present. The dream of success chronically concerns the non-experienced future. To be modern means the constant quest to become better than the person you are at the moment – as Nietzsche maybe would have put it, the hunt to transform from being a fallible human to becoming the "*übermensche*," the superhuman.

Bauman's critical view on the market Capitalist society is inevitable. He painfully concludes that we have left the goal of working towards a just society where solidarity and empathy interlink individuals, and we have embraced an extreme individualistic culture of entitlement, solely focusing on human rights. The individual is no longer bound to the social contract of responsibilities towards others but leaves it all to the state. As we have seen, the ideological attack on traditional values has been quite systematic and has led to massive societal change in the West, causing a deep rift within the culture itself. The symptoms of a society in deep upheaval are too many to ignore.

## The Culture War

\*\*\*

# Conflict and Rage – The Lifeblood of Feminism

There have been several sharply different feminist movements in history. The early women's rights movement fought for equal social and political rights and culminated in the Suffragette movement in the 1920s.

The first wave was defined by an array of free-spirited activism, demanding full participation in public life for women and the right to choose their own way of life, the right to higher education, participation in the workforce as professionals, the right to divorce, claim inheritance, win custody of children, the right to own property and so on. Author Deborah Siegel states in *Sisterhood Interrupted. From Radical Women to Girls Gone Wild* that the movement ebbed after 1920 when women were granted the right to vote.

I would argue that the early movement was based on a constructive realism rather than ideology, and produced better results. Mary Wollstonecraft, who at the entry of the 1800s published *A Vindication of the Rights of Woman*, acknowledged that men and women are different by nature; that the woman is weaker physically and therefore is structured in such a way that she naturally fits into other roles than the man. She states that the woman deserves to be more equal to the man, less dependent on social opinion and reputation, yet, she rendered modesty and chastity as important ideals for the woman.

Wollstonecraft represented a feminism that not only respected modesty and chastity but suggested that women should actively work for men to acquire these attitudes too. Elisabeth Cady Stanton, who died in 1902, hailed the fact that women had entered important professions in society, and was concerned with the legal inequality of the wives. Still, as Harvard University professor, Harvey J. Mansfield points out in *Manliness*, she took it for granted that "nature has made the mother the guardian of the child."

The sexes were not viewed as a social construction that needed to be changed. Social misconstructions and lack of respect for womanhood were that which needed change. In other words, the early feminist movement wished to change society and its outlook on women, not the woman herself. The early movement fought for equal rights and opportunities – with a profound respect for the biological differences between the sexes.

They wished to create equality by raising men to "the higher moral standards."

The second wave or the radical-revolutionary movement of the 1960s had completely different goals and took emancipation far beyond the constructive question of equal political and social rights. This type of feminism was an ideologically motivated cultural reaction against European traditionalism which ended up attacking the whole foundation upon which the stability of Western society was founded: The family. It may be argued that this new feminism was a frontal attack on the traditional role of a woman as part of a family nucleus, an attack on her femininity and on the woman-qualities that characterizes her biologically: she was to dislike even her childbearing ability, her femininity, the very curves of her body, her abilities to form future citizens as a mother.

The movement arguably ended up producing results that weaken the woman's self-esteem, rather than strengthening her. Its theory and focus on the woman as "the weak link" tended to create women who chronically victimize themselves, they find discrimination to be everywhere, chronically angry at men, eager to label those who disagree as "male chauvinists", starkly intolerant of other women who view the world from a non-feminist perspective and who disagree with the 1960s ideology.

It has long been a fashion among stern feminists even to question female beauty – so it seems - deeming openly feminine women as "male-dominated," "trying to look good to please the man." A good-looking woman who takes care of herself has somehow become an offense to the new feminists, who seem to fight the very biological characteristics of their own sex. They fight what they *are*, trying *to become what they are not*.

Maybe the greatest weakness of the radical feminist movement was the assumption that freedom and independence require the woman to step out of the fellowship of men. By disentangling her from the dependency on others – the interdependence that connects us all – freedom became her right to tend to her egoism alone.

This is where neo-Marxist thought found its very best helper on its quest to demolish the traditional, Western societal structure: The woman and her discontentment with life. "Gradually, without seeing it clearly for quite a while, I came to realize that something is very wrong with the way Western women are trying to live their lives today." The quote is from the opening pages of Betty Friedan's *The Feminine Mystique*. I could have said it too, about the radical feminist society that Friedan's ideology produced. Something indeed went very wrong with feminism. It can be argued that due to irrational flaws within the 1960s radical feminist ideology, the movement partly ended up being a counterproductive contribution to Western philosophical thought.

Betty Friedan was born in 1921 and became the founder of American feminism. She wrote about "the problem that has no name," suggesting that which defined the traditional woman – such as her husband, her children, and her home – was the precise problem that limited her. In *The Feminine Mystique* first published in 1963, she addressed the issues of women who "wanted more" – more than what they already had in every aspect of life.

The call for "having even more" resounded quite well among millions of women in the 1950s – ironically the time in American history where women's living standards were higher than ever, with more vocational possibilities, wealth, and freedom than ever before. The economic revolution between 1860 and 1970 represented major changes in society, both culturally as well as economically, with the arrival of electric lighting, television, home appliances, cars and planes and a whole range of other developments in the West.

This was Friedan's chosen time of dissatisfaction, asking for even more. Radical feminism chose its strategy: to urge a whole generation of women to step out of the family bonds and marriage, just at the point when Western culture was at the height of economic power and women were at a historical peak of female liberties. The US was never richer, suburbia never more prosperous. Women were encouraged to rebel against "the boring life as a wife," rebel against the very system that provided her with these historically extensive freedoms. Middle-class women had never before had such luxurious lives, never been as active in the workforce, accessing professional careers and enjoying the benefits of suburban life. The one income family was the norm.

Betty Friedan's call to arms appealed to the burden of life, the boredoms of marriage, the strain of children. She defined the way out, the freedom from all of this: working outside the home. The remedy to the problems within the home was for the women to exit it. She was to find autonomy outside the "boredom of the family." Friedan went as far to describe the American home as a "comfortable concentration camp," hailing the right to be ungrateful and complaining, bitter and angered at family life. The quest of the feminists was to disentangle the woman from her husband and their children – telling her that this was her only way to freedom. To be alone in life became the goal.

It truly is a paradox. The prevailing impression we seem to have of the 1950s, that women were not allowed to work outside the house, "caged" in the house as a servant of the man, is simply not correct. It is part of the current ideologically motivated propaganda which portrays traditional European history in a chronically denigrating light. In the 1950s, many women were participating in the workplace as professors, actors, authors, models, singers, scientists, professors, hairdressers, nurses, etc. After the notorious 1960s and into the 70s, the feminist lobby somehow were able to convince us that women in the 50s automatically were deprived, degraded, discriminated against and demeaned by the man, abused and looked down upon – this is why she now needed to fight him, detest him, deny him sex in marriage, and most of all: confront him.

The German author Dietrich Schwanitz argues in *Bildung* that in the late 1960s, the whole point was to go far beyond the initial women's rights movement. The new goal now became to re-evaluate and change the whole traditional gender issue. Somehow, feminists now found that most of what had happened to the woman in history were discriminatory. Schwanitz states that the new revolutionary ideas implied the end of traditional marriage and the family as we know it. The ideological steps towards the disintegration of the traditional structures in society moved slowly towards its goals of deconstructing society and implementing new norms and a new morality in which old religious concepts of sin and wrongdoing no longer exist. This was seen as progress towards a more just society.

Since the woman was considered "male-dominated," divorce became her way of freeing herself from the "burden of submission to the man" and "the male-dominated marriage." Abortion was legalized in the early 1970s all over the West, children now no longer looked upon as pure asset, but increasingly as a burden. Over fifty million have been aborted in the US alone in the past few decades, with numbers equally high for Europe, according to WHO numbers stated in Pat Buchanan *Suicide of a Superpower*.

The feminist argument is that the woman should have the right to do what she wants with her body. Yet, and this is the point, the child is not the woman's body. It is a new being, the very miracle of life. The growing child is in her body, but not *her body*. The woman stands at the very center of the fellowship of men, through her role as the proud bearer of life, of the new human being in her womb. It is a most miraculous role given her, as her body is gloriously capable of bringing new life to mankind. Without the woman and her childbearing ability, human life will quickly be extinct.

Even here lies another irrationality of the 1960s abortion-oriented feminism which despises its own offspring: How is the Western woman to survive, if she is not to bear children? It means the certain death of her culture, childless as she is. She becomes the lonely last in the line of previous offspring. When she dies, there is no family around her, no sons, no daughters, no grandchildren.

Childless, the Western feminist has to face her lonely future and watch how other ethnic groups, childbearing and child loving cultures, outnumber her. Of this, Samuel Huntington has pointed out in *The Clash of Civilizations and the Remaking of World Order*, that mass migration from cultures that do not share Western values have much higher birth-rates than that of modern Western societies. They will easily end up changing the demographics of our culture dramatically. With no offspring, there is no tomorrow.

Again, it is such a paradox – one out of several irrational building blocks of radical feminism: by demeaning and belittling the biological uniqueness in women, feminists ended up trying to turn her into a man – the man being precisely what they disliked so much in the first place. Friedan managed the unthinkable: to turn feminism into misogyny – the contempt for women and their biological distinctness. These feminists idealized the professional life outside the home, – in the quest of achieving male benefits. Yet, the feminists failed to comprehend that working equally hard outside the home as the man, implied that she would also inherit his heavy workload. While men are biologically stronger than women, she now had to bear the same burdens as him.

It seems that to Friedan, the man's world was a heaven of limitless potential with no hurdles. He was God – the woman his servant. Did it cross her mind that his troubles were precisely the ones she now wanted the woman to also bear? From where did Friedan get the idea that the man's world was one of paradise and bliss? Precisely his extreme workload was what she disliked about him in the first place, complaining about him coming home late from work, too tired, distant and overworked, constantly forgetting the extra chores, ending up sleeping on Friday evening. To her it was boredom. To him, it was surviving the harshness of the world outside the home.

Neither did she reflect much on the strains that the woman puts on the man. Him having to put up with her in the house, her moods, her details, the stressfulness of children, of her professional workload, yet facing his own problems – the male requirements to be good-looking and economically successful, constantly grinding him wherever he turned. Was he not "a servant class" to her too?

In Friedan's attack on the feminine mystique, she ends up throwing overboard the respect for womanly qualities that have traditionally been connected to the female. Arguably, she suggests a new role for women: the quest of becoming "the man." One may wonder how these feminists, with such lengthy arguments for women's right to be selfish, became the epitome of Western thinking. How exactly did women like Friedan expect society to develop to the betterment of all when they so shamelessly gave their lives to fight for the woman's right to be self-absorbed?

This was the age of womanly nihilism, writes Harvey J. Mansfield in *Manliness*. Under the influence of Nietzsche's nihilism – a state in which nothing has meaning and the human himself being the sole source of meaning – came the disappearance of nature and the denial of God. Feminism became the possibility of creating a new order and new identities that may take the place of traditional structures.

Women wanted equality, not for its own sake, but because it gave them autonomy from men, independence from morality, independence from childbearing and the right to abortion. In other words, she was to no longer serve the common good and the future of the species. Ironically, feminism represented an opportunity for her to be more like that which had been considered to be the weakness of the man: irresponsible towards the family, workaholic, adulterous, a sexual predator, a liar, an egoist, a nihilist to whom the world was meaningless, and no one else mattered but himself, an abusive father, raging with fits of anger about the smallest things.

However, surveys continually show that women still do two-thirds of the housework, with little change from 1955 to 2002, as pointed out by Mansfield. The push is for the differences between the sexes to disappear, rendering marriage a dull place where two equally feminine people live together. She is not to be more feminine than him; he is not to be more masculine than her. The quest for sameness completely contradicts the biological sexual attraction, which implies that opposites attract. The man wanted the woman simply because she was *different* from him. He is sexually interested precisely in her physical beauty, that which makes her profoundly different from him. He *wants her femininity;* it colors his otherwise bleak life with excitement and thrill.

Radical feminism ends up pushing for less sex appeal between the two partners. The feminist movement has been criticized for taking it too far, being too strict and fighting the man too angrily, assuming that once male power diminished, all would be well. Assuming, in other words, that women are inherently good, while men are inherently evil.

Friedan ended up breaking up not only the fellowship between the sexes but in the rage of it all – dissolving the woman's joy of female womanhood. The movement ended up enraging girls all over the West, telling them that they were useless unless they managed life without any dependency on the man. Female freedom became the right to break away from the bonds of loyalty to the "old-fashioned family."

✳✳✳

# Cultural Downfall

As we have seen, the ancient Greek philosophers clearly warned of hedonism. If accepted in society as a viable way of determining what is right and wrong, they said, it would cause social and cultural dissolution and the fall of Athenian democracy. They were later proven right.

The ancient Greek philosopher Epicurus has often been misunderstood as an advocate of hedonism, defining pleasure as the absence of suffering. He correctly pointed out that pleasure and suffering seem to correspond to right and wrong, yet he acknowledges that pain sometimes is necessary. This is the kind of pain that causes a man to refrain from doing something that he knows will bring him, even more pain in the future. Thus, choosing pain now, refraining from a given action, knowing that by doing so he will achieve greater pleasure in the long run.

Precisely this is the quest of religion, to help man understand how he is to live in order to achieve the best possible life, both now and in the future. In this sense, religion itself implies an Epicurean moral philosophy of searching, ultimately, for pleasure and a tranquil life, surrounded by good friends and amicable, peaceful living.

Epicurus' goal was that man should strive for an absence of pain and suffering, which would lead him to a life with more pleasure and tranquillity, in which he need no longer fear death or the anger of the gods. Furthermore, Epicurus famously stated that it is impossible to live a pleasurable life without living wisely and justly. He suggested man live a good life, thus avoiding as many of the pains and sufferings as possible.

One of Europe's most widely read authors, the French atheist Michel Houellebecq, created public fury with *The Elementary Particles* and the novel *Extension du domaine de la lutte* (translated into English as *Whatever*), books that can only be described as incendiary literature that brutally focuses on how difficult it is to find true love in a raw, industrialized and cynical world where so many live in utter loneliness following the breakdown of the family. He maintains that in postmodern society, we have neglected the need for human compassion and thereby contributed to the institutionalization of care where the state is responsible for taking care of both the young and the old, in a society characterized by emptiness, lack of empathy and loneliness.

His allegation is that sexuality today consists of a system of differentiation that is as merciless "as Market Capitalism." In the same manner, as rampant economic liberalism, sexual liberalism creates a chronic emotional poverty for those who do not manage to "get it all." Many are relegated to a life of loneliness and masturbation. Houellebecq points out that in such a system some have sex every day, other five or six times in life. Some never have sex. This is the effect of the merciless cynicism of market forces on humanity. However, in a sexual system where the dissolution of marriage is forbidden, almost everyone will find a partner.

In other words, because people's own happiness and satisfaction are dependent on their role as positive contributors in a community, it becomes important for them to maintain good relationships with their fellow man. Precisely this was Aristotle's point of view, that humans are to develop and use their skills to the best of their ability – to function well in the community, is what marks the basis for a lasting happiness or sense of fulfillment. This also affects his self-esteem and helps him succeed in life.

In the postmodern Western society, promiscuity is glorified in a way that few thought possible just decades ago. Alienation, loneliness and the neurotic masturbating culture of the single life have become our most common social phenomenon. More than 50% of Americans live alone now, according to US Bureau of Labour Statistics.[43] In Europe, the numbers are equally high. Houellebecq's cultural pessimism serves as a warning about the long-term effects of product-marketing values dominating the arenas of social bonding. We are not machines, not items of merchandise.

Looking at women's magazines from the 1950s, it becomes clear that something has been lost in the way we nurture our marriages and partnerships. These magazines are full of advice on how to have a spicy relationship, how to handle the children, how to make homemade healthy foods, how to stick to good diets, how to enhance romance, giving each other space, but still making quality time for good sex. It's quite amazing to read these magazines and see how many excellent suggestions they had to give to modern working women or stay-at-home mothers at the time.

Peter Berger maintains that the scent of the transcendental, of reality beyond what can be seen with the naked eye, can be sensed in the multitude of daily experiences. He observes that people tend to be willing to sacrifice some of their own independence and individuality in order to

---

[43] Single Americans become majority for first time (Friday, August 18, 2017) https://www.rt.com/usa/186516-singe-americans-majority-marriage/

receive the benefits of performing their duties to the community. This brings meaning to their existence and becomes the path to a fulfilled life. This unmet need for belonging becomes even more evident in postmodern societies such as the West today, where fragmentation, lack of values and a loss of cultural identity is at a critical level.

The sociologist Zygmunt Bauman asserts that modernity's fluid lack of limits erodes the individual, and creates stress that over time becomes unbearable. He has written compelling books on this: *Liquid Love*, *Liquid Modernity*. The modern world, with a myriad of choices where everything is in free drift, has resulted in a loss of anchoring in a permanent value base. This causes more serious strains on identity than many have recognized.

Bauman discusses the tyranny of the "instant," where modern man has lost his conception of time. Everything must happen in an instant, and preferably with little considerations about the potential consequences of an action. According to Bauman, actions are largely driven by feelings and self-limitation is rare. Momentary pleasures are frequently prioritized above long-term advantages. Many ends up frantically searching for stability, but unable to find it – in a system that idealizes fluidity and permissiveness.

The German sociologist, Ferdinand Tönnies equally addressed these issues, and spoke of the decline of *Gemeinschaft*, the togetherness of the community as it was found in societies based on solidarity, obligations and mutual respect, and the rise of *Gesellschaft* – the looser, individualistic relationships typically found in urban and industrialized societies, at large much more disconnected with the traditional communitarian values.

The criticism against hedonism and its promiscuity is that it does not adequately incorporate the complexity of human nature. It opens society for destructive forces that cause disintegration and self-destruction in the fellowship of men. The body is more than merely the physical and more than an instrument for sexual pleasure. It involves deep psychological mechanisms, a strong sense of reason and a sea of vulnerable emotions as men and women search for acceptance and acknowledgment. Precisely here lie the limits of sexuality. Man consists of deeper dimensions, – a soul and spirit, that cannot be satisfied by titillating sexual intercourse alone. The balance between these human elements is the "middle way" that Aristotle and so many others have spoken of as the desirable way to lasting happiness.

# CHAPTER 16

# Free Speech - Tolerance as Tools of Oppression

*Free speech loses its value when used as a means to bully, blaspheme and belittle those who have other worldviews. It becomes a force of tyranny, of rudeness, of lack of respect for whoever is critical of the extreme liberal agenda. "Free speech" was initially the right to express different political views in the public discourse without being silenced, it was never "every man's right" to shamelessly blurt out foul words.*

## Limitless "Free speech" As a Means to Bully

TO SLANDER AND SPEAK ill of others, harassing one's fellow humans, has been one of the evils of men since the beginning of time. History is filled with examples of horrifying stories of how the lynch mob went after philosophers, politicians and religious leaders alike, killing many, destroying others. The Old Testament of the Bible and the Torah tells the story of many a prophet who stood out from the conformist crowd and spoke words that greatly angered the public and its political elites.

The fate of Jesus Christ serves as an example. There seemed to be no end to the religious leaders' willingness to mock and belittle him, have him condemned based on false allegations, subjugated him to the worst form of torture and, finally, ordered his death.

Something similar happened to the ancient Greek philosopher Socrates. As Plato wrote, in the *Apology of Socrates*, the hatred towards him had become so fierce, that Socrates came to understand that what would sentence him to death was the hatred from the crowds. He was accused of teaching the young virtues in his quest for humility and wisdom, always pointing to the god whom he felt was leading his path and pushing him into the debates. Socrates points out that his accusers condemned the truth, by stating it to be evil and unjust. He lived in a time of massive propaganda, where the truth was called a lie and lies portrayed as truth. Socrates stated that as slander and the hatred of men doomed many before him, it certainly would continue to do so in the future.

"Free speech" is often hailed as a classic, Western value. Yet, this can be debated. During the 1600s, when "free speech" was introduced in the UK House of Commons, it was as a means to ensure that speakers were not interrupted in the middle of a political argument. It did not mean that everyone was allowed to say whatever he or she wished to whomever they wished, disentangled from good manners, politeness, and civility. Today free speech has come to mean something completely else than its original meaning and is often used as a means to bully and harass others in order to silence opposition to the politically correct. Limitless speech is the ideal.

A further historical review of "free speech," brings us quickly to 1949, when the modern ideal of freedom of expression was stated in the Universal Declaration of Human Rights. It is only here that we find "freedom of speech" advocated as a human right. Article 19 of the UN, states: "Everyone has the right to freedom of opinion and expression; this right includes freedom to hold opinions without interference and to seek, receive and impart information and ideas through any media and regardless of frontiers."

Yet, the UN declaration does not thoroughly define the limits of free expression or the required framework of manners when engaging in debates, in order to maintain the respect for one's opponent. The UN charter eloquently speaks of rights, but remarkably less of man's duties and obligations to the fellowship of men. This ideological weakness of the UN's founding principles' partly stems from the neo-Marxist influence on philosophical thought at the time, the organization was founded shortly after World War II.

In essence, man's rights to free expression were established, but not its corresponding obligations and duties. The UN charter failed to acknowledge that free speech is an ideal that needs to work within the framework of morality and ethical boundaries. Rights need to correspond with duties in order to be effective. If these constraints are not addressed and clearly defined, "free speech" might become counterproductive and a tool for the exact same repression one seeks to eradicate. If practiced without the constraints of conscience and civility, politeness and rationality, free speech may be the precise tool to legitimize chaos, weaken democracy and turn it into the rule of a ruthless and merciless mob – known in the ancient Greek world as an ochlocracy. Alexis de Tocqueville argued in *Democracy in America*, as he travelled America in the 1800s and wrote his worries about how easy it is for a democracy to turn totalitarian, that if democracy develops into a tyranny of the majority or the tyranny of the mob, it is in no way dissimilar to any form of totalitarian dictatorship. The anxiety is the same: expressing an unpopular opinion can have frightening consequences, both in democracies and in dictatorships.

Free speech then becomes the very method through which citizens lose their politeness and respect of others and attack them verbally in every thinkable way. The West calls itself liberal but is in effect permeated by an elite with remarkable illiberal values towards those whose opinions differ from their own. Especially mainstream media is permeated by the use of all kinds of techniques to suppress, subdue and silence those considered "enemies of the state," those who think differently and have other worldviews than the extreme liberal establishment. Host of the liberal political talkshow The Rubin Report, Dave Rubin famously speaks about "the regressive Left". As civility and politeness – the bourgeoisie values of old – are waning, it is worrying to see how free speech becomes a tool for the oppressor.

Today, this seems to be the prevalent trend in the American mainstream, a tendency that clearly has authoritarian undertones. The internet and social media being yet another free speech arena without constraints or boundaries, where many engage in debates shamelessly based on the ability to bully the most. There is a deep lack of respect for one's fellow citizens buried in the rudeness practiced in today's Western definition of "free speech." No one seems able to stop it as relativism and nihilism remain the current Western ideal.

Freedom of expression has become the right to mock those you disagree with, those who belong to "unwanted" minorities, such as Christians, for one. In the UK House of Commons, M. Jackson put it bluntly in 2009: "Does fairness and equality only apply to people who are *non-Christians* in this country?"

## Voltaire – Founding Father of Modern Intolerance?

The current Western trend of speaking with a "double tongue" – hailing freedom of expression yet using it to repress those you disagree with – was seen already in the work of the 1700s French philosopher François-Marie Arouet – Voltaire. He became famous for stating the importance of tolerance in Enlightenment political philosophy, saying: "I may disapprove of what you say, but I will defend to the death your right to say it." The sentence has been immensely admired in the West, quoted millions of times as a reflection of a leading secular Western ideal at the dawn of atheism. Apparently, Voltaire spoke highly of tolerance, yet became famous for his immense hatred towards the Catholic Church and the religious traditions in his time. His writings are, ironically, often filled with the very opposite of the respect for others right to differ in opinion.

Precisely the demand for tolerance has been portrayed as a secular ideal, yet it initially copied the Christian view of humanity, based on the belief that all peoples, regardless of class, gender or race, have a fundamental human value. Voltaire did not develop this altruistic ideal in a vacuum, but rather, it derived from Christian philosophy. It was Christian theology in the Middle Ages and Spanish scholasticism that formed the basis of what we today call human rights, as we have seen. Even before that, Athenian democracy spoke of the need for public debates and arenas in which intellectuals could discuss morality, politics and social issues in a civil manner.

Yet, Voltaire's writings are permeated with a reeking dislike of Christianity, Judaism, and Islam. He does not seem to have a shred of respect for religious freedom. It went on to the degree that Wolfgang Amadeus Mozart, upon Voltaire's death, allegedly burst out, saying that "the arch-scoundrel Voltaire has finally kicked the bucket." It may be argued that Voltaire was one of the founding fathers of the mannerless and intolerant slander of religious traditionalists that still today constitute the backbone of extreme secular thought, making him one of the grand hypocrites of his time.

In *Liberal Fascism*, commentator Jonah Goldberg illustrates in a compelling way how the establishment in the US have been willing to go to immoral lengths in order to remove people whose politics they dislike.

The French Revolution was actually a totalitarian revolution that played the populist card to the hilt, he says.

Investigative journalist Sharyl Attkisson, who has been working in the media for over thirty years, tells her sad story in *Stonewalled: My Fight for Truth Against the Forces of Obstruction, Intimidation, and Harassment in Obama's Washington* of the decline in investigative journalism and unbiased truth-telling in America. She points to the multi-billion-dollar corporations that aligned with the government have almost complete control, pushing for a massive surveillance of citizens, journalists, and dissidents alike.

She examines the unseen influences of political figures, special interests, and corporations which manipulate the images you see every day, whether on social media, the news or many other outlets. She strongly advises the public to start viewing the news outlets as TV commercials, saying she has never seen a tougher clampdown on the freedom of the press. People need to start thinking: "Why is that story airing? Who pushed it? What special interest might be behind it?" and "Am I getting the full story?"

A recent European survey showed that there is more fear than ever of speaking one's mind; people simply shut up when in public, not voicing opinions that they know differ from what is considered "politically correct," out of trepidation of the bullying that easily happens in the name of free speech.

Mary Catharine Ham speaks of this in *End Discussion: How the Left's Outrage Industry Shuts Down Debate, Manipulates Voters, and Makes America Less Free*, stating that a growing number of Americans are sensing an insidious strain of self-censorship on topics that break with the politically correct news. They find themselves shutting up and not risking the social harassment of "being the enemy of the system." The radical enforcers who instantly attack anyone who voices opinions or views that are not in line with the establishment are everywhere. At parties, family gatherings, in universities and definitely all over the media. Wherever they are, people feel the fear.

Ham states that the silencing impulse is not born out of normal or healthy self-reflection. It arises out of fear. Neither is it a trait of free societies that debates in which a variety of views presented are forcefully quashed. No, these are the people who wish to *silence* free speech, silence dissent, silence a strong, national debate. This fear of speaking up is actively pushed by leftist radicals who seek to raise the cost of speaking publicly, hoping that slandering others will cause those who have other opinions in society to be silenced. It is a highly undemocratic, authoritarian behavior that seeks to quash free speech, under the pretext of hailing it.

# The Culture War

✳✳✳

# One-Way Tolerance – The Repressive Kind

The term "one-way tolerance" perfectly describes the situation where only one party is required to be tolerant while the other fails to show mutual respect. The term "tolerance" then loses its meaning and becomes a political and ideological tool to silence opposition. This is a cunning game, to use man's desire to be accepted against him, by tainting his name and pushing him out of the fellowship if he does not conform to the politically correct standards.

To call someone intolerant has become an effective weapon, just as the claim of feeling "offended" is used to eradicate opposition. To show respect becomes speaking in such a fashion that the extreme-liberals agree with you. "Disrespectful" is the one that states opinions that oppose the current political elites. The definition of what is deemed to be "tolerant and respectful" is so strict that it quenches plurality and suffocates genuine free thought. In general, the words of C. S. Lewis in *The Screwtape Letters* sum it up. He states that hell must be the state where everyone is concerned only about his own dignity and advancement, where everyone has a "grievance" and lives the deadly passions of envy, self-importance and resentment.

We have seen how the original meaning of the word "tolerance" implies respecting the other person's right to disagree with you, yet retaining your own opinion. It does not require that one party must yield to the other, or that the parties have to agree in the end. The right to disagree is precisely what distinguishes a democratic society from a totalitarian one. Strong disagreement of opinion does not equal lack of tolerance. As a matter of fact, it is an ideal embedded in traditional democracies to value differences of opinion, to encourage it as public debate depends on it. It is considered to be desirable that society is pluralistic, reflecting sub-groups with different values – some religious, some not - all living side by side and respecting each other's right to prosper.

Author and pundit Greg Gutfeld in *The Joy of Hate: How to Triumph over Whiners in the Age of Phony Outrage*, speaks of "artificial tolerance" and "repressive tolerance," stating that most of the time liberals use the mantle of tolerance to disguise their own intolerance. He attacks the double standards – a woman may be called any name imaginable, as long as she's a Republican, a Christian may be widely harassed and ridiculed, but no one criticizes a Muslim, not to mention a homosexual.

He gives a number of examples, among them the strange phenomenon that anyone critical of Obamacare or illegal immigration, almost automatically is deemed to be racist. If one is harshly against the plans for a Mosque on Ground Zero, one is equally attacked for being racist.

Gutfeld points out that we have created a new frantic world of phony grievances and manufactured outrage, professing to be offended by other people's opinions if these are contrary to your own. Tolerance has come to mean something completely different than its original definition: It is a way of slandering people to shut them up, attacking whoever disagrees with the liberal agenda.

By claiming that everyone should be met with "tolerance," it becomes almost impossible to correct bad behavior. Gutfeld takes the example of gangs of youngsters who beat up adults in movie theatres and parking lots, harass girls the same age as theirs on social media and so on, and points to the fact that it becomes almost impossible even to address the issue – as one has to be "tolerant" towards these criminals, as "they have human rights too".

One ends up with a society that respects criminal behavior on the same level as law-abiding citizens, as "everyone has human rights." If someone manages to make it seem like law-abiding citizens are "intolerant," his or her reaction is deemed "offensive," and the criminal wins, without being apprehended. The law-abiding citizen becomes defenseless; the criminal walks free.

According to a 2010 Report on International Religious Freedom of US state department, Christians steadily voice concern about the ability to express their faith in the workplace without being harassed. A revealing example of the bullying tactics used if someone represents a Christian minority opinion – such as the Kentucky Marriage Clerk, Kim Davis, who refused to issue marriage licenses to same-sex couples in 2015, is seen by the abusive article written by an associate religion editor for *Huffington Post*, Carol Kuruvilla, which lists thirteen vocations Davis could never have applied for.

The list was long. The Christian lady could apparently never become a deli clerk – stating Christianity does not allow a believer to eat pork. She apparently could not have been a sales clerk – stating Christianity does not allow one to sell clothes made by several materials. Neither she could have been a church speaker, a school teacher or a men's stylist – stating

Christianity refuses women to speak to men or touch them. Ironically, a number of the commandments are taken from the book of Leviticus.

The writer seems to not even know the New Testament story of Peter, being told by God to "get up and eat" when offered foods such as the creatures of the sea, as "man is not to make unclean that which the Lord has cleansed." Paul and Jesus both made remarks such as "it is not that which enters the body that makes man unclean, but that which comes out of him, from the evils of the heart." Some eat meat, some not. Some drink wine, some not. Everything is to be done in the name of the Lord and to his glory, regardless of whether you eat, drink or do not.

The long list ridiculing the Christian woman does not even apply to a Christian, according to the Bible, which *Huffington Post* must have been fully aware of. It simply was intended as a bullying tactic directed at a person who refused to issue a marriage license. The irony being that most of the cited Old Testament scriptures came from the book of Leviticus – upheld dearly by religious Jews. The *Huffington Post* ends up slandering Jewish eating regulations and systems of beliefs, demeaning the Jewish religion. The editor could have called the article: "Thirteen things practicing religious Jews cannot do, that's how old-fashioned ignorant they are." However, then again, she'd probably have been called in to defend her anti-Semitic comments.

Kirsten Powers' *The Silencing: How the Left is Killing Free Speech* analyses how the American Left has become increasingly extreme and intolerant – illiberal – towards those who do not agree with its opinions. It didn't use to be this way, she states, as the left used to treat different opinions with a much higher degree of tolerance than what seems to be the situation today. Powers, who is regarded as a fair-minded liberal, speaks openly about the current hard-line attack by the extreme left on values such as tolerance and free speech, seeking to silence by oppressing the diversity of views.

She states that this has been cunningly done in academia, politics and American public discourse, where moderate liberals and Conservatives alike have been silenced as extreme left-wingers steadily turn to victimization, claiming to be "offended," "hurt" or "violated" by the opinions of other groups. By claiming to be "offended," it is expected that Conservatives instantly shut up. She calls the current trends the illiberal attack on free speech by the New Left, which now viciously attacks and silences anyone with alternative points of view. She argues that intimidation and demonizing ideological opponents has, to this day, been the left's most successful tool.

By using delegitimization, true free speech is effectively attacked, and tolerance curbed to only apply to "those groups we like." At the same time, opposing voices are refused their right to speak by claiming that their views are "offensive." Powers states that what the New Left does, can hardly be called rational debate. Character assassination, for one, is not a rational argument in any possible way.

Let me, for the sake of clarification, add that it is not only the "illiberal left" that pushes for this type of injustice. As stated earlier, the current left–right divide is on a number of levels outdated and may largely be disregarded, as the Western globalized and internationalized establishment increasingly seems to be unified in both its political as well as economic agenda. Voting right or left, one seems to get the same totalitarian elitist tendencies.

The world-renowned linguist and intellectual, Noam Chomsky, has been quite some beacon of light as an American intellectual who has been practicing "fearless speech" for decades. He has addressed numerous issues over the years, criticized oppressive systems of power in the US, both internally as well as in US foreign affairs. He shows precisely the type of attitude that should have permeated the institutionalized Church and its leaders, actively taking part in society, speaking up for the oppressed, translating oppression into public concerns, voicing the need for a dramatic shift towards solidarity, empathy, and justice, also for those outside of the Western hemisphere.

✻✻✻

# A Culture of Bullying or Rational Debate?

Tolerance signifies *the right to disagree*. Wildly disagreeing parties may mark a tolerant debate, high tempers, loud voices, crossed feelings, yet arguments based on rationality and relevance to the topic discussed. One is to be civil and respectful of differences, earnestly listening to each other as there might be something to learn - the world seen from a different perspective than your own. All parties participating are to be given the space to talk and properly explain their point of view. The expression of criticism and disagreement based on rational arguments in a public debate demonstrates that one respects the opponent as they try to find good solutions to problems in society.

The German philosopher, Jürgen Habermas claims that if public discourse is to be productive and not destructive, it should emphasize rational arguments, based on knowledge. Cold facts should determine the debate. It is the speaker's role to bring new facts to the table that may help the discussion progress towards finding new viable solutions to the problem at hand.

Habermas further requires the debate to be just. The speakers should be given an equal amount of time to speak so that it becomes a real platform for honest debate, not with a prefabricated conclusion. There has to be a just representation. If, for example, one person is placed opposite eight who differ to his views – one conservative versus eight liberals – the debate is not in any way fairly proportionate but rather controlled by the media, as the outcome is obvious. The debate ends up limiting free speech and a just representation.

Habermas further states that those who are unable to state their views or participate should have a representative appointed who may speak on their behalf. For example, animals and the protection of the environment, unborn children, the disabled and so on. If only one group is given the right to speak, we have a dictatorship. The extent to which this tactic is used in Western media outlets today points in the direction that it is willfully done.

Having in mind what Herbert Marcuse, one of the main intellectual instigators of the student revolutions in the 1960s said, pertaining to the need to "curb freedom" in such a way that opponents stop posing critical questions, one may assume that the radical left's intention is to stop free speech and make sure we do not have a fair representation, and thus will not achieve a healthy democracy.

If "tolerance" – understood as a philosophy of licentiousness in the guise of tolerance – is used to unjustly attack an opponent, presenting allegations, rumours, personal harassment or various forms of degradation as though they were "rational" arguments in a debate, the whole arena becomes a totalitarian tool that turns national debates into the Circus in Rome where the point was to kill the opposing gladiator. This is not the definition of rational, civil debate, but rather defines barbarism and chaos.

Sadly, this is the case today, which causes many to say Western society is increasingly authoritarian in structure. Instead of sticking to the requirements for rational, national debate based on qualified knowledge and investigative journalism, many are allowed to reprehensively use character insults, belittling and irony in order to "win the debate." When unable to find good arguments, they resort to bullying. Many complain about the lack of civility and politeness in social media. Yet, watching how mainstream media editors chronically revert to pleasing the mob instead of cultivating a debate based on presenting objective facts – or at least as close as possible to objective reporting - it is easy to comprehend from who "the mob" learn its tricks.

Journalism should not be about dictating to the reader how he or she is to interpret current affairs. Investigative reporting is about finding new facts and presenting them as objectively as possible. The more facts and perspectives on the table, the easier it becomes to grasp a comprehensive understanding of the situation and learn something, not about the ideology of the journalist, but of the reality on the ground. Mainstream news elites instead end up leading the mob on, portraying feelings, sentiments and "offendedness" as rational arguments in debates, pushing for precisely the kind of non-rational debate that produce chaos, hatred and lack of respect for one another's difference of opinion. The one with the other view becomes "the enemy of state."

\*\*\*

# Charlie Hebdo, Terrorism, and Free Speech

The 2015 terror attack in Paris, 2016 in Brussels and the later London attacks have been one of the trigger points of a worsening situation in the escalating culture of fear among Europeans in general. This has been going on for many years, interconnected to issues pertaining to terrorism as well as Western participation in the recent Middle East wars and its brutal effects on millions of civilian lives in Iraq, Afghanistan, Yemen, Somalia, Pakistan, Libya, Syria and so on. During the past decades, terrorism has been well-known to Israel, Iraq, Iran, Pakistan, and others. Terror attacks are a horrendous affair, especially since it affects random civilians. It is a form of warfare which attacks the population, causing fear in the whole nation. What is new is that terror is now also happening in Europe, not only in Israel and the Middle East.

The killing of the French satire magazine, Charlie Hebdo' journalists took the tensions to a new level and brought the question of free speech again to surface. Millions marched the streets of Paris, demanding respect for "freedom of speech" and European values. The "*Je suis Charlie*" slogan became synonymous with the battle for the freedom of expression against radical, Sunni-extremism. The *Charlie Hebdo* magazine was depicted as a magazine that hailed the Western culture's greatest freedoms.

However, when did slander and harassment against religion become one of Europe's trademarks? *Charlie Hebdo* has been known to push the limit to the limitless regarding harassing religion, showing gross disrespect for Christians and people of other faiths. Pope Francis called the *Charlie Hebdo* killings an aberration but also said that the magazine should not make fun of faith and that there is a limit to free speech. When *Charlie Hebdo* on its one year marking after the attack, chose to print a blasphemous picture, depicting God with blood on his clothing, saying he was the real perpetrator of the attack, the Vatican stated, again, that the cover was painful and sacrilegious: "Behind the deceptive flag of an uncompromising secularism, the French Weekly once again forgets what religious leaders of every faith have been urging for ages – to reject violence in the name of religion and that using God to justify hatred is a genuine blasphemy," adding that *Charlie Hebdo* "does not want to recognize or respect believers' faith in God, regardless of their religion".

*Charlie Hebdo* had for years published offensive cartoons and caricatures of the prophet Mohammed as well as Muslim immigrants in general. As no law in France prohibits the ridicule of religious faiths, many French politicians encourage media like *Charlie Hebdo* to continue mocking religions, according to *Newsweek* and others.

Without going into the cultural issues of immigration, Western nations' billion-dollar weapon sale, military engagement and support to various militia and guerrilla groups in the geopolitical conflicts of the Middle East, it is none the less a paradox that *Charlie Hebdo* would never get away with a magazine full of slandering caricatures of Jews. Just imagine. The old slogans from the Nazi era, the long "Jewish noses" caricatured, the allegations that Jews rule the world, that Jews are "filthy rats" and that Israel should be removed from the map: would *Charlie Hebdo* ever publish such depictions?

Alternatively, what about an analysis of "the negro"; mocking everything that is African or African-American, making jokes about the dying in Darfur, portraying "the negro" as an inferior race. *Charlie Hebdo* did, though, make much fun of the drowned Syrian refugee boy who was photographed on the beaches in Turkey, his little face down, small shoes and shorts on. This brings us to the question: What is *Charlie Hebdo*, modern Western barbarism or is this the kind of values and treatment of others we wish to pursue? Does this kind of satire reflect the historical European ideal of respecting diversity and religious freedom, or is it simply a result of the 1960s social revolution and its revolt against societal order?

The *Charlie Hebdo* crew stated their response after the terrorist attack that they from now on would dedicate the magazine to blaspheming religions more than ever. How exactly does that solve the current cultural problems facing Europe? Why did the mainstream media so uncritically end up defending the magazine's right to disrespecting different faiths and religions? How have we come to a position where secularism means the right to bully believers in God? There are many ways to fight terrorism, for one, stopping the Western interference into the internal matters of sovereign states in the Middle East. Freedom of expression does not imply dissolving the respect for religious freedom.

# CHAPTER 17

# Why the Secularized Church Is In Decline

*It's a sad demise, considering how the West used to have a strong spiritual fundament. We are now coming close to the situation that Russia experienced during the Soviet Union era. Even our church buildings are now overtaken by secular state authorities, just like under the Soviets, surveys showing that the vast majority of Europeans – around 80 % - believe in Jesus Christ, but hardly anyone – 2-3 % - go to Church.*

## The Definition of a Church and Spiritual Fellowship

IN A TIME CHARACTERIZED by extreme individualism, with little normative regard for "the other," the guiding ability and public role of the spiritual Church – come in whichever form and denomination it will – is even more important than ever. The values of compassion, humility, self-restraint and orderly conduct pursued by true believers, provide vital corrections to the hedonistic, nihilistic bias of the present. The need for moral reflection on solidarity re-actualizes the need for a firmer message from Church leaders.

Let us, therefore, reflect on what a Church really is, the answer depending on how you define the term "church." Is it a secular entity that is administered by the state with content decided by politicians? Or, is it rather a physical building in which Christians meet? Or again, is it the metaphysical body of Christ on earth, symbolizing God's unity with humans who accept Christ as His gift and thereby joining His kinship? Or, is the Church simply an assembly of believers?

The Greek word for church is "*ekklesia*" meaning "an assembly" or literally "the called-out ones." In a Christian context, it refers to people who consist of a group or body that believes in Jesus Christ. They believe that as evil entered the world, God brought His solution in Christ, so that mankind has the possibility of re-entering paradise, being freed from the burden of living outside of God's light, through accepting the total offering that Christ's death represents.

Christians believe that Christ's holy blood cleanses man from evil and relieves him from the judgment of God, opening up his possibility for oneness and kinship with the Creator through continual repentance. The point being, spiritually as well as physically, the blood of Jesus sifted into matter and into the material world, lifting its curse off the shoulders of whoever bowed before the bleeding Christ – with the corresponding earthquake that ripped the massive veil in the Jewish Temple apart, symbolically tearing from top to bottom, the veil that separated the most holy room from the less holy in the Temple.

By accepting Christ's offering, the believer becomes a member of the metaphysical "body of Christ", united spiritually with God and the believers all over the world in a spiritual kinship, a celestial brotherhood of friends destined by faith to live on after the short years on earth is over, and man enters another realm – the realm of the afterlife.

The Church has, since its early beginning as the disciples began gathering in homes and congregational halls in Jerusalem, been about maintaining and helping these spiritual confidants in Christ prosper, grow and mature, as well as steadily reach out to society. The Catholic Church's beautiful, majestic buildings, with their splendid architecture and craftsmanship, certainly remind the believer of the heavens to which he is traveling. When traveling to the Middle East or to Russia, the equally wonderfully decorated Churches of the Orthodox tradition, ornamented with golden icons and the smell of incense, certainly invoke deep spiritual sentiments and thoughts of the afterlife and the celestial beauty of the heavenly halls of God.

The Evangelical Protestant's more modern and less decorated rooms of gathering, with their modern music and charismatic pastors, are also places where Christians worship, though culturally different from that of the East. Or, as we have seen, the growing number of strong believers who leave the "Churches" in the West, feeling that these congregational halls have become devoid of spiritual power, choose to gather in small home-based churches – in the homes, just as St Paul recommended in his letters to the early Church.

On this, the Orthodox monk and saint, Elder Porphyrios has said:

> We are true Christians when we have a profound sense that we are members of the mystical body of Christ, of the Church, in an unbroken relationship of love – when we live united in Christ, that is when we experience unity in His Church with a sense of oneness. This is why Christ prays to His Father saying, that they may be one.

St Augustine of Hippo also explained the idea of the Church as the spiritual body of Christ, as a spiritual unification between men and God, as illustrated by the Holy Communion. This is one of the deep spiritual mysteries that connects the Church to Christ in a union that gives the carnal man his hope to escape the evils of this world. Pope Benedict XVI speaks of this in *Great Christian Thinkers*.

St Ignatius of Antioch, who was bishop of Antioch from AD 70–107, pointed out in his *Letter to the Smyrnaeans* that wherever Jesus Christ is, there is a universal Church. The body of believers presiding in a particular region, city or nation thus form the unified Church and the body of Christ in that particular geographical place.

The brotherhood of believers may, as we see, come in many shapes and forms and appear in different cultural contexts based on historical tradition in that particular region. Some meet in local churches, be it Catholic, Orthodox or Protestant. Some meet in large convention centers, some have since the early Christian era formed brotherhoods in monasteries and convents, where they consecrated their lives to prayer and intellectual as well as spiritual study of holy text. Others live a spiritual life in the buzzing life of the city, meeting in cafeterias, homes and in churches. The sociological and cultural variations are consequently many.

Again, looking at the example of St Porphyrios' life, in *Wounded by Love* he explains how to be spiritual whether a monk on the Holy Mount Athos – like he was – or a priest in a village – like he also became at one point of his life, or again, working full-time with wounded soldiers and the sick during World War II – which was his vocation in the buzzing city of Athens for over thirty years. Wherever a believer is, he must strive to be a holy man or woman, connected to The Holy Spirit, loving God, caring for others and meeting the needs of those who suffer.

Church buildings or other halls in whichever form they come thus may be said to be, in essence, "just buildings" intended for the congregation of believers to meet, perform mass and share the Eucharist. One may say that the sociological and cultural diversity between manners of congregating varies throughout the world, yet the universal Church, the spiritual body of Christ, is unified through the spiritual brotherhood between all the children of God. From this angle, we understand what the African bishop, St

Cyprian, who was born in Carthage and worked around AD 200, meant when he proclaimed In *De Unit* that God *is one*, the Church *is one*, the faith *is one* and the Christian people are joined into a unity that cannot be severed and cannot be separated. The reason for division is a lack of spiritual knowledge about deeply spiritual truths.

Church buildings are not "the Church" itself, but become "the Church" or "the assembly" once believers gather within its walls and perform sacraments and prayers at that particular location. Secular society calls these buildings a church, where believers come together to pray. Statistics from secular universities may measure who comes in or who goes out of the physical building, but not who is a member of the spiritual Body of Christ.

Billy Graham says of this in one of his TV interviews with Robert Schuller:

> There is the body of Christ, which comes from all the Christian groups around the world, and outside the Christian groups, I think everybody that loves Christ or knows Christ, whether they are conscious of it or not, they are members of the body of Christ. God is calling people out for His name, whether they come from the Muslim world, the Buddhist world or the Christian world or the non-believing world. They are members of the body of Christ because they have been called by God. We must come to a place where we keep our eyes on Jesus Christ and not on what denomination, what church or what group we belong to.

When studying how Christians gathered in the New Testament, it becomes clear that in the spiritual sense, wherever believers gather and seek God, they may be defined as a "church." That is, "an assembly" for "the called-out ones." In the New Testament, we find a number of stories of how the congregation met and prayed together in different homes. This was in the cradle of Christian faith, at the beginning of many of the groups that later grew into large churches, as they quickly spread throughout the Roman Empire and beyond.

People who live in societies where persecution of Christians is regular, and Churches have become politicized to the degree that much of the Christian message is no longer preached out of shame of its content may choose to meet clandestinely. Previously in places like China or Russia, Christians had to meet in secrecy. Today, in places like Northern Europe and in the UK, it seems that this trend is re-emerging while worshipping openly is strongly recommended in today's Russia. Trends change. Today, in the West, many Christians avoid the politically correct churches that in many cases represent the same type of nihilism as society at large; many gather to strengthen each other and receive Holy Communion elsewhere. They may, for example, follow broadcasted TV sessions from other parts of the world, where going to church still means receiving spiritual food or "receiving daily bread" as stated in the Lord's Prayer.

This has become quite a modern trend among many elderly Christians in places like Scandinavia, as the Lutheran Church seems almost totally politicized and reformed to the standards of secular society, that hardly any of the old hymns that they know so well are heard in the service anymore. The liturgy keeps changing and changing, the hymns now even include folk songs with no reference to Christianity, the priest often speaks about purely left-wing political topics. Too many of the elderly, there is little that reminds them of the social and spiritual fellowship that the church used to represent in the local community. Thus, research shows that even the elderly, who in many instances have been the only ones left in Lutheran congregations on a regular basis, now increasingly stay at home in Scandinavia, and watch Christian broadcasts on television.

\*\*\*

## Institutionalized Churches Losing Their Appeal

According to a 2008 ISSP study addressing patterns of change in the religiosity in Norway, only 2% attend church service regularly. This is quite a number, especially considering that over 70% of the same population state that they do believe in a God and the metaphysical dimension. In the ultra-liberal Netherlands, only 1.2% attend church regularly. A 2007 SCP report still indicates that 43% of the population consider themselves to be Christians.

These numbers would be higher if they included everyone that believed in a god, as approximately one million Muslims live in the Netherlands, as well as Hindus, Buddhists, and others. Considering the extensive cultural and religious antagonism that has characterized the public sphere in the Netherlands since the 1970s, it is amazing that so many Dutch still describe themselves as believers.

In the UK, only 800,000 attend church services on a regular Sunday, according to the *Daily Mail*, the number of Christians declining over four million in just one decade. Other statistics such as ISSP 2008 show the number for regular Church attendance being as low as 1.4% in the UK. Still, the number of Christians is as high as 60% – this without counting the growing numbers of Muslims and other faiths. Overall in Europe, statistics show, as we have seen, that around 80% define themselves as Christians, according to Encyclopaedia Britannica. Despite the fact that the percentage of people with some form of belief in God has declined 10% since 1991, statistics show that faith in the spiritual world remains remarkably static. Why then are they not attending church?

The slowing down of church attendance in Northern Europe may very well be happening simply because people feel that they do not find spiritual food there anymore. For how long do you keep going to the bakery if they don't have bread to offer? It is, of course, yet another cunning and subtle way of persecuting the Christian faith, by attacking its leadership which, in the Northern European context, has salaries paid by the secular state. In Norway, for instance, the Lutheran Church was a state-run church until recently. As Bishops are expected to be politically correct – and their payroll and further election to important clerical positions depend on them being so – they have proven to be easily politically swayed away from teaching the traditional, Christian message, readily changing its theological content to fit the anti-religious elite better.

The former death punk band leader, Hans-Erik Husby's brilliant term, "Christophobia" has been, as stated earlier, an anti-Christian plague in Northern Europe the past decennials. There is almost no limit to what agnostics and atheists are allowed to say about the Church, secular authorities sway its content away from the classical Christian message, while public slander is rampant.

In an Oslo Church, a gay singer, Tooji, made a point of performing erotica on the altar in 2014, the later shock being that Church officials dared not deny the singer to perform, out of fear of seeming to be "homophobic."[44] In the aftermath, the issue was hushed down by the quietly "offended" Bishop, probably hoping to return to silence as soon as possible. One may only imagine what would happen if the same was done in a mosque.

Thus, the current Church leadership and its coward bishops end up rendering the Christian followers spiritually homeless, many a priest horrified at the constant liberal, state-run changes; chronic secular reforms which steadily removes its Christian content from the Lutheran Churches, leaving the flock without proper shepherds, without spiritual substance. It has been an anti-Christian strategy that has worked quite well and silenced

---

[44] The bishop reacts to Toojis church-altar-sex music video (Friday, August 18, 2017) http://www.vl.no/nyhet/biskopen-reagerer-pa-toojis-kirkesex-video-1.364968?paywall=true

much of the opposition against, for example, the promiscuity of a heathen lifestyle, which is hailed as the epitome of secular, modern living in Europe.

The new, non-church attending Christians and spiritual individuals now tend to meet somewhere else than in the traditional churches, but where? The study of where and how these Christians assemble in the postmodern structure is quite an interesting endeavor.

Naturally enough, recent sociological studies point in the direction that it actually is the strongest believers who leave. The secular message seems to have little appeal to them as they exit the state-run churches. Many Christians find the secular church a useless place, reduced to merely a beautiful building with no spiritual value. Many seem to feel that modern Christianity is turning away from its traditional roots and becoming some sort of a humanist cult. Josh Packard and Asleigh Hope assert in *Church Refugees: Sociologists Reveal Why People are DONE with Church but Not Their Faith* that the main reason for the exit from American churches is not that the church-goers have become unbelievers. On the contrary, it is often the most believing who get up and leave.

These findings were the result of a major study that concluded that the churches in America are losing their most fervent supporters and their strongest members. It seems to be a trend all over the West: the rapid growth of Christians that are "de-churched" and "done with organized, politicized religion." Exceptions are found within the African-American community, which makes this segment particularly interesting, where trends seem to go in the opposite direction. The same is true for Africans who move to the West. They tend to retain a strong fellowship as church-goers, easily seen in places like London, Paris and other European cities with vibrant African communities where thousands gather to worship on Sundays. The Church somehow has a different and much stronger social standing within these communities and plays a different role with different organizational dynamics.

One explanation for the still strong African-American church standing, may partly be because of the longstanding issues of forced migration and current day lack of a link to "white America" – a cultural disconnect and disapproval of the secular trends within the "white" American establishment elite. As racial tensions traditionally have been high in the US – and growing, even more, today – the church has played in the past and still plays a defining role for many African-Americans as a source of cultural and spiritual identity. It has not been an ideal to these subgroups in society to conform to the standards of secular, liberal America. It certainly looks like the African-Americans have succeeded in positive church-building more than contemporary American society. Packard and Hope seem to conclude with a deep felt sociological point: it is the way religion is practiced that drives people away from Church, yet not from God.

※※※

# Churchless Christians, "cultural religion" and the Lack of Spiritual Fellowship

The Catholic Church in America has gone through a similar decline as its institutionalized Protestant counterpart. The trend is quite new. Under popes such as Pius XII, the number of priests doubled in the US and churches could not be built fast enough. Pat Buchanan points out in *The Suicide of a Superpower* that the 1950s represented a great boost for Catholicism in the US. It was only after the Vatican II council, that sought to reconcile Catholicism with modernity and make it more appealing to the secular world, that Church growth plummeted. Kenneth C. Jones' *Index of Leading Catholic Indicators*, states that in 1965, 1575 priests were ordained, in 2002 only 450. In 1965 only 1% of parishes were without a priest, in 2002, 15% had no priest.

These statistics also show that in 1965 there were 104,000 teaching nuns, today there are 8,200. In 1965, 3,559 men were becoming Jesuit priests, in 2000, the figure was down to 389. The numbers of men studying to enter religious orders as priests were as high as 3,379 in 1965 and only 84 in 2000. This represents a rather stark contrast, stating that almost 4,000 men rushed to become Jesuit priests in the US in the 1960s, yearning to serve God by celibacy and lifelong prayers, spiritual studies and caring for the deprived in society.

Buchanan points out that not since the Reformation had the institutionalized Church undergone such a decline and suffered such a massive blow. By 2007, one in three Catholics had left the Church. Catholics have only seemingly remained at the level of around 25% of the population, due to the large influx of new immigration from Latin America and other Catholic regions. Those remaining in the Catholic Church are much more liberal, *Index of Leading Catholic Indicators* show. Catholics do not attend Mass nearly as often as previous generations, 53% believe that abortion is ok, divorces had soared from 338 in 1968 to 50,000 in 2002. The number, again, significant.

In Europe, many churches are almost empty, especially, as mentioned, within Protestant denominations. It is painful, because what is a Christian to do when major parts of Christianity are hardly mentioned in these still secular-state-controlled-congregations? These "churches" deny the virgin birth of Mary, deny that Jesus walked on water, deny that man will be judged by God in the afterlife, deny the authenticity of the Sermon on the Mount, with seemingly endless discussions on what we may believe in the Bible and which of its content that is based on fairy tales or outdated Jewish customs. Many want a spiritual awakening, but not one that incorporates repentance and the need for a holy life.

At what point do these congregational halls transfer from being actual churches to becoming secular establishments for social gatherings with the goal of avoiding any controversial topic? Today, church attendance is far too often about a beautifully pleasant experience with lovely music, mild speeches by unapproachable, chronically smiling priests and pastors in expensive gowns, where no one is challenged by anything either said or done.

And the mellow, "smiling" message reaches nowhere of importance. A recent poll even showed that 50% of schoolchildren in the UK do not even know why we celebrate Easter, according to the *Mirror*. In America, Easter is increasingly relabelled "Spring Break." Christmas is "a holiday" just like any other holiday as if to hide that its celebration historically has been about the birth of Jesus Christ. Of course, in the ocean of gnomes, trolls and secularized Santa Clauses on their endless rides to and from the North Pole, no wonder many disconnects the celebration of Christmas with the birth of Jesus Christ. The same goes for Easter, with its rabbits crowding every store, as if Easter was a celebration of bunnies. The historical context with its wonderful religious message of hope gets lost in the jungle of advertisements and money spending in overcrowded malls.

The point being, is it the prime minister or politicians' job to help citizens grow spiritually and find spiritual light that might lead them to a better life? Where are Christians to go if all they hear about in Church is ideology and politics? They rather turn on the TV at home and watch the debate in the House of Commons.

This is happening, while the people, in general, wish for more honest, forthright and radical Church leaders. In March 2008, *Foreign Affairs* cited several international studies all of which confirmed that believers wanted religious leaders to focus more on religious core values and spirituality, as well as to articulate distinct opinions on social and ethical questions. Many Church leaders appear out of sync with the non-Western trend where clarity and fearlessness define spiritual leadership. Asians and Africans are even coming to Europe now, as missionaries.

Authors George Barna and David Kinnaman have pointed out that churchless people are growing in numbers in the US. In *Churchless:*

*Understanding Today's Unchurched and How to Connect with Them*, they reveal the results of a five-year study based on interviews with thousands of previous church goers, many saying that they find the church to be a place where one is *not able* to connect to God.

Thus, they leave the traditional congregations, looking for something more genuinely Christian, fellowships that are more outwardly oriented towards society and people in general. They comment on the closedness of many cultural Christian congregations, – of a sectarian focus on "closing the Church door and remaining inside with fellow members" rather than "opening the Church to outsiders."

Sometimes, the Church has reflected approximately the opposite values than those of its humble, yet powerful origin. When the radical element in Christian faith is removed, the Church loses its genuine fervor. It loses its spiritual power. This religion has since its humble beginnings been associated with radicalism. When a nation lacks spiritual leaders that speak out and dare to take unpopular stands, anaemic processes happen, like those presently taking place within the West.

Many, therefore, express the need to relieve themselves of negative religiosity, of a "culturally determined religion with its own set of rules and regulations", often determined by local pastors or leaders, rules that do not necessarily correspond to the commandments of Jesus Christ, but are a reflection of religious heritage within a particular Christian group. Many rebels against this form of "Christian control" done by religious leaders who fail to be spiritual and turn instead to controlling the members of a church. This type of "culturally determined religion" often does not reflect the outward spirit of vibrant Christianity, it is a type of "religiosity" that leads to personal bondage to rules and regulations that have little to do with the genuine Christian faith. The rebellion against these types of religious leaders, make many leave the churches and rather want to live a free life – in purity and repentance as required by the true faith, and in solidarity with the suffering in society, in accordance with the radically relevant message of Jesus Christ.

Religion as bondage is not the type of spiritualism needed in the West today. What we need is genuine spirituality that seeks to enhance society with love for one's fellow man, not religious hypocrisy, selfishness and double standards.

The Eastern Orthodox Elder Paisios of Mount Athos, one of the great spiritual teachers of the Greek Orthodox Church, once said:

> I often see a strange thing that occurs with religious people, reminding one of a vegetable market. There everybody shouts. One says, take oranges; another says

take beets, and so forth, each in order to sell their own stuff. Something similar happens with Christians. Some say if you enter this association you'll be saved. If you go there you'll be saved. However, a spiritual man of God can help. Help, but not strangle.

In *Spiritual Awakening*, Elder Paisios advise those who experience this kind of disentanglement, on how to maintain spiritual fellowship with others even in hard times. The Christian who is struggling in the world is helped when he has relationships with spiritual people. Elder Paisios says that in difficult times, even stronger fellowships are formed among people. It is important that those who live in society maintain relationships with relatives and friends who live a spiritual life. Find spiritual people and stick with them. Form fellowship wherever possible. No matter how spiritually one lives, one needs good fellowship with others. Elder Paisios' advice is to try to become more brotherly and to have a brotherly fellowship. Search for other believers who need fellowship and stick together. That is how we all will be able to walk together on the steep path of ascent towards Golgotha.

In an audience with Eastern Orthodox Church, Patriarch Theophilos III of Jerusalem, he stated much of the same as Elder Paisios, looking at the worsening situation for spiritual Christians in Europe as we seem to enter yet another dark age for believers. When churches become de-spiritualized, it becomes even more important that believers return to the roots of faith to gather spiritual strength, as they did in the early years of Christendom.

Many also find help in consulting priests in the Church whenever it is possible, or when they trust a particular priest to guide them properly spiritually. Some seek the Catholic convents, which tend increasingly to be sources of spiritual light. In the Middle Ages, people sought to the spiritual centers of the monasteries as places for studies, in order to gain information, knowledge, and wisdom. As we know, the university systems grew out of the convents and monasteries which were the main centers of learning in the Middle Ages. In countries where the Church has stronger leaders who are not so easily politically controlled, it may be easier to advise a young believer to go to his local church and get advice from his priest as the Christian message is less tainted by the "cultural religion" described above.

Consequently, the spiritual definition of "the Church as the body of Christ" shows us that modern people who do not attend these extreme-secular Churches still may be attending "the assembly," though in a hidden way. Jesus said that wherever two or three meet, he is among them. Many in the West have spiritual fellowship in smaller communities, meeting in cafeterias, restaurants, in breaks at work, at parties; they pray together and share the Holy Communion in the homes as they did in the New Testament and the days of the ancient church. Others find a source of spirituality in local churches that are still vivid with spiritually awakened priests who may guide and support the believer in his daily walk.

Communism long upheld atheism's repressive attitude in Russia, dictating people's lives and actions, causing a constant, reeking fear. Finally, the anti-religious state lost its power and the Soviet Union crumbled. As stated earlier, since 1989, the Russian Orthodox Church has experienced a remarkably great revitalization. In a governmental survey from 2008, approximately 67% of the population now call themselves Orthodox believers. Among those under thirty, there is an ongoing revival of the faith. People flock to churches which are filled to the brim with praying believers. The President of the Russian Federation, Vladimir Putin is constantly shown during Sunday mass or on holy days to be in church, together with ministers and other leading officials. The Russian newspapers steadily report this, popular as it is to be a Christian in Russia. Countries like Belarus, Georgia, Ukraine, Bulgaria, and Moldova are reporting similar growth in interest in the Orthodox faith. Some say this is done for political reasons, and of course, it is. It is a highly political decision which values you want to push as ideals to your country. Some values strengthen nations, others weaken them.

Churches in Russia are crowded with thousands and thousands, and, according to *Russian Report*, sometimes lines form with parishioners waiting patiently outside for someone to leave so they can enter. The Russian government has for the past years worked to speed up the process of rehabilitating churches, which were used for other purposes after the 1917 revolution, and now return to being sacred halls of worship. Today the Russian people fill the newly restored and reopened Churches where icons smell of fresh paint and Russian Orthodox leaders once again spread knowledge about man's spiritual dimension with a distinctly ethical voice.

As atheism in the Soviet Union eventually fell and the Russians got rid of the totalitarian system they had lived under for so long, the West seems to have implemented the same atheist misery that Russians are fleeing from. We are switching roles. The great paradox is that the Russians embrace what we are trying to extinguish: our historical heritage as found in our main traditional religion and its pillars as ethical cornerstones in society. The increasingly anti-Christian Western establishment and its mainstream media steadily turn our culture in a sharply atheist, nihilist direction, while the Russians, who were denied religion for so long, now flock to return to the Orthodox faith. When they were under Communism, we used to feel sorry for them. Now they feel sorry for us.

# CHAPTER 18

# Post-Modern Christianity Versus Jesus' Simple Message

*It is well-known that the Church, as a normatively authority in society, poses a challenge for extreme liberal forces. To seek political control over the Church and directing it away from Christianity under the banners of "secular Christianity," has clearly been a successful post-war practice. When facing this dark hour of Western decay, let us awaken yet again the spiritual truths that once made our culture great.*

## Church Leaders Have Utterly Failed

In *Decision Magazine*, Billy Graham harshly compares the current status of the United States of America to Sodom and Gomorrah, deserving the judgment of God. He strongly suggests that Christians return to prayer and humility, which used to be a creed in the US that was followed by regular citizens and presidents alike. Graham proclaimed this to be the only saving power for a nation in sharp cultural decay.

It may be argued that one of the reasons for institutionalized Church decline is the tendency to collectively over time become more and more occupied with organizational structures, religious activities, rules, cultural regulations and intricate dogmatic questions. In addition, the Church leadership has, when facing decline, ironically enough turned to secular society for tips on how to liberalize and become more popular among the general public, instead of turning to spirituality and the genuinely Christian message.

The current Anglican Archbishop of Canterbury, Justin Welby, recently described the terrible results regarding the declining church attendance as the effect of being subjected to an "anti-Christian culture," that our culture has been infected with an ideological virus that also is affecting the churches. There may be an element of truth in his statement. Yet, he conveniently neglected to mention, that the responsibility for this decline is his own, and his fellow Church leaders, who so eloquently have chosen to remain silent instead of sounding an angry alarm. They were supposed to be spiritual leaders who showed the way out of social upheaval. The Anglican Church's leadership has quietly conformed to the standards of secular society, omitting subjects of discord; nervously smiling, yet holding on to the prestige of their clerical positions; liberalizing Church theology in accordance with what they knew to be expected by the growing anti-Christian sentiment within the establishment.

Their willingness to comply to the standards of the extreme-liberal society has been remarkable to watch. The Anglican Church has never been more liberal, omitting references to scriptures that are contrary to the secular establishment's views on morality and other issues, even voicing support for the regional implementation of local, Islamic Sharia law in the UK on family matters. The Archbishop may well complain, but it is the Anglican Church' own actions or lack thereof that have caused this spiritual misery. No wonder Europe loses its connection to the metaphysical world when the leaders of the Church are such pitiful cowards.

The passivity of politicized and compromised bishops indicates their relative indifference to the ongoing process of anti-Christianization. If the contrary was the case and they actually cared, we would have heard their voices loud and clear. Yet, the silence is deafening. The complacency is observable even in regular Church services: even if hardly anyone attend, they still manage to portray it as though the service "was successful." Many do not even care if people don't show up, they still seem completely satisfied with the situation and apparently "feel blessed", pointing out in self-glorification that "the choir sang so beautifully today" or "the priest spoke so well of the poor in Africa" and all other kinds of comments that just illustrate the complete lack of care about the empty benches.

Many seem completely at ease with empty benches, bishops smiling as if nothing is wrong. One may assume they care more about avoiding the persecution that quickly would engulf them if they spoke up and defended the true dogmas of faith. This is most unfortunate. The opposition that could have come from vital, spiritual leaders could have helped Europe in her time of cultural decay.

The current situation in the Northern European Lutheran and Anglican Churches are chilling examples to study, as these regions have come far in implementing the extreme secular expectations from the anti-religious political establishment. It is a study on how to de-Christianize the institutionalized churches.

And for decades, bishops and church leaders in Northern Europe have permitted the secular state to control its teachings, as more or less atheistic or non-believing ministers and secretaries of state often dictate its theological direction. In Scandinavia, several of these ministers have openly said they are not even believers in Christ. The Lutheran Church has still obediently accepted their rulings.

The politicization of the Church has turned leaders such as the Archbishop of Canterbury into extreme-liberal puppets of the anti-Christian elites. It is a terrible example on how *not* to defend the faith in an age of social turmoil. Cunning politicians have exploited their position of power and Bishops have been surprisingly submissive to whichever trends they are told to follow, steadily accepting *status quo*. Always with a smile, in meetings with other bishops, as if a meek smile will help them avoid the judgment of their actions.

Due to the weakness of leadership in the Church, the social cohesion has consequently been immense on many priests and laymen. Many a priest has complained about this, fearing losing his job unless he conforms to the secular standards. Others have lost their jobs, been brutally pushed aside for being "too conservative" on for example the issue of abortion.

It is, of course, a matter of the observable to notice that the privileges of the ecclesial elite are maintained only for those prominent bishops who agree to theological liberalism within the Church. Only they get to keep lavish titles and every piece of prestige that comes with it. Only they remain behind its altar and proceed in long, ornamented robes through its halls.

✶✶✶

# Jesus As a "mild, weak, mellow" Creature

In today's politically correct churches, Jesus is caricatured and presented as a fluffy, kind, meek, sweet, smiling creature, who never sets any boundaries or requires repentance from anyone. This is the ideology of liberal inclusion, which implies that all are to be accepted in the Church without being faced with the requirements of leading a life that accords with the message of Christ, without the changing of heart – the entering into a new phase where the old life has to be crucified.

We find that all are welcomed with no need for repentance – or even acknowledgment – of the need to change one's lifestyle when becoming a Christian. Everyone is to continue living just like he did before. Bishops have readily spoken about forgiveness, but we hear little of repentance. The request for an ethical life is steadily toned down, preferably with one of these "meek Christian" smiles.

The focus is on kindness and mildness, but not in righteousness and truth. Citations from the Scriptures are on the sweetness of Jesus, cute stories about his love for children, storytelling about Peter on the water, yet omitting the serious symbolic implications of what these "mild" stories really is about. There is no mention of Jesus' numerous commands "those who love me, must do as I say," "the one that follows me must give up his life," "be filled with joy when you are persecuted" and so on. No one speaks about Christ' Holy ravaging anger against the double standards and fraudulence of the priests, Scribes, Pharisees and biblical scholars of his time. He was shockingly harsh towards the hypocrites and religious leaders of his time, so was St Paul. *The book of Romans* is quite a shockingly tough message.

We are forever reminded that Jesus said, "turn the other cheek," explained as "let everyone slap you around." but never told that He also whipped moneychangers and overturned tables in a righteous wrath that scared the religious leadership to their core. It seems to have been forgotten that there is an important distinction between the fact that Christ loved all people – including murderers and other reprobates – and the Christian demand for an ethical life, a new way of life, a new birth into the spiritual realm in which the force of spiritual light lifts man above his frailties.

Even the concepts of Judgment Day, Hell and other apocalyptic parts of the message of Christianity, have become controversial – and slowly omitted from sermons. One eagerly speaks about the woman who was caught in adultery and Jesus not condemning her, but quickly omit his commandment to her not to return to her former way of life. One must not speak about the Virgin Birth of Mary, of the conscience as God's guiding light in man and of course, never mention the seven deadly sins and their destructive effect on the human beings. One must frankly only speak of that which fits well with the secular, nihilist version of the Christian faith.

Rather than present a manifest Christianity, the extreme-liberal ideology of "inclusion" – which should be relabelled "theology of exclusion" as much of the classical Christian doctrine is removed from its content - consists of reducing the Christian message to a humanistic cult in which no one is to be accountable to anyone – including God. In an eagerness to be "popular," even central dogmas are omitted. With the constantly new translations of hymn books, the Bible and Church liturgy reforms, there is hardly any chance for anyone to remember verses from the Holy Scripture.

The Northern European mess serves as a dire warning to Churches elsewhere in the West and in other regions. The example of the decline of the Northern European churches as well as the Anglican Church, in particular, illustrates how the Archbishop of Canterbury and his bishops were the architects behind this mess. How did they expect the extreme-liberalized Church to develop? Did they think everyone would flock to come listen to the nihilism preached? Did they hope for increased popularity?

The leadership of the Church has allowed the implementation of a "secular religion." allowed regressive forces to change the Church's message, they have confirmed to the standards of the world, concurred with an acceptance of hedonism, and then, when people do not come to church anymore – they lament?

The reason for the Anglican Church's sudden fascination with the Catholics may lie here. The Catholic Church has, at large, been subjugated to the same politically correct pressure, but kept their stance and defended the faith to a much larger degree. Now the weakened Anglicans seem to need the Catholics to help reduce the downfall. A quick glance at what has happened to a country such as Italy under Pope Francis shows that hundreds of thousands have begun going to mass again, the Churches are filled with people. It would have been much better if the current leaders of the Northern European and Anglican Church were honest enough to resign from office. What happens in a company where the CEO loses his employees, while sales are plummeting and consumers complain about the bad quality products? Of course, the CEO has to go. He is incompetent and has not done his job properly. He has led the firm into bankruptcy.

## Christian Selfishness

The renowned Indian leader and philosopher, Mahatma Gandhi, once visited Christian churches in Africa, and was deeply fascinated by the teachings of Jesus Christ, hailing him as "one of the greatest teachers humanity has ever had." However, when encountering Christians, he was deterred from further involvement of Christian communities, stating: "If Christians would really live according to the teachings of the Bible, all of India would be Christian today." Inappropriate and selfish behavior among those who call themselves believers becomes a reason for many to choose to abandon the faith and renounce the spiritual dimension.

St Porphyrios of the Eastern Orthodox Church says: "In fact, the true Christian religion transforms people and heals them. The most important precondition, however, for someone to recognize and discern the truth is humility. Egotism darkens a person's mind; it confuses him, it leads him astray, to heresy."

Many make the distinction – of utmost importance - between religion as a cultural phenomenon where rules, regulations, and traditions are centrefold, and religion as a spiritual reality focusing on the inner man and love for all that which is sacred. The Protestant Christian trend to say that "I hate religion" but "love God" is a statement that tries to explain the difference between "cultural religion" and its fundamentally different, spiritual counterpart. I would suggest that religion as bondage is not spiritualism at all. To be spiritual is something completely different. What is needed in the West today is a genuine spiritual awakening that results in solidarity and love.

Of this, Elder Porphyrios has stated:

> For many people, religion is a struggle, a source of agony and anxiety. That's why many of the "religiously minded" are regarded as unfortunates because others can see the desperate state they are in. And so it is. Because for the person who doesn't understand the deeper meaning of religion and doesn't experience it, religion ends up as an illness, and indeed a terrible illness. So terrible that the person loses control of his actions and becomes weak-willed and spineless, he is filled with agony and anxiety

and is driven to and fro by the evil spirit.

He adds:

> He makes prostrations, he weeps, he exclaims, he believes he is humbling himself, and all this humility is a work of Satan. Some such people experience religion as a kind of hell. They make prostrations and cross themselves in church, and they say, 'we are unworthy sinners,' then as soon as they come out they start to blaspheme everything holy whenever someone upsets them a little. It is very clear that there is something demonic in this.

Respect for human dignity and solidarity towards one's fellow man are cornerstones of civilization, without which states fall into disarray and anarchy. As the French author Victor Hugo, said, to love or have loved, that is enough. Ask nothing further. There is no other pearl to be found in the dark folds of life.

St Augustine pointed out that the believer should scrutinize the truth to be able to find God, who is to be found using reason and a rational outlook on the world. It is He who created the world with its rationality. Thus, man, using his rational mind, does the work of God.

One may say that it is rational to build a society on truth rather than lies, on trustworthiness rather than deceit, on honest payment rather than corruption, on sharing wealth rather than providing only for the elites, as well as on hard work rather than laziness. However idealistic this may sound, the point is nonetheless that everyone will benefit in a society that strives to become the above. We need ideals to stretch out to, in order to better ourselves and reach higher goals. This has also been pointed out by Habermas, that ideals, however impossible to practice, are still needed in order for man to attempt to lift his ethnics to a higher level, be more empathetic and show more solidarity. It is of the utmost importance to determine which values are to be upheld as ideals in a society, as the population will strive to accomplish and live according to precisely these.

Yet, the simple message to "love your neighbor" and to follow the example of Jesus often drowns in ecclesiastical power intrigues that do not glorify God, but instead insult His name. What happens when the "Church" is not the "Church" and ends up becoming a source for blasphemy? When "Christians" reflect almost the opposite of those values prescribed by the radically controversial Jesus?

The linguist, Noam Chomsky, who currently is the most cited living scholar in the humanities, has famously stated that Jesus was the philosopher who defined the notion "hypocrite" – a person who focuses on the crime of others and refuses to look at his own. The Orthodox Bible synonyms' hypocrite to actor, someone who pretends to be something he is not. The religious leaders and ecclesiastical elites at the time were so threatened by Jesus' outspoken call for truth, honesty, and solidarity with the lowest ranks of society, that they persecuted him in the most inhuman way and finally killed him.

Christians have professed, at least in theory, to be the defenders of the message of love. Yet, many Christian communities today do not automatically form the core of modern *socially engaged* Christianity, with a focus on the spiritual person's responsibilities towards the society in which he lives. Some of these communities can best be characterized by a reactionary elements – regressively clinging on to the past – and represent, in essence, an opposition to change in the current religious status quo within their own denomination.

This narrow-minded attitude is not compatible with classic Christian ideology where a dynamic civic engagement and an active social focus is at the very core of the main message. In reality, parts of the so-called conservative Christianity reflect the same postmodern value – relativity that helps to legitimize the development of selfishness as a new secular religion.

Many Christian communities profess to strive for "Christian values." Yet which values are they *really* speaking about? The attitudes that commonly characterize many culturally religious communities? The sum of the "values" practiced by many is gossip, malicious comments, exclusion of strangers, empty words, "religious slang." a frantic compliance with religious regulations, indifference as to what is happening to society as a whole, cowardice, dishonesty, materialism, greed, and hypocrisy. This sequestered, theoretically oriented heresy has justified the cultivation of closed-up, communities, where people receive a religious education that legitimizes their right to let love grow cold in a cynical "God to bless me" status.

This gives rise to accusations of hypocrisy, and the question why Christians so easily forget the most important commandment. The "fight" among some Christian leaders to sit in front pews and adorn themselves with all sorts of self-styled religious titles – eager to be called apostles, prophets or evangelists – carry the main responsibility for the de-Christianization of the West. Even St Paul said one should not be too eagerly wish to become a Church leader, as they will be judged even more harshly.

In this manner, a number of traditional religious communities have become perpetrated by, in essence, the same egocentric, materialistic, self-absorbed attitude as society in general, representing in many ways the exact opposite of what Jesus himself proclaimed. Jesus abandoned the expectations of contemporary traditionalists, sharply criticized established religious practices that focused on outward appearance, opposed class distinctions and showed kindness to disenfranchised minorities.

He demonstrated a deep respect for women and exposed the hypocrisy of the religious leaders. He lived his life as part of the community, not in small, isolated groups and established a new way of viewing humanity based on equality and fairness, which completely renounced the rigid conservatism and hypocrisy of his contemporaries.

We may all lose our spirituality while on the road to the afterlife. There is something about the world's turmoil and its ability to cause us to lose focus on that which is of vital importance. Jesus tells several stories of people who started well but ended up losing "the oil in the lamp" – when the bridegroom arrived they were not included in the wedding celebration.

The story of the four kinds of seed corn illustrates the difficulties of the demands of life. Again, Christianity's existential solemnity is associated with Lucifer's alluring ability to seduce mankind – made possible because the human heart itself is corrupt and attracted by evil, self-destructive desires. Fortunately, there are also many exceptions to these self-destructive tendencies among Christians in the West.

You find it within the denominations, Catholic, Protestant and Evangelical, Orthodox and those rendered to spiritual homelessness in the West, driven out of secular, politically correct Churches that seem to have been reduced to social cults. These spiritually aware believers point the way out of unproductive introversion: Christians must again start to care about each other and the rest of society. This must have practical consequences, both at the individual, at the community level and on national levels.

Again, the Eastern Orthodox monk, Elder Porphyrios:

> The important thing is for us all to enter into the Church – to unite ourselves with our fellow men, with the joys and sorrows of each and everyone, to feel that they are our own, to pray for everyone, to have care for their salvation, to forget about ourselves, to do everything for them just as Christ did for us. In the Church, we become one unfortunate, suffering and sinful soul. No one should wish to be saved alone without all others being saved. It is a mistake for someone to pray for himself that he himself may be saved. We must love others and pray that no soul be lost, that all may enter into the Church. That is what counts.

## Egoism and Lack of Spirituality in Church

The Christian communities in the Western hemisphere were once alive and thriving. For example, in the 1950s and early 60s, the Billy Graham crusades had an immense impact. Millions heard him speak, both in the largest stadiums in America as well as all over the world. It is said that in his lifetime, Graham has explained the Christian faith to more than two billion on earth.

Yet, something soured among the believers into the 1980s and 90s. Materialism took hold, spiritual egoism, self-contentment, and complacency gained defining ground among many. Christians withdrew from engaging actively in "the non-Christian world." A certain sense of isolationism grew out of Christians tending to stay in their own little bubble. They have their own newspapers, their own record labels, their own "Christian" music, their own ministries that for the most part are engaged in Christian shows. There is "secular music" and "religious music" as if the Holy Spirit does not move freely throughout the whole world, among all peoples, creeds, ethnicities, and sub-groups in society, but is confined to only appear within the tiny fragment of "Christian music." The anti-Christian, extreme liberal development in society happening outside of the pleasant congregations, doesn't seem to bother them much. Not even the gross persecution of Christians in the Middle East under Islamist rule seem to reach the heart and produce action.

The religious doctrine of "separating yourselves from the world," has been misinterpreted to legitimizing the Christians' right not to *care* and to *not* go into the world. The art of apologetic argumentation, so well explained by St Augustine and many others, is dying. Many do not quite know what to say to a nonbeliever, apart from "Jesus loves you." They have not been taught much else, let alone have acquired the ability to defend the faith rationally. When questioned, many simply recite Bible verses, yet are unable to link the reference to Scripture to current-day issues in such a manner that the non-believer understands what he is talking about. After all, whoever says yes to the faith, does so through a rational mind, - he chooses to believe. One would expect to find apologetic Christians everywhere, in the marketplace, on the speaker's corner, in lounges and bars discussing Christian philosophy with others, in restaurants, at universities and colleges and at the horse race track.

Christianity has an image problem, write David Kinnaman and Gabe Lyons in *unChristian: What a New Generation Really Thinks about Christianity... and Why It Matters*. They ask: What do people think about Christians and why do these negative perceptions exist? They find, for one, that today's Christianity reflects a Church infatuated with itself. Many Christians have lost touch with the outside world, living in a "cultural religion of Christianity," that focuses on religious rules and regulations rather than the inner, spiritual life with its corresponding love for those who are outside the Church buildings.

Christian communities enforce strict controls with religious restrictions and prohibitions that are based on Christian cultural norms but have no real basis in Christianity. These functions as a "Christian party whip," forcing young believers into an artificial "kindness" and "meekness" seeking to submit them to the corrupt influence of pompous pastors and denominational leaders, who seek to "maximize their ministry" denying people the full expression of their personality and pummelling them into silence.

These movements are often characterized by strong leading religious figures – who remarkably seldom make public statements outside of the Church buildings. It is almost like they are hiding; we rarely see them in the public realm even though Jesus urged believers to "go out into the world." Ironically, the situation can easily be compared to the notorious European "Labour party whip" or "Liberal whip" referred to by many who have dropped out of these political movements, claiming there is no personal freedom to be found within such political segments. Likewise, many Christian groups seem to have relinquished into isolated groups, rather than pressing the message of love on the public stage and in the media.

When was Jesus Christ a boring, weak individual filled with powerless apprehension, sitting pale and silently on Church bench or in meetings, nodding uncritically to everything that was said? Jesus was the kind of person that turned water into wine – to the great delight of the poor bride and groom, as told in the Gospels. He participated in parties and social gatherings everywhere. Many of the stories about him, happened on such occasions.

In light of the above, one can easily understand that atheists initiated the critique of Church priests and Christians who seemed most preoccupied with the art of religious prejudice, hypocrisy and a culture of dishonesty. This strange, self-contained form of "Christianity" so often strictly determined by a whole range of culturally determined rules – not found in the Bible - of what "is allowed" and what "is not allowed for a Christian to do" creates nervously smiling, weak, anaemic and dependent Christians who cringe at the mere sound of a curse word, let alone music from a bar.

How are the outsiders ever to find the spiritual reality of Christ, if Christians hide in their congregations, fearful of resistance, when one should have been out at dinner parties, in nightclubs, at the malls, wherever we all gather and apologetically defending the faith?

Thom and Joani Schultz point out in *Why Nobody Wants to Be Around Christians Anymore: And How 4 Acts of Love Will Make Your Faith Magnetic*, that the institutionalized Church has forgotten its main message of love. "We do not go to Church, we are the Church," Schultz writes, the act of love does not show up beneath stained-glass, but as everyday, ordinary acts done to people you meet throughout the week. Since the Church has come to stand for many other messages, and not loving one's neighbor, the Church itself suffers from its own lack of strategy.

Schulz states that surveys show that as many as 87% of Americans view Christians as judgmental, 85% feel that Christians are hypocritical. That pretty much sums up the general American attitude, pointing grossly to Christians being perceived as what the Bible calls "Pharisees" – individuals with high degree of knowledge of the Holy Scriptures, quoting these here and there, but people who at the same time do not live a life in humility, honesty and love. They are pretenders. Religious pretenders, living as "cultural Christians," bound to the religion and its rules and regulations, not to the spirituality of Christianity.

As Elder Porphyrios, one of the modern-day saints of the Orthodox Church says: "Without Christ, the Church does not exist. Christ is the Bridegroom; each individual soul is the Bride. Christ united the body of the Church with heaven and with earth: with angels, men, and all created things, with all of God's creation with the animals and birds, with each tiny wildflower and each microscopic insect."

The spiritual Church becomes the focal point through which the supernatural Holy Spirit administers and gives man eternal content and power to overcome temptation. This is the assembly of spiritually aware individuals – some meet in the homes, some in institutionalized churches, some meet on stadiums like those of the pope when he travels, yet others meet two by two. These are the ones, ideally, who strive to obey God's commands as stated in the Holy Bible. Their goal is, consequently, to love their fellow man and search in every way possible to further Gods love to all those who live on earth.

The depth of the message being that love is to define how we treat one another. The true role of the Church is intricately spiritual in nature. Man is to strive to lay down his carnal and evil nature and search for spiritual light. The Church's main objective is to help man connect to the spiritual light of God, so that he may come into contact with the Creator and The Eternal One through Jesus Christ.

※※※

# Time to Return to the Roots of True Faith

The Lutheran theologian Dietrich Bonhoeffer was among the very few intellectuals who warned of the coming tragedy in Germany in the 1930s. It cost him his life. The Nazi regime martyred him. It is puzzling to watch how German politicians, intellectuals as well as the Christian leaders failed to oppose National Socialism throughout the 1930s and onward. They watched what was going on, but kept their silence as the state grew into a Socialist totalitarian system, of the repressive kind that Hannah Arendt so vividly described.

We need a new Martin Luther – but one that *unites the Church again.* Spiritual conviction made him cause the uproar in 1517, after which he lost his job, was banned by the pope, was deemed to be a diabolic heretic, was despised among his contemporaries and hated by those he thought were his friends. Yet, today efforts in both the Protestant, Catholic the Orthodox Church have led to renewed strength for the argument of a reunification of denominations. Pope Francis' recent meeting with Patriarch Kirill in Havana, gives hope for a progression towards this goal. Among Protestant leaders, Billy Graham is one of the spiritual leaders who ask for unification and mutual respect between the denominations.

It is appropriate to recall the words of the world-renowned founder of the Salvation Army, William Booth, as his fiery demands for spiritual and moral rearmament redefined England in the 1800s. When he first set out, he was hated by the establishment, spoken ill of, persecuted and harassed; by the end of his career, he was highly respected for what he did to help the many disadvantaged in the decadent British society.

William Booth states in *Darkest England and The Way Out* that the greatest threat in the next century was that England would embrace a religion – a set of beliefs – without the Holy Spirit, a Christianity without Christ, forgiveness without repentance, salvation without changed behaviour, politics without God, introducing the concept of a heaven without hell. Published in 1890, the book quickly became a bestseller. Its radical solutions for the social problems in the English society made it a major reference source for the later development of the UK.

Even today, Booth remains critically relevant and reflects his rock-solid belief in that people through spirituality can rise out of their own misery. His unusually strong ideal of giving people a chance to explore their potential is nothing less than incredible. With the slogan "Soup, Soap, and Salvation," he attacked the English ruling classes with a scathing demand for social and spiritual reforms, in a way that resembles the sharply critical pen of Charles Dickens. Kicked and punched, Booth never lost his fervent engagement. He became the leader of one of the largest popular Christian movements of the nineteenth century and one of the founding fathers of the British welfare state. He laid the foundation for increased self-respect and standard of living among the lower classes in Great Britain.

What we need is a new Socrates, a new Aristotle, a new Augustine who so eloquently spoke of "true religion." We need religious leaders who stand up against injustice and are willing to work hard and suffer until justice is served. Abraham Lincoln once said that America will not be destroyed from the outside, but if we falter and loose our freedoms, it will be because we destroyed ourselves. The descisive factor in order to turn the tide is to hold the moral high ground, as military strategist Sun Tzu implied. The one that has the higher standard according to the moral law, will win the battle. What counts is not the talk, not words, but actions and how you live on a day to day basis. We must, as a culture, reenter the sphere of holding the moral high ground. We need to return to the fountain of spirituality, the source of love, to get a rational and just outlook on life and a conscious focus on the commandment to love God and each other. We must collectively raise the spiritual awareness in society, as has happened in history before, this will be at the core of what will make us great again.

## About the Author

Hanne Nabintu Herland is a Scandinavian historian of religions and best-selling author, founder and host of The Herland Report which reaches millions yearly. She is well-known by the media for sharp analysis, fearless speech and is a strong defender of the historical, traditional values in the West and the Christian faith.

Herland is a fierce critic of current day authoritarian political correctness and addresses a variety of issues such as hedonism, the illiberal and intolerant Left, feminism, the breakdown of the Western family, the lack of respect for religion and traditional values. She is a sharp critic of the Western engagement in the recent wars in Libya and Syria and has written extensively on the failure of the Arab Spring and the US engagement in the Middle East.

She is known for an unusual bluntness which she credits to her upbringing outside the West, often pointing out what people think, but do not dare to voice. Herland works to achieve a higher awareness for qualities such as justice, mercy, and faith, elements that will bring peace between people and nations. She seeks to establish a higher respect for cultural and religious differences, individual freedom, a reduced power of the custodial state and respect for national sovereignty and international solidarity.

She was born and raised in Africa and speaks six languages. Herland moved to Europe when she was nineteen years old and soon commenced her cultural studies at the University of Oslo, Norway. She has lived in South America, the Middle East and her work steadily take her to various Asian countries, Russia, Eastern European nations as well as Europe and the US.

www.theherlandreport.com

## List of References

Adams, James Luther (red.). *What Is Religion?* New York: Harper & Row, 1969.

Admin. "Patriarch Kirill concerned by Christianophobia in Europe." Pravmir. May 5, 2015.

Agora Journal. "Jacques Derrida." Journal for Metaphysic Speculation, 2005.

Allen, John L. "The war on Christians". October 5, 2013. http://www.spectator.co.uk/2013/10/the-war-on-christians/

Allen, John L. *The Global War on Christians: Dispatches from the Front Lines of Anti-Christian Persecution.* New York: Random House, 2013.

Amadeo, Kimberly. "US Military Budget: Components, Challenges, Growth." About News. February 23, 2016. http://useconomy.about.com/od/usfederalbudget/p/military_budget.htm

America's Children in Brief. Key National Indicators of Well-Being 2012. Forum on Child and Family Statistics.
http://www.childstats.gov/pdf/ac2012/ac_12.pdf
http://www.childstats.gov/pdf/ac2013/ac_13.pdf

American College for Paediatricians. "Benefits of Delaying Sexual Debut." https://www.acpeds.org/parents/sexuality/sexual-responsibility-2/benefits-of-delaying-sexual-debut-2

Andrews, Edward D. *Is the Quran the Word of God? Is Islam the One True Faith?*
http://www.christianpublishers.org/apps/webstore/products/show/7489030

Anglican Mainstream. "World AIDS Day: Christian teaching still needs to be heard." November 30, 2014.
http://anglicanmainstream.org/world-aids-day-christian-teaching-still-needs-to-be-heard/

Arendt, Rudolph. *Tænkning og tro. Religionsfilosofi, dogmatikk og etikk.* Copenhagen: G.E.C. Gads forlag, 1998.

Aristotles. *Nicomachean Ethics.* Chicago: The Chicago University Press, 2011.

Aristotle. *Politics.* UK: Dover Publications, 2000.

Attkisson, Sharyl. *Stonewalled: My Fight for Truth Against the Forces of Obstruction, Intimidation, and Harassment in Obama's Washington.* New York: Harper Collins, 2014.
https://www.instagram.com/p/rha2yOPp_9/?modal=true
https://www.youtube.com/watch?v=FzMf2ETp5X8&feature=youtu.be&list=UUvVeMsVltaaACXhlvLoFstA

Baker, Hunter. *The end of secularism.* Illinois: Crossway Wheaton, 2009.

Ball, Terence. "Socialism." Encyclopedia Britannica. http://www.britannica.com/topic/Socialism

Barna, George and David Kinnaman. *Churchless: Understanding Today's Unchurched and How to Connect with Them.* Texas: Tyndale House Publishers, 2014.

Barton, David. "America's Most Biblically-Hostile U. S. President." Wall Builders. June 16, 2015. http://www.wallbuilders.com/libissuesarticles.asp?id=106938

Bauman, Zygmunt. *Postmodernity and its discontents.* Cambridge: Polity Press, 1997.

Bauman, Zygmunt. *Liquid modernity.* Cambridge: Polity Press, 2000.

Bellah, Robert. *The Robert Bellah Reader.* London: Duke University Press, 2006.

Bennett, William. *The Index of Leading Cultural Indicators.* New York: Simon and Schuster, 1994.

Berlin Social Science Centre. "Six Country Immigrant Integration Comparative Survey." (SCIICS) "https://www.wzb.eu/en/research/migration-and-diversity/migration-integration-transnationalization/projects/six-country-immigrant-int

Berger, Peter. *The Social reality of Religion.* Harmondsworth: Penguin Books, 1973.

Berger, Peter (ed.). *The Desecularization of the World. Resurgent Religion and World Politics.* Michigan: William B. Eerdmans Publishing Company, 1999.

Berger, Peter. "Protestantism and the Quest for Certainty". The Christian Century, 26. August 1998.

Berger, Peter and Samuel P. Huntington. *Many globalizations.* New York: Oxford University Press, 2002.

Beyer, Peter. *Religion and globalization.* London: Sage Publications, 1994.

Bible Gateway. "Exodus 20. The ten commandments" New International Version. https://www.biblegateway.com/passage/?search=Exodus+20

Bilsker, Dan and Jennifer White. "The silent epidemic of male suicide". BCMJ, vol.53, nr. 10, 2011. http://www.bcmj.org/articles/silent-epidemic-male-suicide

Boa, Kenneth and William Kruidenier, "Romans", vol. 6, Holman New Testament Commentary (Nashville, TN: Broadman & Holman Publishers, 2000), 365.

Boardman, William. "Obama Drones On: The Slaughter of Pakistani Civilians. Global Research. February 26, 2014. http://www.globalresearch.ca/obama-drones-on-the-slaughter-of-pakistani-civilians/5371002

Bodanis, David. Einstein's greatest mistake: A Biography. New York: Houghton Mifflin Harcourt, 2016.

Bowlby, Chris. "What can history teach us about the credit crunch?" BBC History Magazine volume 10, nr.1, January 2009.

British Humanist Association. "Religion and belief: some surveys and statistics." https://humanism.org.uk/campaigns/religion-and-belief-some-surveys-and-statistics/

Briggs, Catherine. "Porn use can lead to divorce: Study". Lifesite News. 9.06.2014. https://www.lifesitenews.com/news/porn-use-can-lead-to-divorce-study

Brock, Janna. "European Christian Persecution Is Already Here, Is the US Ready?" Freedom Outpost, September 1, 2013. http://freedomoutpost.com/2013/09/european-christian-persecution-already-u-s-ready/#1YKdJHt4IS7GimS9.99

Bromwich, David. *The Intellectual Life of Edmund Burke. From the Sublime and Beautiful to American Independence.* London: The Belknap Press of the Harvard University Press, 2014.

Bruce, Steve. *God is Dead. Secularization in the West.* Oxford: Blackwell Publishing, 2002.

Buchanan, Patrick J. *Suicide of a superpower. Will America survive to 2025?* New York: Thomas Dunne Books, 2011.

Buchanan, Pat interviewed by JP Media, 2012. https://www.youtube.com/watch?v=3GG1rFA_QEk

Business Insider. "These six corporations control 90% of the media in America." http://www.businessinsider.com/these-6-corporations-control-90-of-the-media-in-america-2012-6 https://en.wikipedia.org/wiki/Concentration_of_media_ownership#The_.22Big_Six.22

CBS. "60 Minutes on George Soros". December 21, 1999. https://www.youtube.com/watch?v=p8Ux5b6YM9A http://www.aim.org/media-monitor/60-minutes-ignores-the-soros-drug-ties/

C.G.Jung. *Psychology and religion.* London: Yale University Press, 1938.

Chaput, Charles C. *Render unto Caesar: Serving the Nation by living our Catholic Beliefs in Political Life.* New York: Doubleday, 2008.

Chesney, Robert W. *The problem of the media.* New York: Monthly Review Press, 2004.

Chomsky, Noam. *The essential Chomsky.* New York: The New Press, 2008.

Chomsky, Noam and Edward S. Herman. *Manufacturing Consent. The political economy of the mass media.* New York: Pantheon Books, 1988.

Chomsky, Noam. "The US behaves nothing like a democracy." SALON. August, 17, 2013. http://www.salon.com/2013/08/17/chomsky_the_u_s_behaves_nothing_like_a_democracy/ https://www.youtube.com/watch?v=MeTbDdl7XiE

CNN." War sometimes justified, Obama says in Nobel Peace Prize speech." December 11, 2009. http://edition.cnn.com/2009/POLITICS/12/10/obama.peace.prize/

Cohen, Nick. *How the left lost its way. What's left?* London: Harper Perennial, 2007.

Encyclopedia Britannica. "Positivism", 2016. https://www.britannica.com/topic/positivism

Conolly, William E. *Why I am not a secularist.* Minnesota: University of Minnesota Press, 1999.

Cooper, George. *The origin of financial crises.* New York: Vintage Books, 2008.

Corliss, Richard. "That old feeling: When porno was chic." Time Magazine, March 29, 2005. http://content.time.com/time/arts/article/0,8599,1043267,00.html

Country Progress Report New Zealand. April 2015. https://www.health.govt.nz/system/files/documents/publications/nz_country_progress_report_jan_dec_2014.pdf

Crotty, James Marshall. "7 Signs That US Education Decline Is Jeopardizing Its National Security." Forbes, March 26, 2012. http://www.forbes.com/sites/jamesmarshallcrotty/2012/03/26/7-signs-that-americas-educational-decline-is-jeopardizing-its-national-security/#43fc728f5999

Crotty, James Marshall. "7 Signs That U.S. Education Decline Is Jeopardizing Its National Security". Forbes Magazine. 26.03.2012. https://www.forbes.com/sites/jamesmarshallcrotty/2012/03/26/7-signs-that-americas-educational-decline-is-jeopardizing-its-national-security/#2a9c71d359b6

Cunningham, Hugh. *Children and Childhood in Western Society since 1500.* New York: Routledge, 2014.

Cunningham, Loren and Janice Rogers. *The book that transforms nations.* New York: YWAM Publishing, 2007.

Daniels, Kit. "Ben Stein: Obama "Most Racist" President in History." Infowars. November 2, 2014. http://www.infowars.com/stein-obama-most-racist-president-in-history/

Das, Satyajit. *The Age of Stagnation: Why Perpetual Growth is Unattainable and the Global Economy is in Peril.* New York: Prometheus Books, 2016.

Dedmon, J., "Is the Internet bad for your marriage? Online affairs, pornographic sites playing greater role in divorces," 2002, press release from The Dilenschneider Group, Inc.

Defend Christians.org. "Obama's sins of omission." November 20, 2013. http://defendchristians.org/news/obamas-sins-of-omission/

Derrida, Jacques. *Speech and Phenomena: And Other Essays on Husserl's Theory of Signs.* Evanston: Northwestern University Press, 1973.

Derrida, Jacques. *Of Grammatology.* Baltimore: The John Hopkins University Press, 1997. https://www.youtube.com/watch?v=N8BsnfjtNCg

Dickerson, Kelly. "Five things Einstein got wrong" Business Insider. November 19, 2015. http://www.businessinsider.com/physics-einstein-got-wrong-2015-11/#scientists-now-see-the-cosmological-constant-as-representative-of-a-mysterious-force-called-dark-energy-which-is-causing-the-universe-to-expand-at-a-faster-and-faster-clip-8

Doughty, Steve. "Just 800,000 worshippers attend a Church of England service on the average Sunday." Mail Online. March 22, 2014. http://www.dailymail.co.uk/news/article-2586596/Just-800-000-worshipers-attend-Church-England-service-average-Sunday.html

Drury, Ian. "Extreme internet pornography is driving people to inflict sexual violence and murder, country's most senior judge warns." Daily Mail. January 27, 2015. http://www.dailymail.co.uk/news/article-2928864/Extreme-internet-pornography-driving-people-inflict-sexual-violence-murder-country-s-senior-judge-warns.html

Duduit, Michael. "The 25 Most Influential Preachers of the Past 25 Years." Radical Dicipleship. November 6, 2010. https://4given2serve.wordpress.com/2010/11/06/the-25-most-influential-preachers-of-the-past-25-years/

D'Souza, Dinesh. *America. Imagine a world without her.* Washington: Regnery Publishing, 2014.

Durkheim, Emile. *Suicide. A study in sociology.* New York: The Free Press, 1979.

Dwan, David and Christopher Insole (ed). *The Cambridge Companion to Edmund Burke.* New York: Cambridge University Press, 2012.

Einstein, Albert. *The World as I see It.* New York: Citadel Press. Kensington Publishing Corp., 1984.

Elder Porphyrios. *Wounded by Love. The life and wisdom of St Porphyrios.* http://www.sprint.net.au/~corners/Oct06/ElderPorphyrios.htm

Eliade, Mircea. *The sacred and the profane.* The nature of religion. Orlando: Harcourt Inc., 1987.

Ellis, John. "Nearly Half of Detroiters Can't Read" Business Insider. 5.05.2011. http://www.businessinsider.com/nearly-half-of-detroiters-cant-read-2011-5?r=US&IR=T&IR=T

Encyclopedia Britannica. "Capitalism." http://www.britannica.com/topic/Capitalism

Encyclopedia Britannica. "Worldwide Adherents of All Religions by Six Continental Areas", 2007.

Evans, Martin. "Rotherham council ignored child abuse by Asian gangs because of 'misplaced political correctness', report concludes." The Telegraph. February 4, 2015. http://www.telegraph.co.uk/news/uknews/crime/11391314/Rotherham-child-sex-abuse-scandal-council-not-fit-for-purpose.html

Eurostat Statistics Expained. "Marriage and divorce statistics." June 2015. http://ec.europa.eu/eurostat/statistics-explained/index.php/Marriage_and_divorce_statistics

European Commission, Public Opinion. Discrimination in the EU, 2012 Special Eurobarometer. http://ec.europa.eu/COMMFrontOffice/PublicOpinion/

Folse, Henry (2005). "How Epicurean Metaphysics leads to Epicurean Ethics." Department of Philosophy, Loyola University, New Orleans, LA. http://www.loyno.edu/~folse/Epicurus.html

Fredericks, Bob and Sofia Rosenbaum. "Charlie Hebdo vows to publish more Muhammad cartoons." New York Post. January 12, 2015. http://nypost.com/2015/01/12/charlie-hebdo-vows-to-publish-more-mohammed-cartoons/

Freud, Sigmund. *The future of an illusion.* New York: Pacific Publishing Studio, 2010.

Friedman, Milton. *Capitalism and Freedom.* Chicago: University of Chicago Press, 1962.

Friedman, Milton and Rose Friedman. *Free to choose. A personal statement.* Orlando: Harvest Book, 1990.

Gardiner, Patrick. *Kierkegaard.* Oxford: Oxford University Press, 1988.

Garett, Duane A. "Proverbs, Ecclesiastes, Song of Songs". Vol. 14, The New American Commentary (Nashville: Broadman & Holman Publishers, 1993), 97–98.

Gay, Peter. *Freud: A Life for Our Time.* New York: W.W.Norton and Company, 1998.

Giddens, Anthony. *Sociology* (Sixth Edition). Cambridge: Polity Press, 2009.

Giddens, Anthony. *Europe In the Global Age.* Cambridge: Polity Press, 2007.

Gilhus, Ingvild and Lisbeth Mikaelsson. *Kulturens refortrylling. Nyreligiøsitet i moderne samfunn.* Oslo: Universitetsforslaget, 1998.

Gimse, Lars Martin. "Biskopen reagerer på Toojis kirkesex-video». The Norwegian newspaper, Vaart Land. 08.06.2015. http://www.vl.no/nyhet/biskopen-reagerer-pa-toojis-kirkesex-video-1.364968?paywall=true

Gilje, Nils. "Civil society and the dialectics of modernity." Rapport 9. LOS-Senteret 1996.

Gillespie, Michael Allen. *Nihilism before Nietzsche.* Chicago: The University of Chicago Press, 1995.

Gilhus, Ingvild Sælid and Lisbeth Mikaelsson. *Nytt blikk på religionen. Studiet av religion i dag.* Oslo: Pax, 2001.

Global Research TV. "Obama: Most Pro-War President in Living Memory." http://tv.globalresearch.ca/2011/03/obama-most-pro-war-president-living-memory http://www.globalresearch.ca/more-than-50-of-us-government-spending-goes-to-the-military/18852

Glucksmann, André. *Ouest contre ouest.* Paris: Plon, 2003.

Goldberg, Jonah. *Liberal facism.* New York: Broadway Books, 2009.

Graham, Billy. *Hope for the troubled heart.* New York: Bantam Books, 1991.

Graham, Billy. *The Journey. How to live by faith in an uncertain world.* Nashville: Thomas Nelson, 2006.

Graham, Billy. *The reason for my hope.* Salvation. Nashville: W. Publishing Group, 2013.

Graham, Billy. Interview with Robert Schuller, Hour of Power, May 31, 1997. http://www.youtube.com/watch?v=3WFkb9NkEHE
https://youtube.com/watch?v=7i95RXDyY70#t097

Graham, Billy. Interview with David Frost. "Talking with David Frost: Reverend Billy Graham," David Paradine Television, Feb 18, 1997.
https://www.youtube.com/watch?v=f68IgZruyNI

Graham, Billy. Interviewed by Larry King, Larry King Live. Retrieved July 15, 2011.
http://transcripts.cnn.com/TRANSCRIPTS/0506/16/lkl.01.html

Graham, Billy. Madison Square Garden 1957.
https://youtube.com/watch?v=7i95RXDyY70#t097
https://www.youtube.com/watch?v=f68IgZruyNI
http://4given2serve.wordpress.com/2010/11/06/the-25-most-influential-preachers-of-the-past-25-years/

Graham, Billy. San Francisco News interview. September 21, 1957 and interview with The Star, June 26, 1979 and "The Pilgrim Pope: A Builder of Bridges," Saturday Evening Post, January-February 1980.

Greely, Andrew. "A Religious Revival in Russia?" Journal for the Scientific Study of Religion. Vol. 33, No. 3. September 1994.

Greenwald, Glenn. "Obama's secrecy fixation causing Sunshine Week implosion." The Guardian. March 14, 2013.
http://www.theguardian.com/commentisfree/2013/mar/14/obama-transparency-podesta-sunshine-week

Greenwald, Glenn and Jeremy Scahill. "The NSA's Secret Role in the US Assassination Program." The Intercept. February 10, 2014.
https://theintercept.com/2014/02/10/the-nsas-secret-role/

Grossman, Cathy Lynn. "Conservative Anglican leaders back Uganda anti-gay law." Religion News Service. April 28, 2014.
http://www.religionnews.com/2014/04/28/conservative-anglican-leaders-back-uganda-anti-gay-law/

Grundy, Trevor. "Church of England Sunday attendance continues downward slide." Religion News Service. March 21, 2014.
http://www.religionnews.com/2014/03/21/church-england-sunday-attendance-continues-downward-slide/

Greenspan, Alan. *The age of turbulence. Adventures in a new world.* New York: The Penguin Press, 2007.

Gutfeld, Greg. *The Joy of Hate: How to Triumph over Whiners in the Age of Phony Outrage.* New York: Crown Forum, 2014.

Habermas, Jürgen. "Habermas' speech at the Holberg Price, Bergen, Norway" Aftenposten, November 29th, 2005.

Habermas, Jürgen. *Moral consciousness and communicative action.* Cambridge: Polity Press. 1990.

Habermas, Jürgen. *Religion and rationality.* Essays on reason, God and Modernity. Cambridge: The MIT Press, 2002.

Habermas, Jürgen. *The future of human nature.* Cambridge: Polity Press, 2002.

Habermas, Jürgen and Joseph Ratzinger (Pope Benedict XVI). *The dialectics of secularization. On reason and religion.* San Francisco: Ignatius Press, 2005.

Habermas, Jürgen. *Between naturalism and religion.* London: Polity Press, 2008.

Habermas, Jürgen. *Europe. The faltering project.* Cambridge: Polity Press, 2008.

Habermas, Jürgen. *The divided West.* Cambridge: Polity Press, 2003.

Ham, Mary Catharine. *End Discussion. How the Left's Outrage Industry Shuts Down Debate, Manipulates Voters, and Makes America Less Free.* New York: Crown Forum, 2015.

Harvard International Review: "A path to Recovery. A libertarian Perspective on Economic Crisis." Vol. XXX. Winter, 2009.

Hayek, F.A. *The constitution of Liberty.* Chicago: University of Chicago Press. 2011.

Hayek, F.A. *The road to serfdom.* Chicago: The University of Chicago Press: 2007.

Haywood, Andrew. *Global Politics.* London: Palgrave Macmillian, 2011.

Heidegger, Martin. German TV interview, 1962. https://www.youtube.com/watch?v=3WDmRAASuKc

H.E. The Economist. "Why does liberal Iceland want to ban online pornography?" April 23, 2013.
http://www.economist.com/blogs/economist-explains/2013/04/economist-explains-why-iceland-ban-pornography

Henriksen, Jan-Olav og Otto Krogseth (red.). *Pluralisme og identitet.* Oslo: Gyldendal, 2001.

Hitchens, Cristopher. *God is not great. How religion poisons everything.* New York: Twelve Warner Books, 2007.

Houellebecq, Michel. *The elementary particles.* New York: Vintage Books, 2001.

Houellebecq, Michel. *Whatever.* London: Serpent's Tail, 1998.

Hubble, Edwin (1929). "A relation between distance and radial velocity among extra galactic nebulae". PNAS. 15 (3): 168 – 173.

Hudson, John. "Obama's War on Whistle-Blowers." The Wire. May 24, 2011. http://www.thewire.com/politics/2011/05/obamas-war-whistle-blowers/38106/

Huffington Post. "Religion In Russia Shows Increase In Orthodox Christian Affiliation, But Not In Church Attendance, Reports Pew Survey." Huffington Post. November 2, 2014. http://www.huffingtonpost.com/2014/02/11/religion-russia-orthodox-christian_n_4766753.html

Human Rights Watch." US: Reassess Targeted Killings in Yemen." October 21, 2013. https://www.hrw.org/news/2013/10/21/us-reassess-targeted-killings-yemen

Huntington, Samuel. *The Clash of Civilizations. The remaking of world order.* New York: Touchstone, 1996.

Huxley, Aldous. *Brave new world.* New York: Everyman's Library, 1932 (2013).

International Social Survey Programme 2008: Religion III, ISSP 2008 http://www.thearda.com/archive/files/descriptions/ISSP08.asp

Intolerance and discrimination against Christians in Europe. NGO – Observatory on Intolerance and Discrimination against Christians, 2015. http://www.intoleranceagainstchristians.eu/

Islamic information portal. "Islam as the middle path". Islam.ru. http://islam.ru/en/content/story/islam-middle-path

James, Brendan. "Princeton Study: US No Longer An Actual Democracy." TPM. April 18, 2014. http://talkingpointsmemo.com/livewire/princeton-experts-say-us-no-longer-democracy

Jay, Martin. *The Dialectical Imagination. A history of the Frankfurt School and the Institute of Social Research 1923-1950.* Canada: Little Brown and Company: 1973. https://www.marxists.org/subject/frankfurt-school/ https://www.marxists.org/subject/frankfurt-school/jay/ch01.htm

Johnston's Archive. "Russia abortions and live births by federal subject area, 1992-2008." March 10, 2010. http://www.johnstonsarchive.net/policy/abortion/russia/ab-rusreg.html

Jones, Kenneth C. *Index of Leading Catholic Indicators. The Church since Vatican II.* New York: Orlens Publishing, 2003.

Jones, Peter. *Vote for Caesar.* London: Orion Books, 2008.

Kamala, Nayaswami. "What Jesus Means to Me by Mahatma Gandhi." Practical Spiritual Life Magazine. November 13, 2013. http://practicalspirituallife.com/jesus-means-mahatma-gandhi/ http://www.brainyquote.com/quotes/quotes/m/mahatmagan107529.html

Kaplan, Seth. Fixing *Fragile States: A new paradigm for development.* Westport: Praeger Security International, 2008.

Katusa, Marin. *The Colder War. How the Global Energy Trade slipped from America's grasp.* New Jersey: Wiley, 2015.

Keffe, Simon P. *The Cambridge Companion to Mozart.* Cambridge: Cambridge University Press, 2003.

Kinnaman, David and Gabe Lyons. *unChristian: What a New Generation Really Thinks about Christianity...and Why It Matters* Grand Rapids: Baker Books, 2007.

Kirk, Russel. *The conservative mind.* New York: B.N. Publishing, 2008.

Kluger, Jeffrey. "The biology of Belief". Time. Volume 173, nr. 8, 2009.

Kluger, Jeffrey. "How faith can heal." Time. 23.2.2009. http://content.time.com/time/covers/0,16641,20090223,00.html

Koenig, Harold G. *Medicine, religion and health. Where science and spirituality meet.* Pennsylvania: Tempelton Foundation Press, 2008.

Konstan, David. "Epicurus." Stanford University Encyclopedia, 2014 http://plato.stanford.edu/entries/epicurus/

Kraut, Richard. "Plato". Stanford Encyclopaedia of Philosophy. 2017. https://plato.stanford.edu/entries/plato/

Kramer, Roderick M. 2009: "Rethinking trust". Harvard Business Review, June 2009.

Kuenssberg, Laura. "State multiculturalism has failed, says David Cameron." BBC. February 5, 2011. http://www.bbc.co.uk/news/uk-politics-12371994

Kuhn, Thomas S. 1962 (2012 edition): *The structure of scientific revolutions.* Chicago: The University of Chicago Press

Kuruvilla, Carol. "13 Jobs Bible-Believing Kentucky Marriage Clerk Probably Shouldn't Apply For." Huffington Post Voices. January 9, 2015. http://www.huffingtonpost.com/entry/bible-believing-kentucky-county-clerk-should-probably-not-apply-for-any-of-these-13-jobs_55e5b11ce4b0b7a9633a2d94?cps=gravity_2677_5732701937833073144

Kye-wan, Cho. "South Korea's middle class is shrinking, according to recent report". The Hankyoreh.
http://english.hani.co.kr/arti/english_edition/e_business/678354.html

Lama, Dalai. *An open heart. Practicing compassion in everyday life.* New York: Little, Brown and Company, 2001.

Lama, Dalai and Howard C. Cutler. *The art of happiness in a troubled world.* London: Hodder and Stoughton, 2009.

Lama, Dalai and Jeffrey Hopkins (trans). *Advice on Dying and living well by taming the mind.* London: Ryder, 2002.

Lasch, Christopher. *The revolt of the elites and the betrayal of democracy.* London: Norton, 1995.

Lasch, Christopher. *The Cultural Narcissism. American life in an age of diminishing expectations.* New York: Norton, 1991.

Lenartowick, Kerri and Elise Harris. "Lawyer identifies key groups in European persecution of Christians"Catholic News Agency. March 30, 2014. http://www.catholicnewsagency.com/news/lawyer-identifies-key-groups-in-european-persecution-of-christians/

Lazar, Sara W. "Meditation experience is associated with increased cortical thickness." "Mindfulness practice leads to increases in regional brain gray matter density." US National Library of Medicine. National Institute of Health.
http://www.ncbi.nlm.nih.gov/pmc/articles/PMC1361002/
http://www.ncbi.nlm.nih.gov/pmc/articles/PMC3004979/

https://www.washingtonpost.com/news/inspired-life/wp/2015/05/26/harvard-neuroscientist-meditation-not-only-reduces-stress-it-literally-changes-your-brain/?tid=ss_fb

Levin, Jeff. *God, faith and health. Exploring the spirituality-healing connection.* New York: John Wiley and sons, 2001.

Levin, Mark. *Ameritopia. The unmaking of America.* New York: Threshold Editions, 2012.

Levin, Mark. *Liberty and tyranny. A conservative manifesto.* New York: Threshold Editions, 2009.

Lévy, Bernard-Henri. *Left in dark times. A stand against the new barbarism.* New York: Random House, 2008.

Lévy, Bernard-Henri og Michel Houellebecq. *Ennemis publics.* Paris: Flammarion/Grasset & Fasquelle, 2008.

Lévy, Bernard-Henri. *American vertigo. Traveling America in the footsteps of Tocqueville.* New York: Random House, 2006.

Lewis, C.S. *Mere Christianity.* New York: Harper Collins, 1952.

Lewis, C.S. *The case for Christianity.* New York: B&H Publishing Group, 1999.

Liew, Jonathan. "All men watch porn, scientists find". The Telegraph. 2.12.2009. http://www.telegraph.co.uk/women/sex/6709646/All-men-watch-porn-scientists-find.html

Liptak, Kevin. "Countries bombed by the US under the Obama administration." CNN. September 24, 2014. http://edition.cnn.com/2014/09/23/politics/countries-obama-bombed/index.html

LSE. European Institute. Forum for European philosophy. http://www.lse.ac.uk/europeanInstitute/research/forumForEuropeanPhilosophy/pdf/RichardIveson-text.pdf

Meacham, Jon. "Meacham: The end of Christian America". Newsweek. March 4, 2009. http://www.newsweek.com/meacham-end-christian-america-77125

Magnus, Bernd and Kathleen M. Higgins (ed.). *The Cambridge Companion to Nietzsche.* Cambridge University Press, 1996.

Malik, Kenan. "The failure of Multiculturalism." Foreign Affairs. May 2015. https://www.foreignaffairs.com/articles/western-europe/failure-multiculturalism

Marrinan, Patrick. Paisley: *Man of Wrath*. Anvil Books, 1973.

Max Weber. *The protestant ethic and the spirit of Capitalism.* London: Routledge, 2001.

McLaren, Niall. "Dumbing Down America: The Decline of Education in the US as Seen From Down Under." Truth-out.org. November 22, 2013. http://www.truth-out.org/opinion/item/20043-dumbing-down-america-the-decline-of-education-in-the-us-as-seen-from-down-under

Meland, Kjetil. "Norway does not stop paying benefits after criminal is expelled from the country" Nettavisen. 2016. http://www.nettavisen.no/nyheter/--stopper-ikke-nav-utbetaling-til-utvistekriminelle/3423252430.html

Michell, Stephen (trans). *Gilgamesh, a new English version.* New York: Free Press, 2004.

Minogue, Kenneth. "Liberalism." Encyclopedia Britannica. http://www.britannica.com/topic/liberalism

Moskowitz, Clara. "Einstein's 'Biggest Blunder' Turns Out to Be Right." November 24, 2010. http://www.space.com/9593-einstein-biggest-blunder-turns.html

Munro, Dan. "Med Student Gives Sober Assessment of Future With $500K In Student Debt". Forbes Magazoine. January 30, 2014. https://www.forbes.com/sites/danmunro/2014/01/30/med-student-gives-sober-assessment-of-future-with-500k-in-student-debt/#7067dca85b30

Murphy, Michael. *Multiculturalism: A Critical Introduction.* New York: Routledge, 2012.

Nakata, H. and Sakamoto K and Kakigi R." Meditation reduces pain-related neural activity in the anterior cingulate cortex, insula, secondary somatosensory cortex, and thalamus." US National Library of Medicine. National Institute of Health. http://www.ncbi.nlm.nih.gov/pubmed/25566158

National Association of Social Workers. "Parents, Peers, and Pressures: Identifying the Influences on Responsible Sexual Decision-Making." Volume 2, number 2, September, 2001. http://www.naswdc.org/practice/adolescent_health/ah0202.asp

National Institute of Mental Health, US "Major Depression Among Adults." http://www.nimh.nih.gov/health/statistics/prevalence/major-depression-among-adults.shtml

Newsmag Finance. "Medical School at $278,000 Means Even Bernanke Son Has Debt" 11.04.2013. http://www.newsmax.com/finance/InvestingAnalysis/Medical-School-Bernanke-Son-Debt/2013/04/11/id/498930/

New York Times. "Study finds that 1 out of 3 women watch porn at least once a week" 22.10.2015. http://nytlive.nytimes.com/womenintheworld/2015/10/22/study-finds-that-1-out-of-3-women-watch-porn-at-least-once-a-week/

Nietzsche, Friedrich. *Beyond good & evil*. New York: Vintage Books, 1989.

Nietzsche, Friedrich. *Thus spoke Zaratustra*. New York: Dover Publications, 1999.

Onti, Niki Mariam. "EU wants to abolish cross from Greek flag". Greek Reporter. April 15, 2013. http://greece.greekreporter.com/2013/04/05/eu-wants-to-abolish-cross-from-greek-flag/

Packard, Josh and Asleigh Hope. *Church Refugees: Sociologists reveal why people are DONE with church but not their faith*. Group.com, 2015. https://dechurched.net/2015/12/22/stuck-pastors-who-are-done-with-churc/

Paisios, Elder of Mount Athos. *Spiritual Awakening*. Greece: Holy Monastery, Evangelist John the Theologian, 2010. http://www.orthodoxphotos.com/Orthodox_Elders/Greek/Fr._Paisios/

Palmer, Robert R. Palmer; Joel Colton. *A history of the modern world*. New York: Mc. Graw-Hill Publishing Company, 1984.

Pew Research Centre. Various data from the Forum on Religion and Public Life. "Global Christianity A Report on the Size and Distribution of the World's Christian Population. http://www.pewforum.org/files/2011/12/christianity-fullreport-web.pdf http://www.pewforum.org/2011/12/19/global-christianity-regions/

Pew Research Center: Religion & Public Life (August 7, 2017) http://www.pewforum.org/2011/12/19/global-christianity-regions/#europe

Pew Research Centre Forum on Religion and Public Life, Global Christianity, December 2011.
http://www.pewforum.org/2011/12/19/global-christianity-regions/#europe

Pew Research Forum on Regional Distribution of Christians.
http://www.pewforum.org/2011/12/19/global-christianity-regions/

Rand, Ayn on Philosophy and the Welfare State.
https://www.youtube.com/watch?v=8hoPo86cErs
http://aynrandlexicon.com/lexicon/welfare_state.html#order_3

Piatak, Tom. "The necessity of Christianity." Chronicles. October 2009. http://www.unz.org/Pub/Chronicles-2009oct-00039

PISA surveys and Finland, 2012.
http://www.minedu.fi/pisa/taustaa.html?lang=en
http://www.oecd.org/pisa/

Plato. *The Trial and Death of Socrates: Four Dialogues.* New York: Classic Books International, 2010.

Plato. *The Republic.* New York: Black and White Classics, 2014.

Plato-dialogues.org. "Plato on youth and the excess of freedom."
http://plato-dialogues.org/faq/faq003.html

Pollard, Sidney. *Peaceful conquest. The industrialization of Europe 1860-1970.* New York: Oxford University Press, 1981.

Powers, Kirsten. *The Silencing: How the Left is Killing Free Speech.* New York: Regnery Publishing, 2015.

Phillips, Melanie. *The World turned Upside Down. The global battle over God, Truth, and Power.* New York: Encounter Books, 2010.

Phillips, Trevor. "What British Muslims really think."
http://www.channel4.com/programmes/what-british-muslims-really-think/on-demand/62315-001

Prager, Dennis. *Think a second time.* New York: William Morrow, 1995.

Putin, Vladimir. "Address at the Valdai Forum, September 2013."
https://www.youtube.com/watch?v=HSX2ALtIejw

Rana, Mohammad Usman." Secular extremism." Aftenposten 25.2.2008.

Rand, Ayn. University of Michigan Television interview, 1961. https://youtu.be/JnL9fMjpD90?t=397
https://www.youtube.com/watch?v=8hoPo86cErs
https://www.youtube.com/watch?v=leaAC832gG4

Ratzinger, Joseph Cardinal. *Values in a time of upheaval.* New York: The Crossroad Publishing Company, 2006.

Ratzinger, Joseph Cardinal and Godfried Cardinal Danneels. *Handling on the faith in an age of disbelief.* San Francisco: Ignatius Press, 2006.

Ratzinger, Joseph Cardinal. *Christianity and the crisis of cultures.* San Francisco: Ignatius Press, 2006.

Rauschning, Herman. *Hitler Speaks: A Series of Political Conversations with Adolf Hitler On His Real Aims.* Kessinger Publishing, 2006.

Rawls, John. *A brief inquiry into the meaning of sin and faith.* Cambridge: Harvard University Press, 2009.

Reilly, Molly. "Obama Told Aides He's 'Really Good at Killing People,' New Book 'Double Down' Claims Huffpost Politics. November 3, 2013. http://www.huffingtonpost.com/2013/11/03/obama-drones-double-down_n_4208815.html

Reme, Silje Endresen and Lene Berggraf. "Is religion undermined in the study of psychology?" The Norwegian Journal for Psychology: Volume 46, September 2009.

Schiffer, Peter D. And Andrew J. *How an economy grows and why it crashes.* New Jersey: John Wiley and sons, 2010.

Schlesinger, Jr. Arthur M. *The Disuniting of America: Reflections on a Multicultural Society.* New York: Norton, 1998.

Schwanitz, Dietrich. *Bildung. Alles, was man wissen muß.* Germany: Goldman, 2002.

Siedentop, Larry. *Invventing the Individual. The Origins of Western Liberalism.* Massachusetts: The Belknapp Press of Harvard University Press, 2014.

RT. "Hillary is used to beating, kicking and abusing her own husband – former Nixon adviser." Sophie & Co. February 15, 2016. Interview with Roger Stone. https://www.rt.com/shows/sophieco/332460-hillary-husband-nixon-adviser/

RT. "God a terrorist? Vatican newspaper slams Charlie Hebdo cover." January 6, 2016. https://www.rt.com/news/328080-vatican-god-charlie-hebdo/

RT. "Single Americans become majority for the first time." September, 10. 2014. http://rt.com/usa/186516-singe-americans-majority-marriage/

RT. "Single Americans majority for the first time". September 10, 2014. https://www.rt.com/usa/186516-singe-americans-majority-marriage/

RT. "Extreme porn the cause of rape and violence, claims top judge." RT. January 28, 2015. https://www.rt.com/uk/227147-uk-porn-violence-judge/

RT. "UK teens turning to porn for sex education – study" RT. January 29, 2015. http://rt.com/uk/227451-uk-teen-sex-education/

RT. "1,400 kids sexually abused in UK town, council turned blind eye over 'racism' fears." August 27, 2014. https://www.rt.com/uk/183104-rotherham-sexual-abuse-children/

RT. "Thrown to the lions? Catholic & Anglican leaders say Christians now a minority." February 10, 2016. https://www.rt.com/uk/332048-christians-minority-catholic-anglican/

RT. "Russian patriarch says Christians are oppressed in well-off Europe." January 8, 2016. https://www.rt.com/news/328272-russian-patriarch-christians-christmas/

RT. "Extreme porn the cause of rape and violence, claims top judge". January 28, 2015. https://www.rt.com/uk/227147-uk-porn-violence-judge/

RT. "Christians are under pressure in many developed countries' – Russian Patriarch Kirill to Ed Schultz." February 16, 2016. https://www.rt.com/news/332570-christianity-pressure-world-patriarch/

Ruki, Sayid." Nearly half of all British children do not know about the true meaning of Easter." Mirror. April 16, 2014. http://www.mirror.co.uk/news/uk-news/nearly-half-british-children-not-3419685

Saez, Emmanuel. "Striking it Richer: The Evolution of Top Incomes in the United States." University of Berkley. March 2, 2012. http://eml.berkeley.edu/~saez/saez-UStopincomes-2010.pdf

Saul, Heather. "UK porn legislation: What is now banned under new government laws." The Independent. December 2, 2014. http://www.independent.co.uk/news/uk/home-news/uk-porn-legislation-what-is-now-banned-under-new-government-laws-9898541.html

Schiff, Peter D. *The Real Crash: America's Coming Bankruptcy – How to Save Yourself and Your Country.* New York. St Martins Press, 2014.

Schulte, Brigid. "Harvard neuroscientist: Meditation not only reduces stress, here's how it changes your brain." The Washington Post. May 26, 2015. https://www.washingtonpost.com/news/inspired-life/wp/2015/05/26/harvard-neuroscientist-meditation-not-only-reduces-stress-it-literally-changes-your-brain/?tid=ss_fb

Schultz, Thom and Joani Schultz. *Why Nobody Wants to Be Around Christians Anymore: And How 4 Acts of Love Will Make Your Faith Magnetic.* Loveland: Group.com, 2014.

Seligman, Sara. "Polls." The Hills. February 11, 2013. http://thehill.com/polls/282147-hill-poll-voters-obama-no-better-than-bush-on-security-vs-civil-liberties

Serle, Jack. "More than 2,400 dead as Obama's drone campaign marks five years. "The Bureau of Investigative Journalism. January 23, 2014. https://www.thebureauinvestigates.com/2014/01/23/more-than-2400-dead-as-obamas-drone-campaign-marks-five-years/

"Sexual Orientation and Health Among US Adults: National Health Interview Survey, 2013." CDC. July 15, 2014. http://www.cdc.gov/nchs/data/nhrs/nhrs077.pdf

Shabad, Rebecca. "Poll: Public doesn't want another Iraqi war". The Hill. June 17, 2014. http://thehill.com/blogs/blog-briefing-room/news/209582-poll-voters-support-obamas-approach-in-iraq

Shortt, Rupert. *Christianophobia. A faith under attack.* Michigan: Wm.B.Eerdman Publishing, 2013.

Showalter, Brandon. "China on Track to Have World's Largest Christian Population by 2030". The Christian Post. 21.7.2017. http://www.christianpost.com/news/china-largest-christian-population-world200-million-believers-despite-crackdown-166718/

Skinner, Kevin B. "Is Porn Really Destroying 500,000 Marriages Annually?" "Psychology Today, December, 2011. https://www.psychologytoday.com/blog/inside-porn-addiction/201112/is-porn-really-destroying-500000-marriages-annually

Skinner, Kevin B. "Inside porn addiction". Psychology Today. https://www.psychologytoday.com/blog/inside-porn-addiction/201112/is-porn-reallydestroying-500000-marriages-annually

Smith, Amelia. "French Satirical Magazine Charlie Hebdo Often Mocked Religion." Newsweek. July 1, 2015. http://europe.newsweek.com/french-satirical-magazine-charlie-hebdo-often-mocked-religion-297311

Sinai Speak. "Believe in God in 5 minutes." https://www.youtube.com/watch?v=eQVm8RokoBA https://www.youtube.com/watch?v=aVOLfGDFtH4

Stanford Encyclopedia of Philosophy. "Critical theory." March 2005. http://plato.stanford.edu/entries/critical-theory/

Stanford Encylopedia of Philosophy. "Jaques Derrida". March 2014. http://plato.stanford.edu/entries/derrida/ http://www.egs.edu/faculty/jacques-derrida/biography/

Stein, Rob and Donna St George. "Number of Unwed Mothers Has Risen Sharply in the US," Washington Post, May 14, 2009.

Sharon Jayson, "CDC Study: Birth rates Decline Overall," USA Today, Dec. 22, 2010.

Stern, Fritz. "Hitler: Memoires of a Confidant." Foreign Affairs Journal. Fall, 1985. https://www.foreignaffairs.com/reviews/capsule-review/1985-09-01/hitler-memoirs-confidant

Stoller, Mat. "Growth of Income Inequality Is Worse Under Obama than Bush. Naked Capitalism. April 11, 2012. http://www.nakedcapitalism.com/2012/04/growth-of-income-inequality-is-worse-under-obama-than-bush.html

Surveys on Atheism and Religious Belief, WINGIA, 2012. http:/www.wingia.comweb/files/news/14/file/14.pdf

Squires, Nick. "European Court bans crucifixes in Italy's classrooms." The Telegraph. November 3, 2009. http://www.telegraph.co.uk/news/worldnews/europe/italy/6495252/European-Court-bans-crucifixes-in-Italys-classrooms.html

Stone, Jon. "Just 62 people now own the same wealth as half the world's population, research finds." The Independent. January 17, 2016. http://www.independent.co.uk/news/world/politics/just-62-people-now-own-the-same-wealth-as-half-the-worlds-population-research-finds-a6818081.html

Taylor, Charles. *Multiculturalism: Examining the Politics of Recognition.* New Jersey: Princeton University Press.

The Church of England. "Archbishops recall commitment to pastoral care and friendship for all, regardless of sexual orientation." January 29, 2014. https://www.churchofengland.org/media-centre/news/2014/01/archbishops-recall-commitment-to-pastoral-care-and-friendship-for-all,-regardless-of-sexual-orientation.aspx

The BMJ. "First sexual intercourse: age, coercion, and later regrets reported by a birth cohort". January 3, 1998. http://www.bmj.com/content/316/7124/29.full.print

The Guardian. "Italy is a 'dying country' says minister as birth rate plummets". February 13, 2015.https://www.theguardian.com/world/2015/feb/13/italy-is-a-dying-country-says-minister-as-birth-rate-plummets

*The Holy Bible* (King James version). New York: The American Bible Society, 1980.

The Local Italia. "Italian schools are like a dictatorship." March 25, 2014. https://www.thelocal.it/20140521/italian-schools-are-like-a-dictatorship-cardinal

The Ministry of Foreign Affairs of the Russian Federation. "Speech by Foreign Minister Sergey Lavrov at a high-level event on issues of protecting Christians, Geneva, March 2, 2015. http://archive.mid.ru//brp_4.nsf/0/8F2471AFC72D1B4A43257DFD00340362

"The Perils of Zombie Education". http://www.truthout.org/opinion/item/17103-the-perils-of-zombie-education

The Thom Hartmann Program. "What Do You Do When You No Longer Need Your Slaves?" August 13, 2013. http://www.truth-out.org/opinion/item/18168-what-do-you-do-when-you-no-longer-needyour-slaves-or-your-workers

Toje, Asle. *The Iron Cage. Liberalism in Crisis (Norwegian).* Oslo: Dreyer, 2014.

United Nations. The Universal Declaration of Human Rights. http://www.un.org/en/universal-declaration-human-rights/index.html

UK teens turning to porn for sex education – study https://www.rt.com/uk/227451-uk-teen-sex-education/

US Department of Commerce, Economics and Statistics Administration. "America's Families and Living Arrangements: 2003. Population Characteristics." US Census Bureau. November 2004. https://www.census.gov/prod/2004pubs/p20-553.pdf

Van Buren, Peter." Obama's itchy trigger finger on drone strikes: what happened to due process?" The Guardian. February 17, 2014. http://www.theguardian.com/commentisfree/2014/feb/17/obama-drone-strikes-due-process

Wagener, Otto. Henry A. Turner. (ed) *Hitler – Memoires of a confidant.* Yale University Press, 2005.

Waldron, Jeremy. *God, Locke, and Equality: Christian Foundations in Locke's Political Thought.* Cambridge: Cambridge University Press, 2002.

Watson, George. "Hitler and the Socialist dream." The Independent. November 22, 1998. http://www.independent.co.uk/arts-entertainment/hitler-and-the-Socialist-dream-1186455.html

War Resisters League. "WRL Pie Chart Flyers – Where Your Income Tax Money Really Goes." https://www.warresisters.org/resources/wrl-pie-chart-flyers-where-your-income-tax-money-really-goes

Ware, Timothy. *The Orthodox Church: New Edition.* New York: Penguin Books, 1997.

Washington's blog. "Even Democratic Party Loyalists Starting to Wake Up to the Fact that Obama Is As Bad As Bush … Or Worse." March 17, 2013. http://www.washingtonsblog.com/2013/03/obama-is-worse-than-bush-in-favouring-the-super-elite-bailing-out-the-big-banks-protecting-financial-criminals-targeting-whistleblowers-secrecy-and-trampling-our-liberties.html

Watson, Georg. "Hitler and the socialist dream" The Independent. 22.11.1998. http://www.independent.co.uk/arts-entertainment/hitler-and-the-socialist-dream-1186455.html

Weaver, Mathew. "Angela Merkel: German multiculturalism has utterly failed." The Guardian. October 7, 2010. http://www.theguardian.com/world/2010/oct/17/angela-merkel-german-multiculturalism-failed

Weller, Chris. "This Swedish preschool doesn't use the words 'he' or 'she'." Business Insider. October 15, 2015.
http://www.businessinsider.com/swedish-preschool-doesnt-use-the-words-he-or-she-2015-10

Whitlock, Craig. "Drone strikes killing more civilians than US admits, human rights groups say." Washington Post. October 22, 2013.
https://www.washingtonpost.com/world/national-security/drone-strikes-killing-more-civilians-than-us-admits-human-rights-groups-say/2013/10/21/a99cbe78-3a81-11e3-b7ba-503fb5822c3e_story.html

WHO. "Facts on induced abortion worldwide." Guttmacher Institute. January 2012.
http://www.who.int/reproductivehealth/publications/unsafe_abortion/induced_abortion_2012.pdf

Wilson, A. N. "Lord, how Easter's changed! Nothing better illustrates how much Britain's values have altered in 50 years than the way we'll spend this weekend." The Daily Mail. April 4, 2015.
http://www.dailymail.co.uk/news/article-3025070/Lord-Easter-s-changed-better-illustrates-Britain-s-values-altered-50-years-way-ll-spend-weekend.html

Wright, Wendy. "Christians increasingly persecuted in Europe." Spero News. June 27, 2013.
http://www.speroforum.com/a/ROMKLDSGOZ40/74134-Christians-increasingly-persecuted-in-Europe#.VqDRcVPou71

Yang, Fenggang. "When Will China Become the World's Largest Christian Country?" John Templeton Foundation.
http://www.slate.com/bigideas/what-is-the-future-of-religion/essays-and-opinions/fenggang-yang-opinion

Young-Powell, Abby. "Students turn to porn for sex education." The Guardian. January 29, 2015.
http://www.theguardian.com/education/2015/jan/29/students-turn-to-porn-for-sex-education

Printed in Poland
by Amazon Fulfillment
Poland Sp. z o.o., Wrocław